Legends
of the
Chelsea Hotel

Legends

of the
Chelsea Hotel

Living with the Artists
and Outlaws of
New York's Rebel Mecca

Ed Hamilton

Da Capo Press
A Member of the Perseus Books Group

Cataloging-in-Publication data for this book is available from the Library of
Congress.
ISBN: 978-1-56858-379-2

Published by Da Capo Press
A Member of the Perseus Books Group
www.dacapopress.com

Da Capo Press books are available at special discounts for
bulk purchases in the U.S. by corporations, institutions, and other
organizations. For more information, please contact the Special Markets
Department at the Perseus Books Group, 2300 Chestnut Street,
Suite 200, Philadelphia, PA 19103, or call (800) 810-4145,
ext. 5000, or e-mail special.markets@perseusbooks.com.

*For Hiroya, and for all the residents of the Chelsea,
past and present, living—and having passed on
to that great bohemian flophouse in the sky*

Contents

Introduction

This book came about as the result of a fire. My girlfriend, Debbie Martin, and I were walking up Seventh Avenue one evening, coming home from dinner at the neighborhood restaurant Tello's. As we rounded the corner of 23rd Street, we were met by a cacophony of sirens. A line of fire trucks stretched down the block. Hoping that it wasn't the Chelsea, though knowing all the while that it must be, we approached our building warily. Sure enough, there were firemen running in and out of the hotel. At first they tried to keep us away, but when we explained that we lived there, they let us into the lobby.

Twenty or more of our neighbors had gathered there, in various states of disarray. As the Chelsea is an artistic hotel, they were all writers and artists and musicians—and all wildly eccentric. Someone had brought a jug of wine, and we passed this around as the firemen poured in and out of the building, dragging their equipment with them. No one knew yet what had caused the fire, or the extent of its damages, and we all discussed our theories. Various intrigues played themselves out in the hours we passed before it was safe to go back to our rooms.

An older lady, a former theater actress and a resident of the hotel for more than twenty years, had rescued her good winter coat and her mink hat from the blaze. She sat in her chair with her coat buttoned up, though she soon took the hat off her head and placed it in her lap. A young girl who had lived at the hotel for about a year, working as an artist's model, spotted that hat and just had to try it on. She kept insisting, even when it became clear that the old lady didn't want to give it up. "No, I'm serious. Let me wear that," she kept repeating, until finally the old lady, scowling, was forced to part with her hat. The girl wore it around the lobby for the rest of the night, showing it off to everyone, while the old lady kept a sharp eye on her to make sure she didn't slip away.

At about this point our inimitable proprietor, Stanley Bard, marched the fire chief through the lobby, saying, "This is a very famous hotel. Thomas Wolfe lived here, and the poet Dylan Thomas." It was his usual spiel, though now sounding strangely at odds with the gravity of the situation, and we all laughed knowingly. That was Stanley for you: all was roses when it came to the hotel. He never could see the dark side, even if the place was burning to the ground.

There were several tourists mixed in among us, as the Chelsea also plays host to transients. One man, apparently from the Midwest to judge by his accent, had shared our wine and talked with us, becoming increasingly puzzled as the night wore on. He had caught on that we were all artists, but had yet to wrap his mind around the notion of people living in a hotel. Finally he asked, "How do all you people know one another? Are you in town for a convention or something?"

But the incident I remember best came toward the end of the night when a young guy named Felipe, who had lived at the hotel for less than a week, came limping into the lobby on crutches. Despite our best efforts, everyone in the lobby cracked up laughing when they saw him. Wearing nothing but a red down coat over a pair of briefs, Felipe had painted his face in ghastly shades of orange and red and black. He looked as if had he just narrowly escaped the fire, having scarcely enough time to throw on his coat over his jockey shorts and drag himself down the stairs. But no, as it turned out, he was merely heading out for a night of clubbing. It didn't look like he would be dancing much, but he sure as hell was going to give it the old college try.

Maybe Felipe's appearance was what did it. In any event, it was sometime that night that Debbie came up with the idea for *Living with Legends: Hotel Chelsea Blog* (www.hotelchelseablog.com). We were talking about how interesting and exciting life was at the hotel, and lamenting that, in the face of rising real estate prices and gentrification, all this would soon pass away. Few of the hotel's residents are rich—most of them are far from it, in fact—and though Stanley Bard had kept the rents affordable over the years, there was mounting pressure on him from his board of directors to start charging market rate for the rooms. As our neighbor, the concert pianist Bruce Levingston, says, "It looks like we're on the tail end of the comet here."

We wanted to do something to preserve the history of this unique and vibrant hotel while that history was still ongoing and developing. But since so many disparate events were happening around us at all times—a point driven home by the chaos in the lobby on the night of the fire—a standard academic history of the hotel clearly wouldn't do. We needed a nonnarrative format, where we had the flexibility to record anything that came up, and where residents and former residents could send us whatever material—be it poetry, photography, or artwork—that they had a notion to submit. And that was how Debbie came up with the idea of the blog, a newly emerging format that was made to order for our purpose.

It seemed like a hell of a lot of work to me, and so I tried to talk Debbie out of it. But she said it wouldn't be that bad, at least from a technological standpoint. She knew her way around computers, so she could handle that aspect of the project. What she needed was content, and that's where I came in. Debbie suggested I write a weekly column for the blog.

"No way!" I said. "I don't have time. I'm working on a novel."

Luckily, Debbie was able to persuade me. "All right, All right!"

I finally gave in. "I'll write fifty-two stories, a year's worth, and that's all. And then I'm going back to work on my novel."

Of course it didn't turn out quite that way. Though I was able to produce the fifty-two stories in a matter of a couple of months, in doing so I realized that the ten years I had lived here had given me a lot more to say about the hotel. I found that the lives of my neighbors were what really interested me, and as I became consumed in writing their darkly humorous and often tragic stories, I forgot about the novel and still haven't gotten back to it.

The Chelsea is, to say the least, a unique hotel. Built in 1883 as a luxury co-op apartment residence, the Chelsea was for a brief period the tallest building in New York. In 1905 the building became a residential hotel, catering to the luminaries of the New York theater world, people like Sarah Bernhardt—who reputedly slept in a coffin—and Lillian Russell. Other early residents included Mark Twain and O. Henry, who, often on the lam from the law, gave a different name every time he checked in. In the thirties, Thomas Wolfe stormed and brooded in Room 829 and wrote *You Can't Go Home Again* there.

The forties and fifties were hard times for the hotel, at least in a physical sense. Stained-glass windows, mirrors, and ornate woodwork were torn out, and the large suites were divided into tiny rooms, as the hotel degenerated into little more than a flophouse. Fortunately, many of the old residents refused to move out, and so a lot of the grand architectural detail was preserved. In 1957, Dylan Thomas drank eighteen whiskeys at the White Horse Tavern, staggered back to the Chelsea, and said, "That must be the record," before collapsing and being taken to St. Vincent's Hospital, where he died a few days later. Years later, Brendan Behan would do his best to follow in Dylan's footsteps.

William Burroughs wrote *Naked Lunch* in the Chelsea, and Jack

Kerouac and Allen Ginsberg lived here for a time as well. (Lesser Beats such as Gregory Corso and Herbert Huncke could be found wandering the halls in later years; Huncke died here in 1996.) Arthur Miller lived here, pre- and post-Marilyn, as did Arthur C. Clarke, writing *2001, A Space Odyssey,* in a vain attempt at escape.

The sixties were the Warhol years, and several of his superstars lived in the hotel—including Nico, Brigid Berlin, and Gerard Malanga—and starred in his film *Chelsea Girls,* shot primarily in the hotel. (Viva lived here up until the early nineties.) Bob Dylan lived here from 1961 to 1964, and wrote "Sad Eyed Lady of the Lowlands." Leonard Cohen lived here, received a blow job from Janis Joplin, and wrote "Chelsea Hotel No. 2" to commemorate the experience. Joni Mitchell wrote "Chelsea Morning" about the hotel, inspiring Bill and Hillary—though no one remembers them staying at the hotel—with a name for their daughter.

In the seventies, the Chelsea was home to punk rockers such as Iggy Pop and Dee Dee Ramone. Patti Smith roomed here with the photographer Robert Mapplethorpe. And in 1978 Sid Vicious of the Sex Pistols allegedly stabbed his girlfriend, Nancy Spungen, to death in Room 100, taking his own life a few months later.

Madonna lived here in the eighties and later photographed her book *Sex* in Room 822. The artists Julian Schnabel and Philip Taaffe lived here in the eighties and nineties and maintain studios here to this day. Party hostess Susanne Bartsch moved here in 1981 and never left.

The nineties were another era of physical change for the hotel, this time in the opposite direction. The proprietor, Stanley Bard, took heroic measures to return the hotel to a semblance of its old grandeur, refurbishing the common areas and many of the rooms as well. Notable tenants in this decade included the comedian Eddie Izzard, the director Abel Ferrara, and the singer/songwriter Ryan Adams.

The new century saw the increased gentrification of the Chelsea neighborhood—as literally dozens of condo buildings sprung up all around—and of the hotel. For better or worse, rents have gone up and more prosperous tenants have moved in. Luminaries of the present decade include: Ethan Hawke, Marianne Faithfull, Julie Delpy, Rufus Wainwright, and (until his untimely death) the one-of-a-kind Dee Dee Ramone, who lived here off and on for three decades and never gave a damn if the place was fancy or not.

As Stanley Bard, who took over operation of the hotel from his father in 1957, enters his fifth decade at the helm, the Chelsea has suddenly become a hot real estate property. Stanley has always managed to keep the rents at least somewhat affordable for the writers and artists in residence, but now his partners (represented by a board of directors) are clamoring for profits and ready to move the building in a more lucrative direction. Though Stanley swears he'll never retire, even he can't hold out forever. (We're all hoping he hangs in there through at least 2008, the 125th anniversary of the Chelsea.) Certainly, whatever else happens, when Stanley goes, it will mean the end of an era.

I initially didn't intend to write about the famous people who have lived at the hotel, as I figured enough had been written about them already. Not everyone with a creative dream can be a success, and I wanted this book to be about the no-less-valid struggles of the artists, writers, con men, and lunatics who have lived here over the years, serving as inspiration for those talented and thick-skinned and lucky enough to have hit the big time. Devoting your life to the arts often exacts a heavy toll in bitterness, disappointment, and failure, and I wanted the book to be about this dark side of the creative dream. There's a famous creative energy that pervades the Chelsea. You feel it when you walk through the door, and you never cease to feel it for as long as you live here. Its demands are a lot to live with, and it can come over time to be perceived as a negative energy. It should come as no real surprise that it over-whelms some of the more sensitive among us.

But as I was putting the book together, one thing that struck me was the frequency with which the luminaries of the past seemed to come up. As it was, this amounted to little but name-dropping, though there was a distinct suggestion that these people played a greater role in the lives of the present residents than I was giving them credit for. My agent, Bob Shuman, noticed this as well, and it was he who suggested that I write a bit about the famous people I mention. I told him more than once that I wasn't a historian, that I just write about things that happen in my own life, but he seemed to assume that in time I would come around to his way of thinking, and eventually I did.

And I'm glad I did come around, as it opened up a whole new realm of creativity for me, allowing me to come to a fuller under-standing of what the title of our blog, *Living with Legends,* signifies. For we live side by side with the giants of the past, and it's the influence of these legends that we all have to live up to in our everyday lives. And perhaps that's the real source of the energy that pervades the hotel. The great deeds of the past (and the not-so-great as well) hang on our walls—almost literally—like banners of achievement, haunting and coloring our time here with their pres-ence. And let's remember, too, that the famous haven't all escaped unscathed either. (Nor have I, as you'll see.) The history of the cre-ative arts at the Chelsea as elsewhere represents a cumulative pro-gression, and we inherit the sins of our artistic forebears.

But hey, not to sound too gloomy, most of us here at the Chelsea have a sense a humor about our existential plight. We may all be nuts, but we still have a good time in spite of, or maybe because of, our infirmity, and I trust this comes through in my stories.

Although the book could have been structured in any one of sev-eral different ways, I chose to use a journal form in order to highlight the changes the hotel has undergone in the twelve years Debbie and I have lived here. Basically, from the mid-nineties to today, the Chelsea went from a junky-infested flophouse to something that could almost be called gentrified. Almost, but not quite. Though I wrote most of the stories in the past couple of years, I was able to date them fairly accurately using my notes from those earlier years. The result, a mix of history and biography, myth and legend, fiction (including such ghost stories as "Harry and the Zombie" and "Chelsea Séance") and nonfiction, memoir and anecdote, can most accurately be described as an "alternative history" or perhaps a "history of an idea," the idea being, of course, that of the Chelsea Hotel itself.

Back in the lobby on the night of the fire, it quickly became apparent who had started the blaze. Sitting in a chair behind the front desk was our telephone operator, Shirley Kelly, crying and blubbering incoherently. Though she was wrapped in a kimono, no doubt donned hastily, she had still somehow managed to escape with her trademark wig and her makeup intact. I hadn't seen her come down the stairs; she just suddenly, weirdly, appeared behind the desk, and was just as quickly whisked away to recuperate elsewhere in the hotel.

Shirley had been the nighttime telephone operator for as long as we had lived here. Irascible, frustrating, often downright rude when you spoke to her over the phone, Shirley was a true Chelsea piece of work. In her intricately coifed blond wig and her thick and expertly applied makeup, you could tell she had once been beautiful. Now in her late seventies, Shirley had worked as a performer on the old burlesque circuit and even, to hear some of the older residents tell it, as something a bit more scandalous even than that. She was certainly a colorful, salty character. She liked to drink and smoke and could often be seen on a stool at the bar of El Quijote next door, doing just that. In her tiny room there wasn't anywhere to sit except on the bed, and she must have dozed off with a cigarette in her hand.

Debbie and I, and a few other residents, went up later in the night to look at Shirley's room. Though the smoke had cleared out, a putrid odor lingered. Water was still streaming down the stairwell and standing an inch or two deep on the ninth floor, where the blaze had started. An old janitor was trying vainly to mop up the mess and cursing loudly as he did so; he didn't say a thing to us as we waded through the flood. Shirley's door was standing wide open, though there was some yellow caution tape strung up over the entrance. The room had been almost completely gutted. A blackened and burned-out mattress and box spring lay out of kilter on the floor. There were a few charred scraps of busted-up furniture and wood lying around. Shirley's extensive collection of dresses and gowns and faux furs, which she stored on a rolling rack, had, strangely enough, not burned—a testament, I suppose, to the durability of polyester. All the items had been blackened, however, and everything in the room had been thoroughly soaked through by the fire hoses.

Shirley did come back to work maybe a week or two later, and she was her same old self again, complaining to all who would listen that Stanley—whom she alternately condemned as a ruthless slumlord and praised as the kindliest-hearted man in the world—had placed her in a tiny airless cell. Stanley soon moved her to a larger room, but then he decided it was too risky to have her around the hotel anymore. Some of us were angry over this, but Shirley had a difficult personality and there were others who had never liked her and were glad to see her go. I was one of the former, though upon reflection I guess Stanley did have a point there: Shirley couldn't work much anymore, and perhaps it was time for her to retire to sunnier climes. Perhaps he felt he was just giving her the necessary nudge. She moved in with an older relative in Cleveland, Ohio; but, not surprisingly, that arrangement didn't quite work out. One day Shirley just packed up her few belongings and moved out, and as of this writing we're not sure where she ended up after that.

Culture Shock

Movado

My friend was helping me move some stuff into the Chelsea. I was sitting in his van on 23rd Street, out in front of the hotel. A black guy came down the middle of the street. He was hopping around with a jerky sort of walk, gesturing with his arms at the cars that streamed by him. As he got closer he spotted me. He stuck his head in the driver's window of the van.

"Hey, man, you need a watch?"

"No," I said.

He thrust an open case through the window and into my lap. Then he hopped around to my side of the van, the passenger's side.

"Take a look at it, man. Movado."

I had no idea what Movado was, I didn't care, and didn't want to encourage the man by asking. I was tired from moving furniture and boxes of books, and not in the mood for shopping. But since the case was in my lap, I looked at the watch. It looked pretty good, I must admit. A silver metal band with a black face and one single diamond-like jewel marking the twelve o'clock spot. Still, I didn't want it. I tried to hand it back.

"Sorry, man, I can't use it."

"It's the real thing. Genuine Movado. Not like one of those fake ones you get on Canal Street."

"Oh, I'm sure it's real," I said. "I just don't want it." Actually, I was not at all sure. What did I know about watches? But again, I didn't care. I just wanted to get rid of the guy. I snapped the case shut and tried to hand it back.

He hopped back around to the driver's side. "It's Movado. Look on the back of it."

I was hesitant to tell the guy to get lost. He was just trying to make a buck. Since I couldn't walk away myself, I was forced to open the case back up. Sure enough, there on the back of the watch was etched the magic word Movado. There were a bunch of other words etched there too, but I didn't bother to read them. I closed the case and tried to hand it back, again. He still wouldn't take it.

"You see? You see? Movado," the watch man said.

I didn't see how that proved anything. People who have the technology to make fake watches probably also have the technology to put fake engravings on the back of them.

"That watch is worth a lot of money." He was back on the passenger's side now. I wished he would quit jumping back and forth like that. He was starting to make me nervous.

"Oh yeah, I can tell," I said. "It's a very nice watch. You should have no problem selling it." I had the case closed and was holding it out the window.

"Look at the price tag."

I drew the case in again and opened it back up. He reached in the window and flipped the price tag out from behind the watch. "See that? $450."

Yep, that's what it said. Once again, I didn't see how that proved anything.

The watch man was on the driver's side now, looking around nervously. I sensed he was getting a little bit impatient. "It's not stolen, man," he said. "My wife bought it on a bad credit card." I guess that made it less stolen.

Actually, I didn't care if it was stolen or not. I just didn't need a watch. But now I felt a twinge of sympathy. After all that trouble scamming the credit card people, his wife would be mighty disappointed if he came home without the groceries. She would probably need bail money sooner or later, as well.

"Listen," the guy said. "I'm gonna do you a favor. Only eighty bucks. Movado." I didn't even have eighty bucks on me, only about seventeen. And I needed to buy lunch. If the matter wasn't settled before, it was settled now.

"Where else are you gonna get a Movado for only eighty bucks?"

"Uh, nowhere?"

"Damn straight," the watch man said.

I told him, "Listen, man, I don't have anywhere near eighty bucks. I can't help you."

"Well, what'll you give me for it?"

"I don't want it for any price."

"Make me an offer." I guess he thought I was one tough customer, really haggling. He said, "I might be able to go sixty."

"No way."

"Just make me an offer."

"I don't want it."

"Come on, man, make me an offer. Come on."

I finally gave in. "Alright, ten bucks."

He snatched the watch back and stalked off, back down the middle of the street. "Fuck you, man," he grumbled. "It's a Movado."

Harry and the Zombie

It's well known that underground filmmaker Harry Smith was also a painter, folklorist, and ethnomusicologist and that he collected string figures and paper airplanes. Less well known is that during his time at the Chelsea, Harry kept a Zombie. A disciple of über-Satanist Aleister Crowley—whom he often claimed, much to his mother's embarrassment, to be his real father—Harry was a consecrated bishop in the O.T.O., the Ordo Templi Orientis, a mystical order founded in Germany in 1902 and reorganized by Crowley in 1912. The order is fairly eclectic, embracing all world traditions of magic, and that's what led Harry to the study of voodoo. Traveling to Haiti in the sixties in order to immerse himself fully in the dark art, Harry soon attained the rank of *Houngan,* or voodoo priest, amazing even seasoned practitioners with the ease with which he channeled the spirit of the powerful snake god Damballah Wedo.

Raising the dead, however, is another matter altogether, and it would take Harry the greater part of the next two decades to attain the competence necessary to negotiate the intricacies—and to avoid the myriad perils—of the arcane reanimation ceremony. (In Harry's defense I should note that he *did* have a lot of irons in the fire.) Finally, by the end of the eighties, he was ready to give it a go. Knowing that the only place in New York that would tolerate such an abomination was the Chelsea Hotel, he made an appointment to see our illustrious proprietor, Stanley Bard, and he moved his stuff into the Dowager of 23rd Street that very afternoon. Now all Harry lacked was a suitable subject for his diabolical ministrations.

Luckily, in my early years at the Chelsea, there were still several residents around who remembered Harry and the Zombie, and by questioning them at length I have been able to reconstruct the events surrounding the Zombie's tenure at the hotel. I spoke with a man—for obvious reasons he chooses to remain anonymous—who was involved in the actual ceremony, and what follows is an account, in his own words, of that terrible night:

> At the time I was Harry's disciple, so when he mentioned the idea to me I was all for it, since I figured with a Zombie slave around that meant less work for me. One night this deadhead dude came over, and Harry sat him down on the bed with a big bowl of reefer and a bottle of Jack. I had never seen the dude before and I don't know where Harry picked him up. But while he was busy with the pot and the liquor, Harry went around lighting all the candles in his tiny junked-up room, dozens of them, stuck with melted wax onto every flat surface. Then he put on a ratty yellow robe and a cardboard headdress, and started chanting and dancing around, and it wasn't long before he was possessed by the spirit of Damballah Wedo.
>
> The deadhead didn't seem to care or even to really notice what was going on, until Harry began to anoint him with cat's urine and a greasy, foul-smelling, pitch-like substance. "What the fuck, man!" the deadhead dude said. "Smoke some more reefer, dude," Harry said. "Try some bong hits this time." Harry dragged a bong out from under the bed. Not surprisingly, the bong was a real skull, bored out and fitted with a pipe stem and

mouthpiece. "Try a couple of these quaaludes, too," Harry said. "OK, don't mind if I do," the deadhead said.

Harry pulled a cage containing a live chicken from under his bed and grabbed the chicken out by the neck. It was squawking and flapping and making a hell of a racket, but Harry quickly put an end to that, holding it down and sacrificing it with a sacrificial knife on a sacrificial altar made from the cabinet of an old stereo speaker. "All right, man! Fry it up!" the deadhead said. "I got the munchies like a motherfucker!" Harry squirted blood from the chicken's neck all over the deadhead, and in general all over the room, and then he threw the headless chicken down and it ran around slamming into boxes and rolling in the cat litter. "Hey man, be careful with that thing!" the deadhead said. "Where's the skillet. Put that shit on the stove." Of course, Harry's room had no kitchen, but that's another story.

Taking out a handful of white Zombie powder, Harry blew a huge puff of it in the deadhead dude's face. The dude started sneezing wildly and blowing his nose on the blood-and-urine-stained sheets, but soon he grew quiet. "Far out man," he said. "I'm hallucinating my ass off. Where can I get hold of some of that shit?" But soon he stopped speaking, and his eyes glazed over, and he flopped back onto the bed. I then helped Harry to strip off the dude's clothes and prepare his body for the final stages of the ceremony.

Now of course, as everyone knows, a Zombie must be buried in order to "die" and subsequently be reborn in his new incarnation as the living dead. And further, as anyone who has had to keep dead pets in his or her freezer knows, it is not easy to find a place to bury a mammal—even a small one—in New York City. Harry was able to accomplish this feat in the rooftop garden of the Chelsea. Although he caught hell from the woman whose tomato plants he uprooted, in three days' time Harry was able to dig up the deadhead and reanimate him beneath the light of the full moon as a fully functional Zombie. (As you might imagine, it was incidents such as this that led Stanley Bard to restrict rooftop access.)

Over the next few years, Harry used the Zombie to go out for beer and cigarettes and the occasional sandwich. Sometimes he sent him on more nefarious errands as well—I suppose that goes without saying—such as to stand in line at crack houses on the Lower East Side. Toward the end, Harry's legs hurt him and he didn't like to walk down the hall to the bathroom, so he would take a dump in a plastic bag and have the Zombie take it to the trash bin late at night. The Zombie slept standing up in the hall closet, though sometimes Harry, a drug addict and somewhat forgetful himself, would leave the door ajar and the Zombie would get out and roam the hotel. One time he was discovered huddled in a corner of the basement, nearly catatonic, his eyes glazed, blood and gore caked on his face and arms, the remains of a devoured cat strewn about him. Stanley gave him a stern lecture and sent him back up to his closet.

Now you might wonder at this last incident, as you might also very well wonder why none of the other hotel residents seemed to notice that there was a ravening, bloodthirsty Zombie in their midst. Well, most likely, everybody who encountered him just thought he was a particularly down-and-out junky. For in truth, the Zombie—whose name, by the way, was Paul—was actually quite a bit more cogent and well-put-together than many of the nuts who were running the halls of the Chelsea in those days. And besides, you know how self-involved these creative types can be.

Only the hotel maids, hailing as they did from Old World cultures steeped in mysticism, understood what was going on. They wouldn't go anywhere near Harry's room, wouldn't even clean the transient's room next door to Harry. God-fearing Christian women, they held no truck with voodoo. But eventually Stanley began to put pressure on them to clean the rooms in that corridor, as the area was beginning to smell like a privy on a hot August day. Pushed to extremes, the maids knew they had to act to wipe this ungodly scourge off the earth. Biding their time, they waited until one day when Harry had stumbled into his room and collapsed in a drug-induced stupor, and then, armed respectively with broom, feather duster, and bucket and mop, the three large, formidable women advanced into the dingy corridor to clean out once and for all Harry's filthy den of perfidy.

Knowing enough to go after the master rather than his servant, the maids found Harry passed out on his bed, immobile and seemingly lifeless. They lit sacred deodorizing candles and took up their positions around the bed, chanting the words of darkness forbidden by their religion of light. After several minutes of such noise, Harry still did not stir.

"He's dead," the maid with the duster said, leaning over Harry.

"Don't get too close!" the one with the broom cautioned.

The duster-wielder put her head to Harry's chest. "There's no heartbeat." She poked him with her duster. "He's dead! The bastard's dead!"

"He's dead, he's dead!" the two of them chanted, dancing about the bed, poking Harry repeatedly with broom handle and dust mop.

The third maid, wanting to get in on the fun, raised her sopping mop from the bucket. "Should I give him the holy water?"

"Yeah! Give him the holy water, sister!" the other two sang out.

And the third maid raised her mop from the bucket and swung it over her shoulder in a broad arc, strewing soapy brown water all about the walls and ceiling, and brought it down with a resounding SPLAT! right square in Harry's face.

Sputtering and cursing, Harry sat bolt upright. His detailed knowledge of the occult allowed him immediately to intuit the gravity of the situation. Grimacing at the worst hangover of his life,

Harry reached under his bed and then sprang to his feet. And then the tiny, bearded, gray-haired man chased the three big maids down the hallway in his underwear, wielding a ceremonial Aztec dagger that he had stolen from the Met.

Harry's anonymous disciple had this to add:

> The problem was, they forgot to sacrifice the chicken! Can you believe it! Anybody who watches TV knows that! For anything related to voodoo you gotta sacrifice a chicken! In voodoo you gotta sacrifice a goddamn chicken to get outta bed in the morning! What a hoot! Harry and I spent many a night howling with laughter at their ignorant gaffe.

In the end, however, the maids' spells, amateurish as they no doubt were, seem to have weakened Harry. For he gave up the ghost not long after, singing, "I'm dying, I'm dying, I'm dying!" as he bubbled with excitement at the prospect of moving on to the next plane of existence.

Naturally, Harry made one final attempt to exercise control of the Zombie from beyond the grave. Unfortunately, he had spent too much time on string-figure collecting and ethnomusicology and not enough time on necromancy. It's a competitive art, and those who succeed in it these days are generally narrow specialists. Harry was one of the last of the Renaissance men, and ultimately he paid the price. Alas, his like will not soon be seen again.

After Harry was dead, as is well known, Allen Ginsberg and William Burroughs came to collect Harry's papers and films and other artifacts. Among these items was Paul the Zombie, still holed up in the hall closet. Ginsberg, in an attempt to draw Paul back to the world of the living, coaxed him into a lotus position and persuaded him to chant a few mantras, but this had no lasting effect. Burroughs, on seeing someone so down-and-out that even he could draw no inspiration from his existence, finally decided to sell out, and the result was his infamous Nike commercial. In the end, not even these giants of literature could figure out what to do with Paul, so they just left him in the closet, where he seemed happiest anyway.

Although the rent on the closet was actually fairly low, especially since Chelsea was a depressed neighborhood at the time, Paul the Zombie could not afford it; still believing himself to be dead, and correctly believing himself to be a deadhead, he saw no reason to get a job. And so, after a few months of hounding him, Stanley had no choice but to have Paul evicted. Since then, in between stints in the mental hospital, Paul sleeps in a cardboard box on 22nd Street, sneaking back into the Chelsea periodically or, when he manages to save enough money through panhandling, checking into one of the more modest rooms for a night or two of ungodly revelry.

The Swordsman

I remember my first night in the Chelsea. My girlfriend, Susan, and I had just spent hours moving in all our stuff—more than the guys at the desk had ever seen, they said. I was excited and a bit nervous to be in New York. Though I was dead tired, I couldn't sleep, so as Susan slept I sat up into the wee hours of the morning, drinking beer and listening to the radio.

At one point I had to piss. We shared a bathroom with two or three other rooms, so I put on my flip-flops and walked down the hall. I rounded the corner to the bathroom and came face to face with a huge, fat guy holding a sword. My heart jumped up into my throat and I took a step back when I saw him.

"I was just practicing here in the hall," the guy said, slurring his words, obviously drunk. He had long, coal-black hair that hung in a tangle, obscuring his face and making him look completely psychotic. "I've got a role in a Shakespeare play," he said. "I ducked around the corner when I heard you coming because I didn't want to scare you."

Nah, that wouldn't scare anybody: a big man with a sword lurking in a dimly lit hallway.

Bohemian Flophouse

The Truth about Those Fancy Hotels

Those fancy hotels work like this: first, they take your money, say for a week's stay, in advance. Then they gas you, so you either die or get fed up and leave early. In either case, they get to rent your room out again to some other sucker, thus doubling their money.

One night I was sitting in my tiny room in the Chelsea Hotel, drinking and writing. (My girlfriend, Susan, I think, was away on a business trip.) I had gone out for another six-pack, and had just got back into the hotel and was walking down the hallway toward my room. It was February, and the hall was freezing cold. One of the rooms on the hall had the door standing wide open; I could see inside it, and the window was wide open, too. An old woman with long, dyed-blond hair came out of the room, wearing a long suede coat and holding a sandwich. I had never seen her before.

"Hello," I said. "How are you?"

"I have to eat my dinner out here because my room is filled with smoke!" the woman screamed. Her eyes were darting back and forth in her head like she couldn't see very well. She didn't wear glasses, though it seemed like she needed them. There was no smoke in her room.

17

"That's terrible," I said. "Why is your room filled with smoke?"

"What the hell are you asking me for!? Why don't you ask them down at the front desk?!"

In those days the hotel was filled with crazies. We used to joke that the Chelsea was the last stop on the way to the nuthouse. Sometimes it made me wonder what I was doing there myself. Crazies and creative types: the line was kind of blurred.

But not in this case. "Well, can't talk now. Gotta run," I said, and turned my back on her and walked away down the hall.

She followed after me, screaming: "I don't want to talk to you! I'm just eating my dinner! Why are you asking me about the smoke?! Huh!? Why are you asking me about the smoke?! You've been living here for years! You know what's going on!"

At this point I had only been there for a few months. But I *was* beginning to get an inkling as to what was going on. They would rent these transient rooms out to just about anybody: pimps, prostitutes, con men, street hustlers—people who couldn't get a room elsewhere—often at exorbitant rates. The theory was, that kept the rent down for the permanent residents, the writers and artists and musicians.

Breaking into a run, the old woman hot on my heels, I made it to my door. On the verge of panic, I fumbled around finding the right key, but got it into the lock before the woman could catch up to me. I slipped inside and slammed the door in her face. Goddamn crazy bitch.

Something I had said or done really set the woman off. She screamed for two hours about how there was a conspiracy to kill her. The management of the hotel and the long-term residents were in cahoots in this plot. Unfortunately, the halls wrapped around in such a way that my window was directly across from hers. I couldn't concentrate on my work, and it didn't take long before the old woman was driving me nuts. I was grateful when she went out in the hall and screamed, though I don't think anybody else in the hotel appreciated it.

PART II: GHOSTS OF THE OLD HOTEL

Eventually someone must have complained—or more likely a lot of people, repeatedly, because that's what it would have taken to get a response. Anyway, one of the desk clerks came up and confronted the woman while she was in her room. I recognized his voice: it was a young Chinese man named Joe. I felt sorry for the poor guy for having to deal with this nut. He was obviously low man on the totem pole. He didn't have a very advanced command of the English language, or at least not good enough to talk his way out of this assignment. Joe knocked on her door and said, "Is there problem?"

"Damn straight there's a fucking problem!" the woman screamed.

"What is problem?" Joe asked.

"Can't you see?!"

"No," he said. Then he made a stab at it: "The window is open?"

"The fucking window is open because the fucking room is filled with smoke! I know that smell: you've been spraying for bugs! You assholes can't fool me! My late husband was an exterminator! I better not wake up in the morning with black eyes!"

Apparently, she believed that the inhalation of bug spray causes black eyes. I don't know whether this is true or not. Maybe she was making a faulty association, and the black eyes she had received in the past had been from beatings by her late husband, the exterminator. I could see him now: balding, potbellied, rough and unshaven after a hard day's work, drifting through the halls in his ectoplasmic fog of insecticide.

"No one has sprayed," Joe said. "I smell nothing."

"I know the score, you fucking asshole! I've been around! I know what goes on in these fancy hotels!" In her delusional state, the woman believed the Chelsea to be a fancy hotel.

That was the craziest thing the old woman had said yet. The hallways of the Chelsea were dimly lit by long fluorescent tubes, the linoleum in the corridors was worn, the plaster of the walls cracked, the paint peeling, and exposed wires and pipes jutted out from the ceiling. Even worse conditions prevailed in the rooms themselves. The cheap hotel furniture hadn't been replaced since at least the sixties and was rotting and falling apart. The carpets were stained and dirty. Some of the rooms were better than others, but they were all infested with roaches and mice. That was another thing that made the exterminator story so funny. I doubted there had been an exterminator in the place in years.

It hadn't always been like that. The Chelsea was once a luxury residence catering to the big shots of 23rd Street's bustling theater scene. Late at night, in the flickering fluorescent lights, it was kind of hazy in the hallways, and the past had a tendency to bleed through into the present. Then, if you used your imagination, you could see the lingering traces of the grand old hotel. The layers of peeling paint hid the fancy woodwork, and here and there a stained-glass transom had survived.

So perhaps the woman was remembering the good old days. I caught myself thinking that maybe she had lived here as a young woman, perhaps with her late husband, at the time a virile young exterminator in the prime of his life.

The only problem was that she wasn't old enough to remember that far back. As far back as the time of Dylan Thomas and even Thomas Wolfe, the place had been down at the heels. She would have been young in the fifties or sixties, when the place was a serious flophouse, on the order of a Bowery hotel. By that point the luxury suites had long since been chopped up into cubicles, like the one in which my girlfriend and I lived.

"Please do not curse me," Joe requested of the woman.

"They did this exact same thing to me at the Harold Johnson's!" That's what she said: *Harold* Johnson's. I guess she was under the delusion that that was a fancy hotel, too.

"I am sorry," Joe said.

"I want another room! Immediately!"

"No other rooms are available."

"I paid my $800!!!" That was apparently what they were charging her for a week's rent.

"You can have your money back and go someplace else."

"You're not getting rid of me that easy!"

Then she abruptly changed the subject. Your guess is as good as mine on this one. "And another thing," she screamed, "I want you to turn off this heat!"

"But it is February," Joe protested.

"I said no fucking heat!"

"It is thirty degrees out. You will freeze."

"I paid my fucking $800 and I say no heat!"

Joe went out and got the key that was used to adjust the temperature of the radiator. He came back and turned the radiator off. "There," he said, a tone of perverse satisfaction in his voice. "No heat."

But Joe wasn't getting off that easily. The woman returned to her favorite topic: "Can't you see this whole room is filled with smoke?!"

"You are blind, lady."

"I'm not fucking blind! I'm *legally* blind! That means I can see things up close, just not far away! Who told you I was fucking blind?! I'm not fucking blind, you asshole!"

"Please, you no curse me!" Joe pleaded.

"Can't I get a fucking clerk who fucking speaks fucking English?!"

"You no curse me, please!"

"You fucking foreign asshole!"

Joe finally got fed up with this abuse. "You are crazy lady!" he yelled at her.

"I'm not crazy!"

"YOU ARE!!!"

As Joe walked away down the hall, the woman came out of her room and screamed after him, "I better not wake up tomorrow with black eyes!"

PART III: THE POLICE INVESTIGATION

To save money, we had rented a room without a bathroom. Since I was drinking beer, I had to piss frequently, and since the bathroom was at the end of the hall, I had to walk past the woman several times during the night. The first few times I didn't say anything to her, and she didn't seem to recognize me. But one time, on the way back from the bathroom, I just couldn't help myself: "Sure is smoky in here," I said. Predictably, the woman screamed at me and ran after me again, but this time I had my key out and ready.

The woman continued to yell about the conspiracy—off and on—until about three in the morning. Then she finally wore herself out, closed her door, and was silent for the rest of the night.

But she was up at the crack of dawn. "Jesus Christ!" I said as I thrashed around in my bed. "This shit's gonna drive me to drink!" Since I had been up the night before, writing—and drinking—her rant hadn't completely unhinged me then, but it was a different story when I was trying to sleep. I pictured myself strangling her, shaking her by the neck until her body swung limp and her teeth rattled in her skull.

"You may kill me," the woman raved, as if she'd read my thoughts, "but you'd better dispose of my body good, because there'll be a police investigation!"

Well, I thought, at least she seems to have resigned herself to her fate. I only hoped that somebody would hurry up and gas her to death so I could go back to sleep. With any luck, the police wouldn't wake me up for questioning.

And then she started singing "God Bless America" over and over again. She was being ironic, of course, and so it was kind of funny, but I would have much rather slept. The woman sang poorly, in a hoarse, throaty cackle, and the joke soon wore thin. Once in a while she would switch to "Glory, Glory Hallelujah," and that came as a welcome relief—even though she didn't know all the words.

But then something occurred to me. In her blindness, through the haze of the dimly lit halls, what the old woman glimpsed may not have been the past but rather the future of the Chelsea. The hotel, like the city itself, was on the verge of a transformation. In a year or two the fluorescent tubes would be gone, shining new globes in their place, as would the linoleum, replaced by inlaid wood. Soon there wouldn't be any room for her kind here. Even now, the old bohemians were dying off, or drifting on. Rents were going up. The Chelsea was gradually being gentrified.

The woman seemed determined to sing all day. A jackhammer would have been preferable. A bullet to the head, and then a blissful oblivion.

Giving up on the notion of sleep, I put on my clothes and went out to get a cup of coffee. The woman was leaning against the wall, singing boisterously, but also coughing and sniffling between her verses—probably the result of sleeping with the window open in February.

Along with the coffee, I picked up some beer and cigarettes and a sandwich so I wouldn't have to go out again. Back on my floor, the old woman was still in the hallway. I took a better look at her this time. Her hair had come out of its curl and was dangling limply, its gray roots having worked their way up during the night. Her clothes, the same as the day before, were rumpled. Her makeup was smeared, as if she had slept in it. She had quit singing for the moment. She was looking into a small mirror and smearing some kind of black stuff under her eyes. I didn't speak to her, and she showed no signs of recognizing me from the night before.

PART IV: ANOTHER SORT OF HOTEL

The old woman wore herself out early from singing all day and went into her room and closed the door at about nine o'clock that evening. I was still pissed off about having been deprived of sleep. By this point I was so angry, in fact, that I couldn't even write once it was quiet. As the night wore on, all I could think of was revenge. At about midnight I threw open my window and stuck my head out to see if I could see into the woman's room. Her lights were out and there was no sound coming from within. No smell of gas either. If I had had a smoke bomb, I would have heaved it in through the woman's window. I've got to remember to keep some of those suckers on hand.

I thought about dressing all in black and going over there to perform an exorcism, but I would have needed a suitable text. (I wished I had held onto my copy of *Naked Lunch*, written by William Burroughs while he was living here. That would have scared that bitch!) Unfortunately, I had sold off most of my books before I moved into my closet at the Chelsea.

Anyway, I had a better idea. I drained my beer for courage and headed out into the hall. I got the fire extinguisher down off its hook, walked over to the crazy woman's door, and banged on it good and hard. Harder than necessary. It was taking her a while to answer, so I banged some more. She appeared at the door in her bathrobe, with her coat over the top of it. A blast of cold air hit me in the face.

"What the hell?!" she screamed, her eyes darting back and forth. "Who are you?!"

I held the fire extinguisher in one hand and the hose in the other. "I'm the exterminator," I said.

For just a moment, her face showed terror. "What?! What do you want?!"

"I'm here to spray your room."

The woman just totally went off: fucking this and fucking that. I thought she was going to attack me for a minute, the way she was thrashing her arms around. I got away from her quickly, almost running. The time I took to hang up the fire extinguisher probably would have given her a chance to catch me, but something must have given her pause. She just screamed; she didn't chase.

And really, I don't know what she had to complain about. You'd think she would have appreciated this independent confirmation of her theory. But maybe she just hated her late husband, the exterminator, so much that she couldn't bear to be reminded of him. Poor man, at least now he's at rest. For the second night in a row, the woman screamed long into the night.

They got rid of the old woman when her week ran out. I was surprised: I thought she was going to be one of those who barricade themselves in their rooms and refuse to leave. We get a lot of those cases around here, people whom they just keep on gassing, but who never seem to take the hint. Anyway, she went on her way to cause trouble elsewhere: hopefully to the nuthouse, but most likely just back to the good ol' Harold Johnson's.

Indie Rockers Cash In:
Ryan Adams at the Chelsea

There's a phenomenon my girlfriend, Susan, and I have noticed of late: young singers check into the Chelsea, write a few songs, then use the hip cachet of the hotel to sell records. Good for them—so long as they get out while the getting's good. Examples include Rufus Wainwright, Keren Ann, and Hank Williams Jr.'s daughter Holly Williams.

Recently, as well, a singer named Ryan Adams has become very popular. Actually, I guess he's been popular for a while, but I didn't pay any attention to him until now, since I usually only listen to jazz. But the other day I saw his picture in a magazine and said, hey, didn't that guy used to live at the Chelsea? In fact, if I'm thinking of the right guy, he lived next door to us about ten years ago when we lived on the third floor. A slender fellow in his early twenties, he only lived there for a few months, and in that time I probably spoke to him about two or three times, at most. We were both pretty reclusive. He stayed in his room, and once in a while I heard him plucking on his guitar. I stayed in my room and typed on my computer.

Born on November 5, 1974, in Jacksonville, North Carolina, Ryan had a brief run-in with punk rock before setting out on the alt-country road to fame. He formed his first country band, Whiskeytown, in 1994. They disbanded in 1999, and Ryan released his first solo album, *Heartbreaker*, in 2000. Since then he has been extremely prolific, releasing at least seven albums and a couple of EPs in addition to numerous bootlegs. Due perhaps to his love affair with the bottle, Ryan has a notoriously unstable temperament, a tendency illustrated by a couple of fairly hilarious incidents. Once, at a concert, some guy in the audience jokingly requested that Ryan play the song, "Summer of 69" by the bad eighties rocker Bryan Adams. Ryan was not amused; he freaked out and had the guy thrown out of the building. (The guy should have just requested "Freebird" like he does at everybody else's shows.) Another time, a music critic named Jim DeRogatis had the temerity to pan one of Ryan's shows, saying he was tired of Ryan's bad-boy behavior and the whole troubled-artist routine. Understandably upset, Ryan self-medicated with Jack Daniels and left a ranting message on DeRogatis's answering machine: ". . . fuck you man, like fuck you, you asshole. . . . You obviously have a problem with me. Not with the music, because you can't refute it. Because it's too fucking good, and you know it is . . . you are really, obviously, one of those guys who comes to gigs and bums people out and just stands around with your fucking notepad." Yeah, I hate those guys. They know where they can stick those fucking notepads.

Ryan Adams definitely lived in the Chelsea at some point, perhaps on a couple of different occasions. Although, addled by drink as I typically was in those days, I can't swear it was him, for the sake of argument I'm going to refer to the guy next door as Ryan. So anyway, one day I noticed I hadn't heard Ryan moving around in his room for a while. A couple of weeks went by, and I just figured he had moved out. But then one afternoon I came back from the deli and saw him in front of his door loading up a luggage cart. Looked like he had an amp and some other musical equipment.

"Hey, you moving out?" I said. "Sorry to lose you. You need any help?"

"No thanks, I've only got a few things," Ryan said.

"All right, well, good luck," I said. He seemed like an okay guy, and I thought, well, too bad I never got to know him. I went into my room and closed the door.

Ryan was very productive during his stay at the hotel and wrote a whole album of songs, entitled *Love Is Hell.* It's not a very original title, but it is a good album. Although on the album Ryan seems bored and depressed, at times nearly suicidal—lying in bed without the energy to close his window as the snow and rain blows into his room—and acts like he can't wait to get out of this God-forsaken place, his time at the Chelsea appears to have been well spent.

There are two songs on the album that reference the hotel directly. On the best of these, "Hotel Chelsea Nights," Ryan implies that he was involved with a girl who lived up the hall from him in the Chelsea. Discounting the schizophrenic old ladies on the floor, I can't imagine who this muse might have been. Then, as now, there seemed to be an unending stream of attractive young would-be starlets sashaying through these halls, doing the bohemian trip, living here a couple of weeks or a couple of months—in rare cases never leaving, growing old and weird along with the rest of us. Perhaps it was Parker Posey or Alanis Morissette, or Beth Orton, or even Winona Ryder, all of whom Ryan dated at one time or another—though I sure as hell don't remember seeing any of them around here. I like to think it was Brooke Humphries, who lived on our floor at about the same time. Brooke was the one who hid club kid Michael Alig in her room after he murdered that drug dealer and cut him up and threw him in the river. Love would have been hell indeed.

In the same song, Ryan says that 23rd Street is "strung out like some Christmas lights, out here in the Chelsea night." I think this is an apt description of the street as seen from above at night from the windows of the Chelsea. But Ryan also uses this as a metaphor for his emotional state—that is, he himself is strung out—suggesting some familiarity with the use and abuse of drugs. All of which leads me to wonder if he was one of the junkies nodding off in my bathroom in those bad old days. Were those his dirty needles I had to pick up? Was that his blood left strewn about on the floor and the fixtures? Son of a bitch!

(Actually, I'm only joking about the drugs. I have no evidence for that, and Ryan seemed saner than the majority of the people around here—which is probably why he was so eager to leave!)

Another thing I wonder is if Ryan was influenced by *The Willie Nelson Christmas Album,* which some lunatic who lived above us was in the habit of playing over and over at around this time. This fact alone could account for the bleak tone of Ryan's album.

Not long after I talked to him in the hall, I heard somebody banging on Ryan's door. It took a while—Ryan was probably sacked out in bed, too depressed to move—but he finally opened the door. It was Stanley Bard's voice I heard next.

"I want my money," our proprietor said, pointedly.

"I have to wait for my advance check from the record company," Ryan replied.

I almost burst out laughing. Yeah, right! Now I've heard everything. I had to move away from the door lest they hear my stifled snickers. In any event, though he didn't crack up laughing like me, I doubt that Stanley believed the story about the record contract either. Certainly, he didn't let the guy out of the hotel with any of his stuff that day. So maybe it was Ryan and maybe it wasn't, but if it was, I guess in the end he showed us.

Herman Melville at the Chelsea
(or Close, Anyway)

Around the corner from the Chelsea on Seventh Avenue, a homeless man, apparently drunk, was mediating a dispute between two of his similarly situated buddies: "Nah, you know the story of Moby Dick, don't you? They didn't call him that because he bit his dick off! He bit his leg off! That's why he walked with a peg leg."

Well, that clears things up. No need to use a peg leg just because you got your dick bit off. I noticed, however, that the man seemed possibly to be confusing Ahab with the white whale. More importantly, if the name "Moby Dick"—as applied to either man or whale—doesn't refer to a bitten-off dick, then to what on earth does it refer? I guess I should have stopped and told the men that I, too, was interested in literary criticism. Perhaps together we could have solved this riddle.

The Willie Nelson Christmas Album: Harry Smith at the Chelsea

There are a lot of musicians living at the Chelsea, good ones as well as bad. They practice all the time, day and night, and most any type of music is tolerated, from jazz, to classical, to rock and roll.

Even so, there are limits. One holiday season, the person living directly above me acquired *The Willie Nelson Christmas Album*. This album involves Willie singing the old standards—"Jingle Bells," "Silent Night," "The Little Drummer Boy"—only with a guitar and a country twang. It was a little bit interesting, maybe, the first couple of times. But it got old really fast. Like the traditional holiday season, the playing of this album began around Thanksgiving and went on from there—not just once or twice a day, but repeatedly, morning, noon, and night.

It was a young guy named William who was playing it. I could tell by his voice, as he often sang along. Apparently, he was really trying to get into the Christmas spirit, psyching himself up. A rich kid who fancied himself a poet, William was the kind of guy who went from one fad to the next and didn't do things in half measures but really went all out. As soon as one side of the album would finish, he would flip it to the other, over and over again. The pauses between sides were maddening: maybe this will be the end, I prayed each time.

But I had only been in New York a year or so, and I still had plenty of patience. Knowing William, I knew that sooner or later he would get sick of the album, and then he would never play it again. In the meantime I tried to keep my window closed.

Come to find out, I wasn't the only one who was annoyed. When I came out of my room to go to the bathroom one afternoon, I saw Ray standing in the open door of his tiny room, 328, which also happened to be Harry Smith's old room. As he was a painter, Ray had replaced Harry's stacks of boxes with stacks of canvases. I had become accustomed to thinking of Ray as the archetypal New Yorker, I guess because of his gruffness, though it turns out he was from Minnesota. Ray had been working on a canvas, and he wore his paint-spattered work clothes. His long black hair, too, was speckled with paint.

"Who in God's name is making that infernal racket?" he asked crossly. "How in the hell am I supposed to work? I have my art to do, my painting. How can I maintain inspiration with this insipid garbage echoing through my brain. Who is doing it?" he demanded. "Who!?" He acted almost like I was responsible.

"I think it's William," I said.

"That figures! I'd like to go up there and wring his scrawny neck! It's driving me fucking crazy. It's like cats yowling! What is his problem? Listen to it once, then give it a rest, you asshole! And turn down the fucking volume, for Christ's sake. Jesus. Has he got the record player in the window or something?" Ray gestured toward his window.

Ray's window, I could see, was wide open. He had to keep it open when he was working to avoid being asphyxiated by the paint fumes. In general, there was too much heat in the back of the building anyway. In the brief pause in our conversation, we heard strains of Willie's guitar as he crooned, "Have a holly, jolly Christmas. . . ."

"Who the hell wants to hear that shit?!" Ray said. "Nobody could! It's inconceivable!"

I.T.

He seemed to be implying that William was doing it purposely to drive him crazy. "Yeah, it is kind of annoying," I said, chuckling.

Ray scowled at my levity. "I'd like to tear his head off and shit down his neck!" he said, like some kind of demented bohemian drill sergeant.

"I wouldn't go that far," I said.

"Yeah, but you're from Tennessee, right?"

"Uh, yeah," I said. Close enough, I figured, for the sake of argument.

"For you it's different," Ray proclaimed. "For you, that music is a way of life."

It made me wonder what sort of misconceptions he was harboring, of Southerners in general and of myself in particular. Like most of my friends, I had grown up listening to the Beatles and Led Zeppelin.

"You mean Christmas music?" I asked.

As I mentioned, Ray lived in Harry Smith's old room, 328, the room that shared the corridor with our room and Ryan Adams's room. Ray had lived there since they had cleared out Harry's room, which took them some time, apparently, since Harry was a notorious pack rat. Unjustly obscure, Smith was perhaps most influential as a filmmaker. A book called *American Magus*, consisting of interviews with Harry's friends and acquaintances, came out on him a few years after his death, and that's where I've gotten most of my information about him—though sometimes older Chelsea residents tell stories about him as well.

Harry was born in 1923 in Portland, Oregon, and grew up on an Indian reservation, where his mother was a teacher. His parents were Theosophists, which no doubt contributed to his lifelong obsession with magic and the occult. Short and slight, with his wisp of a beard, he actually looked like a troll or a gnome or some sort of elemental being. After a year or two studying anthropology in college, he settled in San Francisco, where he established a reputation as a painter and underground filmmaker. But he soon moved to New York, where he was to live, for the most part, for the rest of his life.

Harry's paintings are mandala-like, composed of weird swirling colors and alchemical symbology. He was uncannily attuned to the rhythms in life and music and based many of his early paintings on the jazz of Monk, Parker, and Gillespie, attending their club dates and painstakingly recording each note of their performances, then reproducing these in brushstrokes on the canvas. He used much the same method in many of his early animated films, the most famous of which include *Mahogany, Heaven and Earth Magic,* and *The Tin Woodsman's Dream,* and was the among the first to develop frame-by-frame hand painting of films. Sadly, Harry stopped painting once he started drinking heavily, as his style required precision and a firm hand. In the sixties he switched to live action in his films.

In the fifties Harry compiled his *American Folk Music Anthology* for Folkways Records. Recorded mainly from old 78s—some of them very rare, with only a few copies in existence—which Harry collected in used record stores in San Francisco, the anthology introduced a new generation of musicians to the music of such folk masters as Doc Boggs, the Carter Family, and Mississippi John Hurt. Some say Harry single-handedly brought about the folk music revival of the early sixties, but in any event he had a profound effect on the musicians who gathered in the coffee shops of Greenwich Village in those days. Bob Dylan, another old Chelsea resident, based several of his songs on recordings from the anthology. In the last year of his life, 1991, Harry was awarded a special Grammy for his work on the anthology.

Harry was an ethnomusicologist and made field recordings as well. One of Harry's most famous recordings is of a Kiowa Peyote ceremony, which he attended on the invitation of Indians he met while in jail for drunkenness in Oklahoma. Back in New York, he recorded the ambient sounds of the city, sticking a microphone out the window of his room at the Chelsea to document the daily rhythm of the street life below. (He listened to the tapes over and over in order to discern patterns.) While living in a Bowery flophouse, he recorded the sounds of the down-and-out men in the surrounding cubicles, including the death throes of the old and sick. Here, too, he found a certain rhythm.

Harry obsessively collected and cataloged records, books (including a large number of pop-up books), cassette tapes, gourds, Ukrainian Easter eggs, tarot and playing cards, folk crafts, cheap plastic toys, and all kinds of pop ephemera. Of special interest are his collections of mounted string figures, of which he had thousands, and paper airplanes from all over the country, which he donated to the National Air and Space Museum. He stored these collections in whatever apartment he was living in at the time, and with friends, and basically with whoever would have them. (As I, too, am a pack rat, this makes Harry a character dear to my heart.)

A true polymath, in his early work Harry seemed on the verge of synthesizing his myriad influences. But alcohol and amphetamine abuse weakened him: though basically good-natured, in his later years he became ill-tempered and belligerent. An all-around weirdo, Harry had an abiding interest in magic and alchemy, the cabala, and all things occult. As I mentioned earlier, he was a disciple of Satanist and fellow drug abuser Aleister Crowley and a bishop of the Ordo Templi Orientis, Crowley's mystical society. He liked to keep birds as pets, and when they died he stored them in the freezer. Asexual, Harry didn't like for people to touch him. However, he once took a "spiritual wife." To consummate their marriage he marched the young girl up the Bowery, instructing her to kiss each of the hundred or so derelicts they encountered on their walk. They were both rip-roaring drunk, however, and the girl didn't seem to mind.

Harry refused to sell his work for money, although he was willing to trade it for drugs or for the books and records he was constantly buying. He was known to destroy his films and paintings in fits of rage, and a lot of his best work (and boxes of his collections as well) was thrown out or stolen by landlords when he was evicted from various places for not paying his rent. Always virtually penniless, he survived by bumming money off Allen Ginsberg—with whom he lived in the East Village for a time—and the rest of his friends. In his later years the Grateful Dead (who, legend has it, once performed a concert on the roof of the Chelsea) gave him a ten-thousand-dollar-a-year fellowship to honor his work on the folk anthology.

Harry lived here at the Chelsea off and on in the sixties, seventies, and eighties. In the seventies he lived on the seventh floor but moved out because he thought the building was becoming too violent; he had apparently been assaulted by one of his acquaintances. Becoming increasingly frail in his final years, he died in 1991, coughing up blood, in Room 328 of the Chelsea. Harry famously faced death singing: "I'm dying, I'm dying, I'm dying!" Not too original, admittedly, especially for a genius of his caliber, but still not bad, considering the circumstances. It takes a real man to go out singing.

The guy who sublet us Room 332 knew Harry Smith. Gerald told us when Harry lived there, his room was piled to the ceiling with boxes of junk, so that there was hardly any space to move around. Harry couldn't even open the door all the way because there were boxes stacked behind it. He said that after Harry died his room remained sealed up for several months, since nobody could figure out what to do with all the stuff, and of course Stanley—by no means your average run-of-the mill landlord—knew better than to just throw it away.

One day, Gerald recounts, he came home and saw several people standing in the corridor outside Harry's room. Others were inside the room, moving boxes around. As he squeezed through the men to get to his door, who should come out of Harry's room but Allen Ginsberg himself: round-bellied, bespectacled, gray-haired, and bearded. Gerald stood there staring at him for several moments but was too shocked to say anything.

"I could hear them out there for a long time talking," Gerald said. "And I could hear them moving things around, and I wanted to go out there and introduce myself to Ginsberg, but I was kind of intimidated. Here's this guy I've idolized my whole life, I mean, this great poet! But I really wanted to tell him how much I admired his work. Finally, I had to go out anyway, and so I worked up the nerve and opened my door.

"There were some guys standing around and they had some boxes on a luggage rack, but I didn't see Ginsberg. I said hi to those guys and tried to get a look in Harry's room, but I couldn't see anything. I walked on down the hall, disappointed that I had missed my chance.

"I was cursing myself for not talking to Ginsberg," Gerald went on, "and not really paying attention to what I was doing. I guess I must've had my head down, because I remember looking up, and when I did, who should I see coming through the door at the end of the hall, but William Burroughs!"

Ginsberg and Burroughs both lived in the Chelsea in the late fifties and early sixties, as did Jack Kerouac. Burroughs wrote *Naked Lunch* here. (And I don't know why he doesn't have a plaque on the front of the building!) But anyway, when two-thirds of the Holy Trinity of Beatdom turn out for a shot at the spoils, you know you've got a significant figure here. And Kerouac, of course, was indisposed at the time.

———————

Harry didn't collect everything, however. Notoriously—several people around the hotel have mentioned this to me—Harry used to throw his trash out the window onto the roof of the synagogue next door. Some think this was a symptom of anti-Semitism on his part, while others maintain that Harry himself was part Jewish, so who knows? Personally, I think it was probably just the easiest way to get rid of his trash. Which leads me to suspect that part of his collecting, too, had to do with the fact that he just didn't feel like walking the paper airplanes and string figures down the hall to the trash bin, so he cataloged them and put them in boxes. Disgusted that there were certain things he couldn't collect, like rotting fruit and old containers of Chinese food, he flung these from his window. On the other hand, it would have been easier simply to throw them down into the courtyard below. As his window faces south, and the synagogue is to the west of the hotel, he would have had to lean out the window and sling the trash in order to get it onto the roof. In his later years, Harry had trouble with his legs and couldn't walk so well, but I suppose there was nothing wrong with his arms.

(Years later, the folks at the synagogue had their revenge—if not exactly on the right person, at least on a resident of the offending corridor—an episode which I recount later in the book in my story "The Transformative Power of Dirt.")

Not only nutballs lived down this corridor. Later, after we were gone, a very nice girl with pink hair moved into Room 328. She wore pink clothes and painted the room and everything else she came in contact with pink as well. (Come to think of it, that's a little nutty too.) You can see her picture, taken in Harry Smith's old room, in Rita Barros's photo book, *Chelsea Hotel: Fifteen Years*. She was a painter, she said, but mostly I think she was just a walking work of art herself. I wonder what Harry would think of his room now: pink. He'd probably put a hex on the girl. Or maybe he'd marry her—spiritually, of course.

And, oh, as far as I know, Willie Nelson never lived at the Chelsea.

How to Score a Pad at the Chelsea

Whenever we tell people we live at the Chelsea, they invariably ask us, "How the hell did you get a place there?" It's very difficult, you see, and most people get turned away. Here's the story.

We had always dreamed about moving to New York, my girl-friend, Susan, and I, but we just could never get around to it. I had always wanted to be a writer and I knew that New York was the place to achieve my goal. I had been teaching philosophy, becoming more and more frustrated because it wasn't what I really wanted to do. I finally got fed up at the university and quit, and then—luckily, it turns out—Susan's job ended too, so there was nothing to keep us in Washington, DC. This was toward the end of 1995.

Susan found a job in New York, so she went first to find us an apartment while I stayed in DC and wrapped up our business there, finished the semester of teaching, and got our stuff ready to move. She stayed at a place down on the Bowery called the Pioneer Hotel, in a little room only big enough for a bed and a TV mounted on the wall.

The first place Susan tried was the Chelsea Hotel. We'd dreamed of living in the Chelsea Hotel for almost as long as we'd dreamed of living in New York. We knew it was where Thomas Wolfe had lived, where the Beats and the Warhol people had hung out. She spoke to Stanley Bard, the owner, and unfortunately—though predictably enough—he didn't have anything available.

Outside of that, there was nothing in our price range in even moderately decent neighborhoods. Susan visited a lot of places on the Lower East Side that were little more than crack houses, and converted factory buildings in the garment district where you surely would have been killed coming home late at night.

Finally, somewhat desperately, Susan started looking at sublets. She answered an ad for one in our price range, and it turned out to be at the Chelsea Hotel. The guy who was renting it was a singer and guitar player named Gerald. Gerald was making a living as a studio musician in Nashville but still holding onto the dream of big-time success in New York with a band of his own. Susan told him of her love for the hotel and how she'd always dreamed of living there. Gerald wanted somebody who appreciated the hotel, as that's important to most everybody who lives here. His only reservation was that she was a woman, since women tend not to like the idea of a shared bathroom, he said. It was a tiny room, but the rent was ridiculously low since Gerald had been living there since the seventies.

The only catch was, two or three times a year we had to move out for two weeks so Gerald could come back to town and play a few gigs with his band. This was really less of a problem than it seemed, since the room, though small, had abundant storage space for our stuff in a loft Gerald had built above the bed. And since the rent was cheap, we had plenty of money left over for a hotel room—at the Pioneer, anyway. It was like a little vacation in Chinatown twice a year.

Once we were in the door of the Chelsea we probably could have gotten our own place at any time: so badly did Stanley Bard hate the idea of subletting that I think he would have rented us a place just to thwart this abuse. But we had agreed to stay in Gerald's place for at least a year. In February 1997, Stanley gave us our own place, which, though still small, was much larger than Gerald's room. Our new room was on the eighth floor, with a view of Uptown and the Empire State Building. We got what we wanted after all—our first choice.

As for Gerald, he was back to square one; he kept it up for a few more years after that, subletting his room for a few months at a time, coming to town a couple of times a year to re-form his band and play a couple of gigs. We went to see Gerald and his band play a couple of times, and they were pretty damn good, real professionals, a lot better than most of the kids who are getting record contracts these days.

A big Italian guy whose hair was once long and black, Gerald was now balding and graying. He was self-conscious of that fact and wore a wig for performances. One time I commented on it jokingly—I don't remember what I said, but I'm pretty bald myself, so I'm sure my remark was meant to be self-deprecating—and he took it rather badly and had to cut me down in return. He called me a red-faced Irishman, not very nicely. He was sensitive about it, obviously, and I think he felt his age was what was holding him back.

We haven't seen Gerald in many years. I guess he gave up the room in the end. But he allowed us in, allowed us to live our dream, and so, in a way, his dream continues, as we've taken it up for him. And no matter what happens from here on out, we did get to the Chelsea, at least. That counts for something in my book.

Bathroom Hijinks

The Manatee: Hiroya, Part I

Hiroya was a fat young Japanese man with a broad, round, jovial face. He wore red, paint-spattered overalls over a striped T-shirt. His coal-black hair was long, wild, unkempt. "I be famous painter," he told us when we met him, about a year after Susan and I moved into the Chelsea. "I come to Chelsea for art. Now I paint. I make money. I be famous." He didn't speak English well—though he spoke it quickly and at length—and at first we couldn't understand him at all. He was raving, manic: a lunatic. It wasn't long before he was dragging his paintings out into the hallway on the eighth floor, setting up a show for us, explaining his technique and his symbolism in as much detail as we could bear. We loved his work, however, and—because Susan insisted; I was far too cheap—we were among the first people in New York to buy his paintings.

Hiroya's art was like his person: wild, colorful, unrestrained; he splashed it over large canvases. He had his own symbolic language that he used in his paintings: railroad tracks, ghosts, crosses, coffins, all in giddy profusion. Graffiti-inspired, Hiroya's art could be somber and eerie or buoyant and playful, but it was never less than energetic.

Hiroya's capacity for work was huge, as was, apparently, his budget. (He was from a wealthy Japanese family, who had sent him to New York—it's my theory anyway—to get him out of Japan. Obviously he would have been an embarrassment to any halfway respectable family.) Every day he would set out rows of canvases that I had never seen before, large, ambitious paintings, stringing them all up and down the hall, and there would be an art show in the hotel. Hiroya's art may not have been strictly original, but he had enough vitality in his person to make up for it and to lend to his art a reflected life.

I, too, inspired by the thrill of being in New York, was going through a period of heightened creativity at this point, writing story after story, and I think I saw something of myself in Hiroya.

Hiroya's true originality, and the thing I envied in him the most, lay in the art of self-promotion. He would lurk in the lobby and pounce on the unsuspecting, trumpeting his artistic talents and achievements, his one goal being to lure his hapless victim upstairs to look at his paintings. He would show his work to whomever he could convince to look at it: art critics, rock stars, tourists, auto mechanics, didn't matter. "You buy now, soon won't be so cheap," he would tell these people. "I be in gallery, then you talk with dealer. He charge much, much more. A hundred times." If you had come into the Chelsea looking for a colorful bohemian character, then this was your lucky day. And if you were really lucky, Hiroya would perform a Butoh skit for you right there in the lobby. Many people, including some famous ones, bought his paintings, even though Hiroya had a perverse, self-defeating habit of refusing to sell to anyone he didn't like, no matter what the price.

As you might imagine, Hiroya was a polarizing figure, and opinions of him soon fell into two camps: those who loved him, or at least tolerated him, and those who flat-out despised him and could scarcely bear the sight of him. His energy and his talent and his playful sense of humor were what people loved about him. Because he *was* quite funny. He was a trickster; he knew how to press people's buttons. He had a talent for ridiculing people who took themselves too seriously, a rare gift for exposing their pretensions. He would find out what they were sensitive about and keep harping on it until it drove them crazy. For instance, if you were a pompous, self-important artist, he would find a really stupid picture in a magazine, and insist that your work was just like that, and that that was why he admired it so.

There was a dapper man named Jimmy who used to hang around the lobby a lot, waiting for it to get late enough to go to a bar and get drunk. (Not a bad guy, though rather long-winded and self-important; I myself drank with him many a night at the El Quijote next door.) One time Hiroya asked him, "What you do?" and Jimmy, one of the few people in the hotel who had no creative pursuit, made the mistake of saying, "I'm rather a man-about-town." Forever afterward, that was what Hiroya called him, mockingly, every time he saw him.

The desk staff, in particular, disliked Hiroya, I would almost say loathed him, with a passion that knew no bounds. It was understandable, I guess, since they had to deal with him every day, and over time his act must've worn quite thin. When there was nobody else in the lobby to talk to, Hiroya would pester them mercilessly.

When Hiroya first arrived in New York, he didn't know anyone in the art world. The New York art scene is an insular one, and they don't just automatically let people into it because they say they're great artists. So Hiroya needed some sort of publicity stunt to draw attention to his work. He found his gimmick in the Bunny paintings. These are just what they sound like: generally small in size, but ranging from 8-by-12 inches up to, say, 23-by-48 inches, these canvases, in bright neon colors, depict a bunny, simply drawn and usually holding a carrot, above Hiroya's overlarge signature. Sometimes these paintings also bear a slogan, such as 180% Cool, or I Love Chelsea Hotel. Hiroya produced hundreds of these in a range of color combinations and of varying degrees of complexity. First he handed them out to anybody in the hotel who wanted one and then he started hawking them around the neighborhood. He gave them to all the shopkeepers, and soon you couldn't step into a deli or a dry cleaner or a shoe store anywhere near the hotel without seeing a Hiroya Bunny, sometimes displayed proudly in the window or behind the counter, at other times wedged in behind a cooler or a cabinet.

It seemed that no one could refuse the Bunnies: they were cute, after all, and Hiroya was such a friendly guy, so insistent, and so weirdly charismatic. The culmination of this phase of Hiroya's career was what he referred to as "The Seven Hundred Feet of Bunnies." In the Barnes and Noble store on Sixth Avenue Hiroya hung dozens of bunnies, in all the shades of the rainbow, from the railings of the second floor overlooking the retail floors of the book and music departments. I can't imagine how he convinced them to let him do this, but in the end it was indeed quite a spectacle.

But Hiroya was impatient. When nothing seemed to come of the Bunnies, when they didn't get him the attention he craved, he started drinking heavily and put on even more weight. Hiroya had never been much of a drinker before, and so this was a surprising development. He seemed desperate for some sort of artistic identity: he drank because he became convinced that that's what painters were supposed to do, and he drank even more once he saw that it annoyed people. Unfortunately, he couldn't hold his liquor well, and at one point he got so drunk that he passed out in the lobby and couldn't be revived, and they had to take him to the emergency room. I, too, was drinking heavily, smoking, getting fat and unhealthy myself, and I contributed to Hiroya's problem—more knowingly than I really like to admit—when I gave him a quart of bourbon one Christmas. I liked to see people in the same boat as myself, I guess. Hiroya was even more of a clown, more entertaining, when drunk. But I think it's likely that the drinking affected his judgment and weakened him for what was to come.

───────────

Hiroya's fatal flaw was his desire to please. That was the flip side of his relentless self-promotion. He needed to be tough, as self-promoters usually seem to be, but for Hiroya, his self-promotion was a fragile thing. He was desperate for approval—you could see it at times—in a rather pathetic and ultimately self-defeating way.

One afternoon I came home to find that Hiroya had mounted yet another of his impromptu exhibits in our hall. Hiroya himself was nowhere to be seen, but a tall, skinny, fortyish, blond-haired woman, in a long skirt and Birkenstocks, was standing there amidst his paintings. "I've commissioned your neighbor, the artist Hiroya, to undertake a painting for me," she said, speaking in a pompous, affected tone.

"That's great," I replied.

"He is absolutely a wonderful artist. I just admire his art so much."

"Oh, I do too."

"That's why I've commissioned him to undertake a painting of a manatee."

"A manatee?" I asked, incredulous.

"A manatee is a large sea mammal," the woman informed me, condescendingly.

"Yes," I replied.

"I simply adore sea mammals," she explained. "I think they're among the finest sort of mammals. Don't you? Especially manatees. So noble and intelligent."

I almost burst out laughing. But the woman was serious, and I didn't want to upset her. "They *are* pretty high up there on the list," I said. Despite the fact that there were a dozen large canvases spread out in the hall, I wondered if she had even really bothered to look at Hiroya's art.

The woman was obviously disturbed. Not that it was any surprise to meet a disturbed person wandering our hallowed halls, but this woman was disturbed in an unusual way for the Chelsea: she was a New Ager, a nature lover, the kind who go around with T-shirts with pictures of lovable wolves on them. And that's the

49

kind of thing she wanted Hiroya to paint: a cuddly T-shirt portrayal of a manatee.

I found the whole thing rather hard to swallow. When I talked to him about it later, Hiroya, sensing my disapproval, was apologetic. "She pay five hundred dollars," he said. "It no good, I know. But I make what people like."

The New Age woman was the kind of person Hiroya would have ridiculed if he had had his wits about him. Instead, befuddled by his craving for approval, seduced by the least show of attention, he produced a cartoonish gray manatee, frolicking beneath a yellow sun in a foamy sea of aquamarine. The woman even made him paint the noble sea mammal on an oval canvas, of all things! The result, predictably enough, was a complete piece of junk.

Ironically, Hiroya kind of looked like the manatee he had drawn: fat and rather sluggish, yet cute in a roly-poly sort of way. I came to view the manatee painting as a tragic self-portrait. Intentional or not, Hiroya always did have a good sense of humor about such things.

Nanny by Trade

One of the coolest places in the hotel is the El Quijote, the Spanish restaurant in what used to be the Chelsea's dining room. Decorated with garish murals of Don Quijote jousting with windmills, it opened in 1936 and looks like it hasn't been remodeled since.

One night my girlfriend, Susan, and I were drinking at the El Q's ancient wooden bar when in walked a girl in her mid-twenties whom we had seen earlier that night in the hotel. She was scantily clad and heavily tattooed. She had a huge tattoo on her arm of a naked devil girl: bright red, voluptuous, with horns and a tail. "That's a nice tattoo," Susan said. It really was a fine piece of work. The girl said her name was Courtney. She said that although she wanted eventually to become an artist, in the meantime she was a nanny, as she said, "by trade."

The bar was filling up. A family came in and stood behind us: a father and mother and three children, the oldest a teenage boy. As they waited for their table, Courtney struck up a conversation with them. In particular, she seemed interested in the teenage boy and flirted with him, at one point actually asking him to come visit her later that night in her room at the Chelsea. The boy was much too shy to talk to her, though he did smile and seemed to relish the attention. But she was making the rest of the family extremely uncomfortable, and they were visibly relieved when the waitress finally came to seat them.

We thought Courtney had just been joking, and we laughed and told her it had been pretty funny. But after a few minutes she said, "I think I'll go over and talk to those people some more."

"I don't think that would be a good idea," Susan said.

She went anyway, and sat at the family's table with them. We couldn't hear what was going on, but after about five minutes the father stood up and appeared to say something cross to her. Courtney came back and sat down beside us once more.

"What happened?" I asked.

"Oh nothing," Courtney said. "They invited me out to their home for Thanksgiving."

At about that time, Dexter, a man in his late fifties, a documentary film director we knew from the hotel, came in and sat down at the bar a few stools away from us. He seemed depressed, and slumped down on his stool, hanging his head over the bar before he had even ordered.

We called out to him and waved, and Dexter looked up and muttered something about it being his birthday. On hearing this, Courtney squealed with delight, and ran over to him and gave him a big fat birthday kiss, right on the mouth.

This did manage to cheer Dexter up. "Let me buy you a drink," he said, smiling.

But for some reason that pissed Courtney off. "Who the hell do you think you are?!" she yelled in his face, and stormed away.

Courtney's change of mood came so quickly that it was jarring. Dexter looked more confused than disappointed.

Scowling, Courtney sat back down next to us. "He's a dirty old man!" she told us, disgustedly.

Of course, there is the obvious irony. But besides that, the funny thing is, Courtney was right: Dexter had a girlfriend who was almost as young as she was.

The First Punch:
Stormé DeLarverié at the Chelsea

I first ran into Stormé (her name is pronounced "Stormy")
DeLarverié in my first few months at the Chelsea. Susan and I
were subletting our room on the third floor with the bathroom
down the hall. Gerald, the guy we were subletting from, told us that
our key also worked in the seventh-floor bathroom. Since our
bathroom was often occupied—by other residents or by junkies or
the homeless—I started going up to the seventh floor more and
more. Why not? I had no idea there could be any objections. It was
nicer than our bathroom, more homey, with pictures on the walls,
soap dishes, air fresheners, little touches like that. There was a rug
on the floor and even, I believe, a matching toilet seat cover. I used
this bathroom for a while but, I guess, mainly at night; then one
time for some reason I made the mistake of going there in the
afternoon.

As soon as I got in there, the Jamaican maid started knocking
insistently on the door, saying she needed to get in to mop the
floor. But that was about standard, so I didn't pay much attention.
But soon I heard another woman loudly exclaim, "Somebody's in
there!?" as if that were the damnedest thing she'd ever heard of.
Still, that was her problem, I figured; I wasn't going to rush. Though
I knew the two women were waiting out there, I finished up,
flushed the toilet, and even washed my hands.

When I opened the door, there was Stormé, blocking my way.

53

In her mid-seventies at the time, Stormé was stocky though not fat. A light-skinned, mixed-race person, she wore her white hair closely cropped. She was dressed, as always, in jeans and a sweatshirt, topped off by a floppy hat. On that day she was wearing sunglasses, partially masking her expression, which was nonetheless recognizable as a scowl. "Use your own bathroom, honey," she said, an intimidating presence, staring me down.

I could have been a junky or a nut, for all she knew. In this hotel—especially back in those days—it was a good bet that I wasn't the most savory of characters. The maid stood well back, breathlessly waiting to see how this potentially explosive confrontation would end.

"Excuse me," I mumbled, squeezing past Stormé and hurrying away down the hall.

Back on my floor, I ran into a guy I knew—in fact, it was Jimmy, Hiroya's "man-about-town" —and, still confused and a bit angry from the encounter, I said, "Some old lady just told me I couldn't use the bathroom on the seventh floor."

"An old lady?"

I described her, and Jimmy said, "Oh my God! That's Stormé! You're lucky she didn't pull a gun on you!"

Apparently Stormé had the reputation of threatening—with a gun—junkies who tried to shoot up in her bathroom. I don't believe I've been back since.

––––––––––

Born on Christmas Eve, 1920, in New Orleans, Stormé worked professionally as a drag king and torch singer. Pictures of her in drag show her to be suave and handsome, uncompromisingly androgynous; you could mistake her for a man trying to look like a woman. In the forties through the sixties she was the emcee—or, better yet, the ringmaster—for the Jewel Box Revue, a traveling gay drag show, the first in America to be integrated. Playing to mixed-race as well as mixed gay and straight audiences, the revue gained mainstream acceptance in larger cities around the country. In this context, Stormé was the subject of the 1987 film, *Stormé: The Lady of the Jewel Box.* Produced by DC filmmaker Michelle Parkerson, the movie emphasized Stormé's appropriation of male symbols of power, such as suits and ties, in furtherance of the gay rights struggle.

But Stormé's real claim to fame is that she's the person who threw the first punch at Stonewall, the rebellion (named for the bar on Christopher Street) that gave birth to the gay rights movement. Prior to Stonewall, gay people were subject to arrest pretty much arbitrarily for such offenses as kissing or holding hands in public or for dressing in the clothes of the opposite sex. The police staged raids on gay bars at unpredictable times, arresting whomever they pleased. The night of June 27, 1969, was seemingly like any other, with one exception: earlier that evening the city had mourned the passing of gay icon Judy Garland in a funeral attended by twenty-two thousand people. Whether this had anything to do with what happened next is open to speculation, but this time, when the police raided the Stonewall Bar in the early hours of June 28, they soon found that the gay people had had enough and were ready to fight back—in particular, one formidable drag king.

I doubt that Stormé went there that night looking for trouble, but she wasn't going to run from it either. When a plainclothes policeman punched her outside the bar, she retaliated, slugging him in the jaw. When asked what the policeman did next, Stormé, in an interview for the gay TV news magazine, *In the Life,* replied, with characteristic terseness, "He was on the ground. Out."

At that point all hell broke loose: gay patrons flooded out from the Stonewall Inn and other bars in the area, and up to two thousand gay people held off the assaults of four hundred police officers that night. The next night they waged a similar battle, and then five nights after that another, putting the authorities on notice that gay people would no longer consent to be their doormats.

Though several people witnessed the incident, for years no one was quite sure who had thrown that first punch. Most were under the impression—understandably, given Stormé's appearance—that it was a gay man who had started the fracas. And Stormé is not one to brag. It took author Charles Kaiser, in his book *The Gay Metropolis,* to ferret out the truth: that it was a certain cross-dressing lesbian who had done the honors.

Stormé may not have been a great leader, but like Rosa Parks before her, she had what it took to ignite a movement, and I believe her action is destined to grow in significance as history bears out the legitimacy of the gay rights struggle. In a place where, let's face it, most of us are pursuing highly self-aggrandizing activity, she's one of the few people in the Chelsea Hotel to have done something that will continue to resonate down through the years.

———————

Now in her mid-eighties, Stormé has lived at the Chelsea since 1972. Though I've made her out to be quite a tough character, if you met her, you'd have to agree she's one of the nicest people around. Just as long as you don't cross her. I've thought for a while—and told people half-jokingly—that Stormé must have taken a vow early on never to take any shit from anyone. For most of us this sort of thing would require walking around on edge, constantly vigilant, with a perpetual chip on our shoulders. But Stormé seems to have mastered the art without losing sight of what's most important in life. So maybe after all that's just her character; maybe she didn't need a vow.

In later years Stormé worked as a security guard at a bar in the Village. Though she now spends most of her time on a corner stool in a bar closer to home, I believe she still works a couple of nights a week to this day. After years of obscurity, she's finally begun to be recognized for her role in the gay rights movement. On the last Saturday of every June, she rides in a big white Cadillac with other veterans of Stonewall at the head of the Gay Pride parade.

Recently—that is, in 2006—one of the Japanese painter Hiroya's paintings was stolen from the walls of the Chelsea Hotel stairwell. When I mentioned this to Stormé, now eighty-six years old, she seemed troubled that someone would do something so despicable; we had all grown attached to the painting, which had become something of a monument to Hiroya's passing.

"They got my fur hat too," Stormé said, as if to suggest that we were in the midst of a crime wave here.

"How'd they get your hat?" I asked.

"Stole it right out of my bathroom," she said, incensed. "It makes me so mad. I wish I could catch the person who did it."

"Was it a nice hat?"

"A hundred dollars!" Stormé exclaimed, "That's what I paid for that hat." But her mood lifted a little and she smiled a wry smile as she went on to say that she had left a note in her bathroom that read:

> To the thief who stole my fur hat:
> if I catch you, your ass is grass and I'm the lawnmower.

So here's fair warning: if you're the thief who stole that hat, it might be best not to come around the hotel for a while. And as for the rest of you, if you know what's good for you, stay out of Stormé's bathroom!

The Revelatory Work

I found a purse in the shared bathroom one morning. It contained the usual junk that women carry around, and a wallet with an ID and forty dollars in it. From the picture on the ID, I could tell that it wasn't anybody who had any business using our bathroom. I suspected the worst, that the woman was a junky who had broken in to shoot up, and that made me feel like taking the money and throwing her purse in the trash just to teach her a lesson.

Instead, I asked a couple of people on our floor, and one of the prostitutes knew her name, and said she lived in the hotel. I asked for her room number at the front desk and took her purse down to where she lived on the second floor.

The woman who answered the door was tall, middle-aged, with long, dyed-red hair. She wore bracelets and a flowing, robelike, Turkish hippie shirt. She had apparently been sleeping or otherwise indisposed, and at first she didn't understand what I was saying, but when she caught on she was really grateful: "Oh my God! I didn't even know that was gone. Oh thank you so much. Let me give you a reward."

"That's okay," I said.

"No, no. I should give you something for your trouble. I'm so scatterbrained!" She checked her wallet, then said, "Oh, I'm afraid I'm kind of short right now. I'm unemployed at the moment."

"Don't worry about it."

"Actually," she said, "I'm a poetess. At the moment I'm composing a long revelatory work of scope and vision that I believe will open the eyes of a great many people around the world."

"Wow," I said, and then, mercenary son of a bitch that I am, asked, "You think you'll get some money for that?"

"Perhaps," she said, with a touch of condescension. "Certainly I'm not in it solely for the money."

"Of course not."

"Cynthia Blair, by the way," she said, extending a long, thin hand.

I didn't hear anything more from Cynthia for a few weeks after that, but apparently it had been bothering her that she couldn't give me a reward, because one day she showed up at my door. "I still don't have any money," she said, "but I have this coffee pot. It's a nice coffee pot, don't you think?"

There was nothing nice about it whatsoever. It was an old, used coffee pot. I must have looked rather bewildered, because she clarified her offer: "You can have it if you want."

I took the pot. "Thanks," I said.

"I just wanted to give you something for your trouble."

Now the strange thing about it was, it was a very small coffee pot, apparently for espresso. I had never seen one before. "Uh, how do you use it," I asked

"I don't know. I've never used it before," Cynthia said. "I think you just put it on the burner."

"Hmmm." It had a plug for an electrical cord.

"It needs a basket or something to go inside, but maybe you can find one of those."

"Oh yeah, I'm sure that'll be no problem," I said, unable, despite myself, to suppress a hint of sarcasm. "Thanks. It looks real good."

We stood there in the doorway for a moment, not knowing what more to say to one another. Finally, I asked, "How's the revelatory work coming?"

"What? Oh, very well, thank you. I believe it's being well received."

"Good," I said.

"However, as I'm sure you must realize, these things take time to be resolved, and in the meantime the mold and the fungus are growing thick all around us."

Cynthia turned to go. But then she thought of something and turned back and said, "Oh, by the way, I'd rinse that pot out if I were you. I had bleach in it."

To clean needles, perhaps? I wondered, but I didn't ask. Something for the trash after all.

The Eighth-Floor Bathroom: Herbert Huncke at the Chelsea

When Susan and I moved from the third to the eighth floor of the Chelsea Hotel, it was a big upgrade in terms of living space. And we were much closer to the shared bathroom as well; in fact it was almost next door instead of way down at the end of the hall. Susan, especially, appreciated that. But it was that bathroom—so convenient on the face of it—that turned out to be the problem.

The third-floor bathroom had been somewhat bad, but our new one was a mess of a whole other order. The floor, the sink, the shower curtain, and the tub were generally caked with black, greasy grime, and there was always an inch of water slopped out on the floor. Sometimes there was blood strewn over the toilet and floor and old needles and baggies scattered about, making it clear that junkies were shooting up in there. We also suspected the homeless of making use of the facilities, as we would often find piles of reeking, fetid clothes.

Besides the mess, it was inconvenient. Nearly every day someone would steal the toilet paper—and not just full rolls either, but half rolls, quarter rolls, every last scrap. The junkies would nod off and sit in there for hours. We couldn't get in at all in the early morning hours, which was tough when we woke up and needed to piss. The junkies, when we ran into them, were never very friendly, and it seemed risky to confront them—especially since they knew where we lived.

I didn't want to make waves by complaining immediately. Susan and I both felt we were lucky to get into this place. And when I did finally mention it at the front desk, the suggestion—implying as it did that they weren't doing their job, that they were letting in unauthorized persons—was met with resistance and disbelief; they treated me like I was crazy.

The obvious solution was to keep the bathroom door locked. But it was difficult to get everybody to cooperate with this plan. Hiroya, the eccentric Japanese painter who shared our bathroom, was no problem: he was deathly afraid of sticking himself with a dirty needle and contracting AIDS. ("One time all it take!" he would rave in his broken English. "One time! You history!") But we also shared the bathroom with two transient rooms; people stayed in these rooms for anywhere from a couple of days to a couple of months. Sometimes it was hard to tell if the junky in the bathroom had come from outside or had actually rented one of these rooms. In any event, many of these people simply did not see the importance of keeping the door locked.

But no matter what we did—even when we were lucky enough to get some responsible tenants in the transient rooms for a couple of months—the junkies always managed to get into the bathroom sooner or later. And once in, they knew how to disable the lock so they could come back whenever they wanted. Of course, when I woke up in the morning and found the lock broken, I would call maintenance, but it might take them a week or more to get around to fixing it, and in the meantime our bathroom was open full-time as a shooting gallery. What bothered Susan was that the place was always a mess, but for me it was more the principle of the thing: it was driving me nuts that I couldn't control my own bathroom.

What I decided was that I was going to keep complaining, keep getting the lock fixed, until maybe the staff got sick of it and started keeping the junkies out of the hotel. I would just keep calling everybody: I would call maintenance, and if they didn't respond, I'd call housekeeping, and if that didn't work, I'd call the front desk. I would call about once an hour until the lock got fixed. And if a junky broke the lock that night, I'd be back on the phone the next day. (Hiroya, too, complained constantly—as he had from the day he moved in— but since he was pretty much clinically insane, the management never paid much attention to him.) For variety, I had Susan call sometimes.

The upshot of this was that they decided to renovate the bathroom—hoping, I guess, that that would shut me up. Oh well, I figured, it needed it. In the meantime—for about two weeks—we had to use a bathroom on another floor, which was inconvenient, but well worth it if it fixed the problem. (It was Stormé's bathroom, by the way, and you can bet she had something to say about that!) Stanley Bard, our beloved proprietor, stopped in from time to time to oversee the work, promising us a nice modern bathroom. When the workers were done, it did look a bit newer but otherwise the same. I had thought for sure they would put a new lock on, and I told Stanley and the desk manager and the workers that that was the most important thing, but in the end they just spray-painted the old one and stuck it back on there. It was broken within a week, and so all the renovation accomplished was to give the junkies a nicer place to shoot up in.

It was frustrating to watch the new bathroom start to go downhill again so quickly. I didn't know what to do except to keep complaining. But now the staff was more hostile, since they figured the renovation had somehow solved the problem. Now they demanded to know who was breaking the lock. I knew not to say anything about junkies, the forbidden topic, the dirty little secret. So I said, simply, "I don't know."

"We know it's you who's breaking the lock," Stanley Bard said to me one day, implying, I suppose, that I was doing it out of sheer perversity. His calm assurance almost made me doubt my own sanity. Stanley, who flat-out refuses to entertain any sort of bad news about the hotel, was the last person on earth you wanted to mention the junkies to.

Looking at the matter objectively, what Susan and I noticed was that the bathrooms on other floors didn't have this problem, at least not to the same extent. That was the funny thing: although some of the bathrooms were kept sealed up tight, others were regularly left unlocked, even standing wide open, and yet they'd be perfectly nice inside. I'd heard many of the other residents say that junkies used their bathrooms too, but from talking with them I got the sense that this was mainly an old problem, that they were talking about the eighties or even the seventies. For some reason our bathroom was a holdover from the bad old days.

I can't say it was really a revelation, not like a bolt out of the blue. It was just that the truth of the matter gradually dawned on us, becoming clearer with each passing night that a junky nodded off on our toilet: it was Herbert Huncke's bathroom.

Herbert Huncke, the legendary junky, petty thief, and Times Square hustler who inspired Burroughs's character Herman in *Junky,* Kerouac's Elmo Hassel in *On the Road,* and appeared as himself in Allen Ginsberg's *Howl,* was born in Greenfield, Massachusetts, in 1915 and grew up in Chicago. (He tells his story in his various writings, including his autobiography, *Guilty of Everything,* published by fellow Chelseaite Raymond Foye's Hanuman Books.) Molested in a Chicago park when he was a young boy, Huncke started using heroin in his early teens, supporting his nascent habit in part by hustling on the streets of Chicago. He ran away from home when he was twelve, seriously intending to make it to New York City, but the cops caught him in upstate New York and sent him home. Huncke never seems to have had a regular job of any sort. He spent his later teen years and early twenties riding the rails and hitchhiking around the country.

In 1939, when he was twenty-four, Huncke made it to New York City and immediately hit Times Square. He was already well trained for a life of hustling and petty crime; he says the city was the only place he had ever felt that he truly fit in. He soon made the acquaintance of jazz greats such as Charlie Parker and Dexter Gordon, men to whom he was drawn as much by a love of junk as of music. When Alfred Kinsey came to town in 1946, gathering material for his study of sexuality, Huncke was one of the first people he interviewed. In the forties Huncke met the Beats as well: to him Ginsberg and Kerouac looked like clean-cut college kids. He thought Burroughs, who was a little bit older and wearing a suit, was a cop, but he warmed up to him sufficiently to give him his first shot of heroin. For these nascent writers, Huncke represented the sort of lumpen authenticity to which they aspired. He taught them what it was to be "beat" and may have even coined the term.

Huncke pretty much sat out the fifties, serving three years in Sing Sing and Greenhaven for burglary, and then, after less than a year on the street, five more years in Dannemora on another burglary charge. When he got out in '59 the Beat scene was in full swing, Kerouac, Ginsberg, and Burroughs were big names, and Huncke was famous by extension. He hung out in the bars and coffeehouses of Greenwich Village and later the East Village, trading off his newfound notoriety to separate the more gullible hipsters from their money. He roomed with the poet John Wieners in the East Village in the early sixties; besides that, he hopped around from crash pad to flophouse, sponging off whoever would have him and supporting his heroin habit with various scams. He seems to have rarely had a place of his own in those days.

Huncke moved into the Chelsea Hotel in his last years, after the death of Louis Cartwright, his companion of twenty-five years, who was mugged and murdered in the East Village. He was too sick to make a living for himself by this point, so his small room was generously paid for by the Grateful Dead—frequent Chelsea Hotel visitors themselves over the years. Though he was in a methadone program, Huncke's heroin habit continued up until his last days at the Chelsea.

Our first full year in the Chelsea, 1996, coincided with Huncke's last, for that was the year that he died. We moved up to his floor the year after that, when his room was being used by transients. To tell you the truth, I was hoping that it was Thomas Wolfe's bathroom we were sharing, as that was the writer I was most interested in at the time. But Huncke was certainly good enough: though better known as a muse to the more famous Beats, Huncke was a fine writer in his own right. His straightforward, unadorned prose was an inspiration to the Beats, as it was to me. I remember Huncke as a gaunt, emaciated old man slumped in a chair in the lobby. He was very sick at the time, so I didn't see him often. Though I would have been intimidated by such an eminent literary figure anyway, I was doubly so because of his reputation as a scam artist. Perhaps I would have introduced myself eventually, but he was gone before I could work up the nerve.

———————

Over time we learned Huncke's room number and made the connection that that was a room that shared our bathroom. But we didn't think much of it. He was dead, after all, and so wouldn't be shooting up—or doing anything else for that matter—on our toilet. However, his spirit was strong and still drew heroin and its aficionados to our floor. His various friends and connections, accustomed to using our bathroom when they came to visit Huncke, now considered it their property. We were in a turf war.

The situation continued in this way for perhaps another two or three months: the lock would get broken, the bathroom would get trashed, I would doggedly complain, and they would eventually fix the lock. And then, unbelievably, the management decided to renovate the bathroom again. And so, for the second time that year, we were forced to make the trek to another floor. This time it was clear that the intent was to punish me. The message from the management was that they didn't want to be bothered; they wanted me either to fix the problem myself or else to shut up about it.

I began to have dreams and half-waking visions of finding dead junkies in the bathroom: blue-skinned, glassy-eyed, ODed with needle in arm and slumped down on the toilet or floating in the bathtub. These were frightening but also in a way strangely satisfying visions.

I like to think I'm one of the saner characters at the hotel, and yet it's funny the way psychosis can creep up on you unawares. By this point I was totally obsessed with the bathroom. Susan, wisely, told me just to let it go, but that was something I couldn't bring myself to do. The situation finally got so bad that I decided I had to take some action—for my mental health, if nothing else. Late at night I would listen for the sound of the door being opened, and for the click of the lock when it closed. I placed my chair by the door so I could hear better. I sat there reading, even though the light was bad and it made me sleepy.

It took a few nights. These junkies were really sneaky, and somehow, one night, somebody had gotten in there without me knowing it. But I heard the soft click-click-click-click, that I had learned to recognize as the sound of the lock being disabled. When I opened my door—though I did it as quietly as possible—the sound abruptly ceased. I knocked on the bathroom door.

"Occupied." It was a woman's voice. I hadn't expected a woman.

I knew that if I just waited there, she wouldn't come out. She was waiting for me to go away. So I pretended to go back in my room, closing the door firmly and then tiptoeing around the corner of the corridor and hiding.

When she was sure I had gone, the woman came quietly out of the bathroom. Rounding the corner, she saw me and I startled her. She looked to be about fifty and was wearing leopard-print pants and a black leather jacket. She looked like either an old prostitute or a refugee from the New Wave scene of the eighties. Her ratty black hair was pinned up on her head.

She walked right past me. "What room are you in?" I asked.

"I'm visiting my friend," she said.

"What room is she in?"

"I don't have to answer your questions," she snapped.

I quickly went to the bathroom door, which she had left standing open, and checked the lock. Yep, broken alright. That pissed me off further and I ran after the woman to yell at her, but by the time I had got to the elevator she had already slipped away, probably down the back staircase. She knew her way around.

I was caught unaware the next time as well. I had been drinking liquor all night and had passed out in my chair. When I woke up hours later I had to piss. I knocked on the bathroom door.

"I'll be out in a minute." It was a man this time.

I got a book and sat there reading in my chair by the door. I was almost starting to drift off to sleep again, but I really needed to piss. About half an hour or forty-five minutes had passed when I got up and knocked on the bathroom door again.

"I said, I'll be out in a minute!" the guy yelled.

I stood there in the hall and waited a couple of minutes and knocked again. This time I kept pounding.

The junky jerked open the door. "What's your problem?" He was bald, with a shaved head, dressed all in black, like a guy from the art world.

"You've been in there for an hour."

"No, I haven't. I just got in there."

"I timed you!"

"Fuck you!" he said as he brushed past me.

I didn't chase after him. To tell you the truth, I hadn't really thought this through too well. I didn't know what I was going to do when I confronted these people. All I really knew was that they didn't like being seen. If it had been the eighties, I probably would have been knifed, but as it turned out, I got lucky and the junkies I confronted didn't come back.

For a while after that we had relative stability, because a semi-responsible girl had moved into one of the transient rooms and we were able to keep the bathroom door locked. We had the lock changed entirely, since it had become clear that some of the junkies had their own keys—copies obtained, perhaps, from Huncke himself. As the Chelsea insanity began to consume me, I became the Crazy Bathroom Person of the eighth floor. My senses became preternaturally attuned to the click of the lock, the vibrations of the closing door. The other residents were soon accustomed to my habit of bursting wild-eyed out of my door at any hour of the day or night—often scaring the shit out of them—to see who left that goddamn door open.

I had thought all along that the junkies getting into my bathroom were all from outside the hotel. But one incident in particular made me rethink this. One afternoon as I was puttering around in my room, I heard a crashing sound coming from the hallway. Then, as I approached my door, I heard it again. Throwing open my door, I saw a guy who I knew lived here, because I always saw him hanging around the lobby in a bathrobe. He was a skinny little old man, and he was trying desperately to bust down the bathroom door. When he heard me he looked up. His eyes were bloodshot, watery, sick. It was kind of pathetic, and I almost felt like offering to help. But I was more annoyed than anything, and so I said, "What the hell are you doing?!"

He didn't answer. Instead he lowered his shoulder, and, with a final burst of strength, crashed open the door. He was inside in a flash, and threw the bolt behind him.

I stood there for a moment wondering what to do, then turned around and went back to my room. I felt sorry for the old man and didn't have the heart to confront him. When he came out, he closed the door so quietly that I didn't hear it.

Toward the end of the nineties we finally got the situation under control. It required constant vigilance on my part. I learned a trick to keep people from damaging the lock, so now I don't have to fight to have it fixed every other day. We got permanent residents in the formerly transient rooms, people who shared my concerns about keeping the bathroom clean and needle-free. But more than anything else, the city just changed: it gentrified, and the junkies either cleaned up their acts, died, or moved away. The hotel changed too, in the same way: they raised the rent on the junkies who lived here, and most of them moved out. In a way it's a good thing—in many ways, actually—though they raised the rent on the rest of us too, and I fear that crazy writers may be next on the list to go.

A few years ago, in 2003 or so, Carla, the girl who was living in Herbert Huncke's old room, threw out a worn suitcase full of papers. I was standing in the hallway when she tossed it into the trash, and when she explained that she had found the suitcase stashed in the back of her closet, I snatched it out of the can immediately. Rushing back to my room, I breathlessly opened the suitcase and spread the papers out on my bed. Unfortunately, the papers consisted mainly of the ravings of the aforementioned insane woman, author of the revelatory work, Cynthia Blair. Now I saw that at some point she must have lived on my floor. Either that or Huncke stole her suitcase! She was by this point long gone from the hotel. Typed in rhymed verse, virtually all of the papers concerned the same subject: a sinister mold that was spreading across the country, robbing unsuspecting people of their health and sanity. The papers did smell, in truth, somewhat moldy, so perhaps Cynthia's fixation was understandable.

However, folded once and tucked into the inside pocket of the suitcase—thus protecting it from the mold—was a broadsheet of a story by Herbert Huncke, autographed by the great man himself and dated August 30, 1995. It shows a photograph of an emaciated Huncke holding a beer and a cigarette. Titled "Again—The Hospital," and published by White Fields Press, based in, of all places, my hometown of Louisville, Kentucky, the story is somewhat despairing, and describes how Huncke has come to the end of his rope, both physically and mentally. Though taken from an earlier book, it perhaps approximates Huncke's state at the end of his life:

> The ordeal of having to face people while walking along the street is almost beyond endurance—and accompanied by the awareness that it is self-inflicted is so humiliating—at this point I can only wish for death—or that by some miracle or other I'll become invisible and pass through the crowds of people unnoticed.
>
> Today is the third day I've spent trying to get into the hospital and if I don't make it in today I can't even guess what I'll do to get by until tomorrow. My habit continues to make the usual demands—and I've run out of people who are in a position to help me—or willing to do so. Allen claims to have run out of money—and Panna has reached the end of her patience—and there is no one else I can think of.

When the girl who lived in Huncke's room saw how much I wanted that suitcase, she started to think that maybe those papers might have been worth something. Carla had no idea who Herbert Huncke was, but when I explained it to her and showed her the broadsheet with Huncke's autograph, she was mad at herself for throwing the suitcase out. She wanted the broadsheet back, but I wouldn't give it to her. Huncke's spirit nearly drove me insane, so maybe he figured he owed me something.

Vicky and Keanu

PART I: A BIG MISTAKE

Vicky had auburn hair and a round, dimpled face. You could tell she had once been quite pretty. But now she was nearing fifty and had lost her looks. I thought she must've had a pretty good body too, in her younger years, but now she was rather heavy. An actress, Vicky had worked sporadically in plays and commercials, but lately the work had dried up, and now for the most part she was unemployed, living off food stamps and various forms of public assistance. She lived in a tiny, junked-up apartment with her little boy, Keanu, a child she had had late in life. The father was no longer in the picture, nor had he ever really taken much interest in the child.

Vicky was pretty much helpless, having relied on her looks to get men to do everything for her throughout her whole life. One day I was helping her put an air conditioner in her window, since the maintenance people no longer responded to her requests.

"It's impossible to get anybody to do anything around here," she said.

"Yeah, I know what you mean. I keep asking them to put a better lock on the bathroom door so the junkies can't break in, but they ignore me."

"Do you pay your rent?"

"Uh, yeah," I said.

"There's your biggest mistake. Don't ever give them a cent. I haven't paid my rent in seven years."

"Seven years!?" I exclaimed, incredulous. "And Stanley Bard hasn't said anything? He hasn't tried to throw you out?"

"Well *of course* he's said *something,* " Vicky said, as if I were an idiot. "Stanley bothers me all the time. But he wouldn't dare throw me out. He knows I'd sue the pants off him!"

Seven years was approximately the age of her little boy. I found myself wondering if maybe Mr. Bard had refrained from evicting her because he didn't want to put the child on the street. (Less charitably, I wondered whether in fact Vicky might have had the child in order to avoid being thrown out.) Vicky said that Stanley was overcharging her on her rent and therefore she didn't have to pay anything.

One time Susan and I were drinking in the bar of the El Quijote. Vicky came in, Keanu in tow, and sat next to us and ordered a martini. After a while, a man started cursing and carrying on at the end of the bar.

Keanu looked around his mother and asked me, "Why is that man acting like that?"

"He's drunk," I said.

Keanu nodded his head in assent.

Strangely, Vicky got mad at me. "Don't talk that way in front of my child!" she snapped. "He doesn't know what that means."

Actually, Keanu did seem to understand. And he had made a point of asking me instead of his mother, as if perhaps he couldn't expect a straight answer from her.

PART II: THE PAYOFF

A few months afterwards, Vicky asked me to help her carry some boxes down to a friend's car; she was moving most of her stuff to storage. "We have to move out, but I got ten thousand dollars out of the old skinflint," Vickie said. "I could have gotten more if I'd decided to take him to court. That's what he was really afraid of."

So Stanley paid her off to get rid of her, I thought. "Ten thousand dollars," I said. "That sounds pretty good."

Actually, while it appeared quite generous under the circumstances, it didn't seem all that good for Vicky. She would have to find a job pretty quickly, since her new landlord was probably not going to be quite so understanding as Stanley Bard. I thought it would probably take her a considerable chunk of that money just to get established. And I had a feeling she might have been exaggerating the amount as well. "So what are you going to do now?" I asked. "Do you have any leads on any apartments?"

"I'm going to Hollywood to work in the movies," Vickie said.

It didn't make much sense to me: here's a forty-nine-year-old woman, out on the street with a young child, and she's planning to move to Hollywood to become a movie star.

"I've always wanted to do it, and now I'm just going to go for it," Vickie said. "I know it's going to be tough, but I have a lot of experience in the theater and I'm really going to work hard."

"Good luck," I said. "Break a leg."

"She's so cute," Keanu said, expressing his faith in his mother, I suppose, or perhaps just repeating what she had told him.

Three months later Vicky and Keanu were back in town, having run through the ten thousand already. She told me that she and the child were sleeping on fold-out cots in a friend's kitchen on the Upper East Side. But they were already wearing out their welcome, and Vicky was wondering where they would go next. I got the distinct feeling that she was hinting around that maybe I should let them camp out for a week or two in my apartment.

By the end of that week, Vicky and Keanu were hanging out in the lobby of the Chelsea. When I talked to her, Vicky seemed kind of defensive, as if people had been asking her—though I hadn't— what she was doing back in the hotel. "I told Keanu that this wasn't our home anymore, but he wouldn't accept that. He kept wanting to go home. He kept saying, Mommy, when can we go back to the Chelsea. I had to bring him here to show him that this wasn't our home anymore."

Keanu wasn't saying anything. He was looking at the ground and seemed embarrassed. I doubted that this had really been his idea.

It soon became clear that Vicky had come to ask for her old room back. "I have to let Keanu see that there's no possibility of us coming back to live here again," she said. "He made me promise to ask Stanley if we could come back, and I agreed in order to show him it was impossible. I think it's important for him to have some closure so he can move on."

I don't know what Mr. Bard said to her, because he wasn't around at that moment. Vicky went up to the front desk to try to persuade the desk clerks to take her side in the matter, but they laughingly told her not to bother, since there was no way in hell Stanley was going to let her come back.

1998

Crime and Punishment

Twilight of the Club Kids:
Michael Aliğ at the Chelsea

When we moved in, it was Susan who rented the sublet from Gerald the musician. She didn't say anything about me, and I just moved in later in the middle of the night. I didn't know what the rules in New York were. I didn't know if Gerald was allowed to sublet to more than one person. But I found out pretty quickly that Stanley Bard hated sublets with a passion. So in the beginning I was worried that he would find out I was living there and throw me out or, more likely, raise Gerald's rent. I tried to keep a low profile. But it turns out I was just being paranoid. It turns out the Chelsea is an excellent place to hide out.

We had been living on the third floor for a few months when Brooke Humphries moved in across the hall. She was hard to miss, as she dyed her hair various combinations of blue, green, and pink and had multiple facial piercings. Brooke was very heavy and not too attractive. She was, however, always pleasant and polite when I spoke with her.

Brooke served as the den mother to a large group of club kids, mostly young, skinny gay boys. She quickly had a dozen or more of these kids living with her in her room. I saw them sometimes late at night when—outlandishly outfitted in frilly lace and glitter, their hair dyed and their faces painted—they were on their way out to the clubs, or else very early in the morning when they were returning, much ruffled, after a night of partying. They slept all day, allowing Brooke to function as their point person to the daytime world, a world into which they were too weird and dysfunctional to venture. I looked into Brooke's room one time, and the floor was covered with five or six mattresses heaped high with piles of clothes. There was virtually no other furniture except maybe a couple of chairs and a small table. Overflowing ashtrays and bags of trash accented the minimalist decor.

The kids apparently kept reptiles in the room, or at least one reptile. One time an iguana escaped the apartment: it got out on the balcony and climbed up a trellis to the floor above. That was as far as it got. It was cold out, and it just stayed there, clinging to the railing, and froze to death. The old woman who lived in that apartment came out one morning and found it hanging there, and it almost gave her a heart attack.

Another time, I was coming down 23rd Street when I heard a cacophony of shrieking above me. I looked up, and a group of three or four club kids were bustling about on the balcony of their room. One of them had a broom, and all of a sudden he lunged and swept something off the balcony. As it fell I could see, it was a little gray mouse. But the mouse was lucky. It landed in the fluffy pillow of a woman's thick, curly, black hair, becoming entangled there. The woman screamed, threw her hands to her hair and shook it vigorously. And then, inexplicably, she ran, still shaking her hair, down the street and straight through the open door of the El Quijote.

I came into the hotel one afternoon and the place was crawling with cops. It was like Sid had stabbed Nancy all over again. Up on my floor it was the worst, as the police activities centered around Brooke's room, the door of which was standing wide open. The cops didn't give me any problem about walking down the hall, but then one of them stopped me and asked me if I had seen any unusual activity on the floor—I think he meant drug dealing—and another cop asked if I knew Michael Alig, or if I had ever seen him around the hotel. By this point Alig's picture had been in the papers, so I knew what he looked like, and I hadn't seen him. Or at least I didn't think so; though a bit older than most of them, he had apparently been able to blend in with the other club kids. I looked into the room and saw Brooke sitting in a chair, surrounded by cops. The club kids appeared to have fled.

Michael Alig came to New York from South Bend, Indiana, in 1984 to study at Fordham University and later at the Fashion Institute of Technology. But what Michael really enjoyed was the New York nightlife, and he soon dropped out of school to devote his energies to partying full time. He became a party promoter and was hired by Peter Gatien, who owned the Limelight and other venues, to bring the celebrities and the cool people into his clubs and make sure they had a good time there. This involved ensuring that everybody had lots of drugs on hand—such as ecstasy, special K, cocaine, and heroin—and, apparently, doing lots of drugs himself. Michael quickly gained a reputation as someone who really knew how to throw a party, and he became famous for pushing the scene to new heights of outrageousness and bad taste.

In 1996, the Drug Enforcement Agency (DEA) was investigating Peter Gatien on charges that he had allowed his clubs to become havens for the selling and using of drugs. If you were into drugs, now was the time to lie low, but for Michael Alig, nearly out of control on various drugs, that was not an option. The DEA apparently caught him with something, and in exchange for immunity, he agreed to cooperate in the investigation of Gatien. Far from sobering him up, this close call gave Michael a feeling of invulnerability.

It was against this backdrop that the events of March 17, 1996, took place. Michael was living with a drug dealer named Angel Melendez who had saved up some thirty thousand dollars and was keeping it in the apartment. Together with another drug dealer, who went by the name of Freeze, Alig decided to kill Angel and take his money. Freeze hid behind a door and hit Angel in the head with a hammer, then Alig injected Angel with Drano and smothered him with a pillow. Apparently due to laziness, they kept the body in the bathtub for a week as they continued their nonstop party—now intensified by the infusion of Angel's cash. Finally, because he was unable to take a shower, Michael hacked the legs off the corpse with a knife from Macy's, bagged these and boxed the rest, and then the two killers hauled the corpse over to the Hudson River and threw it in.

Since he didn't think the police or the D.A. could touch him, Michael bragged openly about the killing, turning it into a joke. He was at least partly right about this, as the DEA was able to protect him for quite some time. But not forever. Although the cops initially didn't worry too much about the disappearance of a gay Latino drug dealer, Angel's family came to town and pressed the investigation, and reporter Frank Owen wrote an exposé for the *Village Voice* asking where Angel was and recounting the rumors of Alig's involvement. Alig went out of town for a while, but then came back and shuttled between the Chelsea and various other hideouts for a few months. When Angel's body turned up in a potter's field in Staten Island in September, that forced the D.A.'s hand. That's what the cops were doing in the Chelsea on December 10, 1996: looking for Michael Alig. Although they didn't find him here that day, they tracked him down somewhere else not long after.

Once again they went easy on Michael for cooperating in the investigation of Gatien (whom they never could pin anything on), and he got only ten to twenty years for manslaughter. He was thirty-two years old in 1998 when he was sentenced, and I guess he should be up for parole soon. And so—unfortunately for the rest of us—he's got a good part of his life still ahead of him once he gets out.

When Brooke wouldn't tell the police where Michael Alig was hiding out, they busted her for cocaine possession. A few days later she was released on bail and came back to her apartment, only to find that that Stanley Bard was completely freaked out over the whole situation. He said he didn't want her staying here any longer, and she would have to pack up and get out right away. She'd been breaking the rules by keeping all those kids in her room, and though it was fine when she was paying the bills and not attracting any attention, when one of the kids turned out to be a nutball murderer, that was a different story. Brooke probably could have fought Stanley, but by this point she had enough to worry about. She was facing twenty-five years on the cocaine rap.

Junky Joe and the Europe of the Mind

The most beloved—and enigmatic—character ever to grace the halls of the Chelsea is, of course, our illustrious proprietor, Stanley Bard. Among his many endearing qualities, Stanley possesses a congenital inability to admit that anything bad has ever taken place in the hotel. There are no roaches or mice, and certainly no junkies have ever lived here. If pressed, he might be willing to admit that Sid and Nancy had a slight altercation one night back in the seventies, but absolutely nothing untoward has happened since. The writers and artists living here are all brilliant, contented, and wealthy. The magnificence of the Chelsea's luxury accommodations is scarcely rivaled even by the Plaza or the Waldorf-Astoria—perhaps not even by Buckingham Palace itself.

We were talking to a friend in El Quijote the other night, someone who used to live here back in the eighties and nineties, and he told us a tale that's perfectly illustrative of this tendency of Stanley:

> I was going up to the ninth floor to visit my friend one time. The elevator was slow, probably somebody was holding it up, so I walked up the stairs. As soon as I turned onto his wing I saw cops all over the place, about eight or ten of them. They were coming in and out of an apartment. There was a stretcher in the hall with a body in it in a black body bag.

I knew whose apartment it was—it was a guy I knew, I'll call him Joe—and I assumed it was him in the body bag. Joe was a junky, so of course I immediately suspected that he had ODed.

One of the cops finally noticed me standing around and said, "Don't come up here yet. Go back downstairs. We'll let you know when you can come up."

The elevators still weren't working, so I walked back down to the lobby. It was full of people. They weren't allowing anybody to go up. Stanley was standing behind the desk and so I went up to him and said, "What's going on up on the ninth floor?"

"Nothing, why would you say that?" Stanley said.

"There were cops all over the place!"

"No there weren't."

"Yes there were!"

"You may have seen one or two policemen," Stanley admitted. "They probably have a room here."

Stanley's manner was so matter-of-fact and convincing that he made me doubt the evidence of my own senses. I began to think that maybe I was becoming one of the crazy people wandering the halls here. Still, I'm not that far gone, so I said, "Stanley, you can't tell me *nothing* is going on."

"Well, I don't know what you want me to tell you then."

"That was Joe, wasn't it?" I said. "Joe's dead, isn't he?"

"Joe?" Stanley said. "Oh, no. Joe's fine. He just went on a little vacation. Europe, I think. He'll be back in a couple of years, I'm sure."

In the days that followed there were plenty of rumors circulating around the hotel, but nobody ever got any definite information, and nothing about the incident ever appeared in the papers. Stanley has his ways of keeping things like this quiet.

It's difficult to discern how much of Stanley's act is a con and how much a sort of rosy-spectacled tunnel vision. Whatever his secret, he's a brilliant magician whose sleight of hand has allowed him to conjure up the infinitely seductive shadow reality of the Chelsea. Who but a philistine, a sworn enemy of art, would think to mention such trivialities as heat or running water? It hardly matters that Joe—or whatever his name was before he passed into myth—has yet to return from his sojourn abroad.

Dietary Tips of the Homeless

Around the corner from the Chelsea, on Seventh Avenue, I was waiting for a friend to ride the subway uptown. There were two homeless men camped out near the entrance to the subway. They were old, or at least they appeared old, their faces worn and weathered.

"Fuck the salad," the bigger one said. He was paunchy for a homeless man, and had wavy, gray, uncombed hair. "Roast beef and mashed potatoes, plenty of gravy. Fuck the salad," he repeated, for emphasis.

"Gotta eat the salad," the smaller, thinner one said. "Gotta have your vegetables, fresh vegetables, or else you'll get sick. 'Specially with all the drinkin' we do."

"What are you talkin' about?" the big one said. "Sick how?"

"Just sick, that's all. How the fuck do I know? Your teeth'll fall out! Your fuckin' dick'll shrivel up and drop off!"

The bigger man paused to reconsider his position in the face of these threats. "Still, it tastes so bad," he said.

"That's what the dressing is for, you dumbass," the smaller man said.

They were too preoccupied with their discussion to even bother hitting me up for money.

Chelsea Death Cult: Sid Vicious at the Chelsea

For better or for worse—and most, including certainly our proprietor, Stanley Bard, would say for worse—the defining event of the Chelsea Hotel occurred when Nancy Spungen was found dead in the bathroom of Room 100, stabbed to death with a hunting knife belonging to her boyfriend, former Sex Pistol Sid Vicious. Sid himself, upon awakening from a drug-induced stupor, called the police at around 10:30 on the morning of October 12, 1978, to report Nancy's death. When the police arrived, Sid was in a confused state, alternately denying and confessing to the killing, and so he was immediately arrested and charged with Nancy's murder. We were deprived of an official inquiry by Sid's own death less than four months later, when he ODed on heroin while out on bail awaiting trial. The circumstances of Sid's death—it was unclear whether it was accidental or a suicide—only deepened the mystery and enhanced the punk rocker's burgeoning legend.

We'll probably never know what really happened to Nancy, but that hasn't stopped people from speculating over the years. The simplest theory holds that Sid just went crazy, stabbed Nancy over some petty disagreement, and maybe didn't even remember in the morning. Though Sid did seem actually to love Nancy, he was in the habit of beating her with some regularity, and he was prone to other acts of violence as well. On the other hand, some believe that a drug dealer who visited that night may have killed Nancy, perhaps in a disagreement over money, while Sid was passed out. Lately, the dealer, now dead, has even been identified by the writer Alan Parker (*Vicious: Too Fast to Live*) as Michael Morra, an actor known by the ridiculous moniker of Rockets Redglare. (Rockets later appeared in over thirty movies, mostly in bit parts, including *Mystery Train* [1989], *Basquiat* [1996], and *Trees Lounge* [1996].) Others speculate that Nancy may have accidentally fallen on the knife or that she may have committed suicide, perhaps as part of some sort of pact with Sid.

While Sid was out on bail, he continued to live as recklessly as ever, his behavior becoming increasingly violent and bizarre. He tried to commit suicide twice, once by slashing his wrists and another time by trying to jump out the window of a hotel room he was sharing with his mother. After the second attempt they put him in Bellevue Hospital, where he was forced to withdraw from heroin. It was this withdrawal that may have been his undoing, for as soon as he got out of the hospital he immediately shot up and, probably because his system was no longer used to it, ODed and died. Complicating the picture, however, is the fact that Sid left various suicide notes and so may have ODed on purpose. Finally, as Parker alleges, Rockets Redglare may have provided the heroin that killed Sid, perhaps giving him a "hot shot" of unusually pure heroin in order to keep him from telling his side of the story at trial.

Sid's fans certainly favored the suicide-pact interpretation—and who wouldn't, really? It's much more romantic; the probable truth is so banal. But in any event, the ambiguities of the case allowed the legend to thrive. Not long after Sid's death, the punks started coming to the Chelsea from all over the States and Europe in a morbid pilgrimage to the sight of the slaying. Sid represented for them the true meaning of punk: he was a rebel to the end, dying for their sins in the ultimate act of defiance, offing himself in a final, flying fuck-you to this uncool world of lamers and squares. Sid's fans idealized his relationship with Nancy, which in reality was, by most accounts, a codependent union of the damned: the two were miserable apart and even more miserable together. The legend and the death cult were aided by the movie *Sid and Nancy*, which came out in 1986 and portrayed the couple as the Romeo and Juliet of punk, battling to break free of the straightjacket of conformity forced upon them by society. The punks carved their initials into the door of Room 100 with their switchblades and set up makeshift memorials: roses in empty liquor and beer bottles, cigarettes, joints, used needles, love notes. The more ambitious carved slogans: Too Fast To Live, Too Young To Die; It's Better To Burn Out Than To Fade Away; Don't Let Them Take You Alive; I Did It My Way; and the ever popular, Love Kills. If there was anyone staying in Room 100 at the time, they must've been puzzled when they opened their door to discover such cryptic tokens of misplaced hero worship.

It quickly became apparent to the management what was going on. After replacing the wooden door several times, they decided to employ more drastic measures. They tore out the walls and split up the rooms of the apartment between the two adjacent rooms, effectively wiping Room 100 off the face of the hotel map.

But that didn't stop the punk rockers from coming. Though in the eighties it was supposedly much worse, even by the time I got here, in the mid-nineties, it was a common sight to walk in the front door and see a group of punks in black leather jackets and ripped clothing, even the occasional mohawk, lounging in the lobby chairs. Though affecting a look of ennui while gazing at the paintings, they were often scarcely able to contain their excitement at being in the famous Chelsea Hotel, a place of such darkness and mystery. Because they were generally so young, the tattoos and piercings, the chains and the metal studs, the black eye makeup and lipstick only managed to make them look pitiful and vulnerable.

(On the other hand, Sid, with a mean streak a mile wide, looked just like them and was in fact their prototype.) As they approached the desk, you waited to hear the inevitable question: "Can we stay in Room 100?" And the desk clerk's no less inevitable reply: "There is no Room 100." Any inquiry specifically about Sid and Nancy was met with feigned ignorance and stonewalling, perhaps even a flat denial that the couple had ever lived here.

Sid Vicious was born John Simon Ritchie on May 10, 1957. His mother, Anne Beverly, was a heroin addict who, at least on some occasions, supported her son by selling marijuana. (Sid's father was not in the picture.) Not surprisingly, Sid took to drugs early and was shooting speed by his mid-teens. Sid was initially a hanger-on in the London punk scene, more interested in punk fashion than in music. He hung around with the members of the Sex Pistols and went to their shows, where he engaged in violent and self-destructive behavior such as throwing glasses, swinging a chain to clear the dance floor, burning and cutting himself, and assaulting anyone who criticized the band. His biggest contribution to punk music seems to have been his invention of the Pogo, a dance where you jump up and down and hurl yourself against other members of the audience with the dual purpose of getting a better view of the band and pissing people off. Besides that, Sid made a few half-hearted attempts to form his own band, with himself to serve as drummer, though nothing ever came of these efforts.

Sid had known John Lydon, a.k.a. Johnny Rotten, for some years before Johnny started the Sex Pistols. And in fact it was Johnny Rotten who had given him his nickname: Sid was named after Johnny's pet hamster. When Glen Matlock, the Sex Pistol's bassist, quit the band in the spring of 1977, Johnny hit upon the brilliant idea of hiring Sid to replace him. As everyone knew, Sid had no idea how to play the bass, but that was beside the point. Johnny's aim was to shock and upset people by showcasing Sid's bizarre and asinine antics. Sid did not handle his newfound fame well. The punk rock scene was, and remains, a magnet for the troubled and even the psychotic. Deranged fans egged Sid on to new lows of self-destructive behavior. Sid would dive into the audience with little or no provocation, brawling with fans and security guards alike. However, in a refreshing bit of poetic justice, Rotten's inspired personnel move backfired on him, as Sid proved the more charismatic of the two and came to challenge Rotten's status as front man for the band. Sid had a rare talent for mayhem and was able to disrupt the functioning of even so notoriously anarchic a band as the Sex Pistols. Through the sheer force of his own unstable personality, he managed to drag the band down with him, as it imploded during its 1977 to 1978 American tour.

Sid met Nancy, the Yoko Ono of punk, in London soon after he joined the Sex Pistols. Nancy Spungen, a heroin addict from the New York punk scene, had led a privileged childhood in the upper–middle-class suburbs of Philadelphia. According to her mother, Nancy was never quite right: she was given to violent outbursts from a very early age—once attacking her babysitter with scissors—and had to be sedated with prescription drugs from the time she was five. By the time she was a teenager, she was sedating herself. Nancy had the true punk attitude: belligerent, confrontational. A predatory groupie, Nancy's stated ambition was to meet and hookup with a rock star and, failing to find the rock stars so gullible in New York, she traveled to London with that aim in mind. Nearly everyone on the London scene hated her immediately for her exceedingly nasty, abrasive personality. She was known as a parasite: even her name—the "g" is soft—fit her to a T. Apparently, Sid was one of the few people Nancy was even remotely civil to. Theirs was a violent love—literally as well as figuratively—a truly volatile union. Nancy introduced Sid to heroin and used it to push him over the edge. For what it's worth, Nancy was a true muse, inspiring Sid to germinate the seeds of all that was genuinely nasty and loathsome in his being.

———————

No matter how they're dressed, you can't stop people from sitting in the lobby, especially if they're minding their own business and not hurting anyone. The punks don't look that much weirder than a lot of the residents here, and sometimes they tone down their costumes for checking into the hotel. Stanley likes the money, and so plenty of them have been able to get a room in the hotel over the years—just not *that* room—especially if they show up in the off-season. (Perhaps some of them even have the foresight to call ahead for a reservation.) Once in, the punks inevitably make their way to the first floor, generally late at night, to the approximate site of Sid's old room, where they pass the wine somberly and burn candles hazardously beneath sloppily tacked-up British flags.

But one time a group of punks actually managed to rent Sid's room—or anyway what they considered the closest thing, a room which actually contains at least the bathroom, though now even that's been renovated. Maybe they sent one of their number dressed like an Ivy League prep in a pair of khaki pants and an alligator shirt. Or maybe one of them got his mother to rent the room. In any event, they lucked out. Predictably, they invited all their friends over and partied all weekend—the various punks coming and going—playing the Sex Pistols over and over, and the Ramones and the Clash. I had a friend on the floor (he was the one who gave me the details for the story), and he said he was curious and peeked in the room a couple of times: he said on the last night they kept the room dark, the shutters drawn, and burned candles in there, perhaps even attempted a séance. But by Monday afternoon they were gone.

Except for one guy, who decided to stay on. Discovering that he was still in the room, they called him from the front desk and told him he'd missed checkout time, but he said he was staying a few more days. And that's just what he did: he barricaded himself in the room and wouldn't come out. He would phone out for food and cigarettes from the deli down the block, and when they delivered, he would open the door just a crack—the chain still on—and shove the money out and pull the bag back in before anybody could get a look. He wouldn't open the door for any other reason and he wouldn't let the maid in to clean the room.

After a couple of days the maid got a bit pushy. Maybe she had been ordered to get a look in the room, or more likely she just thought it would make her job all the harder the longer she waited. "Housekeeping!" she called out in her thick Jamaican accent, rapping with her key, and, without waiting, trying the lock and finding her way barred. The man had moved a chest of drawers against the door.

"Go away!" came a faint voice from within.

"When can I come back?" the maid demanded. The maids around here don't take no for an answer.

"Later," the man replied, his voice a hoarse croak.

"When later? I have other work now, but I can't stay here all day. You want me come back at noon?"

He opened the door, barely a crack: "Go away!" He sounded British, my friend said, or maybe Irish.

"It smell like urine in there," the maid said, disgustedly, as she turned away from the door. "I know it be bad."

They might have left him alone longer, but the punkers had reserved the room for the weekend, and beyond that they hadn't paid. Toward the end of the week Stanley was no doubt getting a bit nervous. He had been talking to the guy on the phone and receiving unsatisfactory answers, so now he sent one of the bellmen, an Italian guy named George, up to the room to pay the recluse a visit.

When he got up to the room, George banged forcefully on the door. "Hey, you okay in there? Open the door," he said.

"Go away," the recluse said from within.

"Your friends only rented the room for the weekend," George said. "You can't stay here."

"I'll pay later, when I check out."

"I'm sure you will, but they need the room for somebody else. You got to go."

"I can't go anywhere now."

"We'll get you another room," George said, and when that didn't work, he said, "Okay, you can stay here, but you have to come down to the desk and talk to Stanley."

The guy in the room wasn't falling for that. "I'll talk to him on the phone."

"He doesn't want to do that, he wants you to come down."

The recluse didn't say anything.

"Let me at least see you," George said, "to see that you're okay."

Several moments went by as George stood before the door. There was the noise of the heavy moving of the chest, and then the door, with the chain on, opened the slightest crack.

"You don't look too good," George said.

"I'm sick," the man said.

"Let me in and I'll call an ambulance and get you to the hospital," George said, but the guy wouldn't go for it. "Just trying to help you out here," George said, as the recluse closed the door in his face.

George stood there for a moment, not knowing what else to do. "We don't want to have to get the cops involved," George said to the closed door. And though he meant it as a threat, it was no less true for that: the management really doesn't like to have the police wandering around in the hotel.

They let him stay on a couple more days and kept coming back to check on him, with similar results. Sometimes he wouldn't come to the door at all but just called out weakly from far within the room. Staff and residents on the floor began to speculate that maybe he had come up with the idea to kill himself in Sid's room but then couldn't quite bring himself to take the plunge. (It's not uncommon for people to check in and then commit suicide here, hence the concern.) He stopped phoning out for food and seemed to be lying in bed, attempting to will himself to die.

Finally, fearing disaster (and of course wanting to rent the room out again), the management gave in and called the police. Two cops arrived and—accompanied by several members of the staff—they knocked on the door and announced their presence.

With predictable results: the recluse simply refused to get out of bed.

"We're not trying to hurt you," one of the cops called out. "We just want to check on you." He waited a minute and then said, "Okay, you leave us no choice. We're coming in."

Using a passkey, one of the maintenance men opened the door a crack and clipped the chain, but the door was well barricaded, and even the two big cops couldn't force it any further. But the maintenance man knew what to do: he busted out one of the top panels of the door with a mallet so one of the smaller staff members could climb in and move the obstruction. The guy inside didn't protest at all as this was done.

The cops went in to talk to the recluse and then, after a while, they called in the manager. They were in there for a long time talking to him, but he must've been pretty bad off, because finally they called an ambulance, and the paramedics came and looked him over. They brought a stretcher and left it outside the room in the hall, but in the end the guy walked out under his own power. Much older than the punks who had rented the room, probably in his mid-forties, the man appeared sick and wasted away, perhaps with AIDS or cancer, and he walked with a limp, supporting himself with a cane. His pale, wispy hair was thinning, and he had a week's growth of gray beard on his face. He seemed alert, my friend said, though he moved slowly. It was a mystery how he had had the strength to move that chest of drawers against the door, but I guess where there's a will, there's a way. The man's worn leather jacket, hand-painted with symbols of dissent, was the only outward sign of his punk allegiance.

When the maid got in there, the room was close to the worst she'd ever seen—and that's saying a lot around here. The room reeked of cigarettes and pot smoke and urine, and much worse. There were piles of garbage all over the place: liquor bottles, beer cans, Chinese takeout containers, and pizza boxes crawling with roaches. The toilet was backed up and filled to overflowing with vomit and shit. The mattress and the box springs had been dragged off onto the floor, burned with cigarettes and soaked with urine. The carpet, too, had been saturated with urine and beer, and the gang of punk hooligans had burned holes through the carpet and into the floor. Candles had been melted down to wax on every flat surface, and graffiti was spray-painted all over the walls. Much of the furniture had been busted up and burned in the fireplace. They'd even attempted to chip off or pry up the bathroom tiles— though of course these were different tiles from those Nancy had expired upon.

The maid refused to touch the room. It was a job for the wrecking crew. Once they had lugged out all the trash, they threw out the mattress and box springs too, along with the rest of the wrecked furniture. They ripped up the sodden carpet and hauled it out to the curb.

These days, the kids don't ask for Room 100 so much anymore. It's partly because the young people coming to New York in this zero decade are no longer the misfits and outcasts who made this city great. Now it's the very people they ran away from, the popular kids who grew up watching shows like *Friends* and *Sex and the City* and thought New York looked about as threatening as a shopping spree at the local mall. The Chelsea still has a certain cachet, but a radically different one: it's no longer, *I want to move to the Chelsea and make art;* but rather, *I want to move to the Chelsea and make money.* Now there are Room 100 key chains for sale at the front desk, and even Stanley Bard seems to miss the attention. It feels like the end of an era, and I just want to scream at these kids: hey, don't you know Sid's the James Dean of punk! I want to say, look, he's the Jim Morrison of your generation. The Chelsea is your Père-Lachaise. But their generation has grown up too. The kids have moved on to Kurt Cobain, though I guess even he is yesterday's news by now.

And yet the old ghosts refuse to rest. Recently, Susan and I were involved in planning a reading series in conjunction with the Algonquin Hotel. We were going to call it *Lobby Legends: From the Vicious Circle to Sid Vicious.* Patti Smith had recently come out with a new book of poetry, and we wanted to ask her if she would read at our event. One of the greatest performers associated with the punk movement of the seventies—a brilliant singer and song-writer, as opposed to the talentless Sid—Patti lived here at the Chelsea with the photographer Robert Mapplethorpe in the seventies and then once again with her children in the nineties. It seemed possible that she might do it, because she often reads in small venues, and we hoped to appeal to whatever lingering traces of affection she might still feel for the old hotel. We went through several people around here who are still in contact with her, and we waited and waited, but she wouldn't get back to us. Everyone was puzzled as to why she wouldn't at least respond. (We contacted Leonard Cohen, by contrast, on the off chance that he might read, and his response was a prompt and polite no thanks.)

We couldn't figure it out. But then, while I was researching this story, I stumbled upon what I thought might be at least part of the answer. On December 6, 1978, while out on bail awaiting trial for Nancy's murder, Sid attended one of Patti's concerts. At some point during the show, he assaulted Patti's brother Todd, shattering a glass beer mug in his face and kicking him in the nuts. We hadn't stopped to consider that Patti had moved in the same circles as Sid and that we might be dredging up unpleasant memories. It was our title, with its unintentionally insensitive reference to Sid, that had scared her away.

I ran into Patti once here at the hotel, by the way, in the mid-to-late-nineties. It was in the early morning hours, when the hotel is quiet and at its most mysterious. I had awakened after a night of drinking, unable to go back to sleep, and had got up to take a piss. After I came out of the bathroom, still restless, I wandered out into the main hallway. Looking through the glass door into the stairwell, I saw her descending the stairs, moving ghostlike behind the florid iron balustrade, her figure gaunt, her hair scraggly and gray. I did a double take: Is that Patti Smith? They had kept her residency quiet, and I hadn't even known she'd moved in. I watched her as she paused on our landing to examine a painting. She appeared haggard, though she still possessed that unique, uncanny sort of beauty that transcends outward form.

Patti had fled the doomed punk scene not long after Sid's death, trading in the fast life of New York for the domestic stability of marriage and motherhood and a life in the suburbs. She had returned to New York after the tragic death of her husband, Fred Smith, to heart failure, to pick up her career where she had left off more than a decade before.

Maybe she, too, was having trouble sleeping and had set out to explore her past in the hallways of the old hotel. At that moment she turned and, without surprise, saw me, and our eyes met. I could feel her searching my face for a token of memory, looking within herself for a spark of recognition, hoping perhaps that mine was a face from the old hotel of her youth. I was, of course, too young to have been there. But whatever she saw in my face—and maybe I just had that mad, deathless, Chelsea look—in that uncertain time of her life she smiled, and I smiled back, before she continued on her way down the stairs.

Cowboy Doc

We used to have a doctor in the Chelsea. I needed a flu shot one fall and, since I had seen his fliers in the elevator, I went to his office on the second floor. It was eleven in the morning. It took him a long time to answer the door, and when he did, a cloud of pungent, exotic smoke wafted from the room. The doctor wore army pants and a T-shirt and spoke in a southern drawl. Classic rock was playing on his stereo. Though his office hours began at nine, he said he had just got out of bed.

I believe I must have been one of his first patients, and he showed me around the office proudly. He had remodeled the place to look like an old-time doctor's office, complete with antique equipment, like apothecary cabinets and examining tables from the fifties, all very cool. (There's a particular Chelsea aesthetic that many residents seem to share: grandly trashy, worn chic, whatever you want to call it, and he had that down pat.) I was impressed.

I told him I was a writer, and he said he'd written a novel: a sort of combination of *Star Wars* and the occult. I had begun a novel of my own that year, along the slightly more realistic lines that I tend to prefer, but I lied and said I'd like to read his. (No sense in riling someone who's about to stick you with a sharp object.) I got the flu shot, and he called me back several times afterwards to make sure I hadn't had a bad reaction.

Soon after that, somebody took to defacing the fliers he had put up in the elevators, writing "Cowboy Doc" all over them, among other things. There's a dark side to the Chelsea: wherever you have a lot of creative people, there are bound to be some who are bitter about their careers not quite panning out. The flu shot worked, however. I didn't get sick all winter.

I kept meaning to go back and visit the guy but as a rule I never go to the doctor unless I absolutely have to, and so it wasn't until the next fall that I ventured back down to his office. He wasn't there, but the door of his office was standing open and movers were carrying out all of his antique doctor's equipment. He just never got enough business. Though to my mind he fit right in, probably for a lot of people he didn't really inspire confidence as a doctor.

I remember our conversation the day I got the flu shot. He said he had been trained as an all-purpose doctor by the army, and he gave me a long list of the specialties in which he had attained competence. The one that stands out in my mind is "Emergency Psychiatric Intervention," and I told him that sounded like it should go over pretty well at the Chelsea.

Declining Fortunes

Run: Virgil Thomson at the Chelsea

The ancient, groaning elevator is one of the best places in the hotel to meet interesting people. In fact, you may get to know them better than you'd like to if, as occurs with some regularity, the elevator breaks down between floors.

One day I was in the elevator with Gerald Busby, a classical composer and pianist. We had just gotten on in the lobby, and the door was nearly closed when an arm shot into the small crack, and the door sprung back open again. A young man bounded onto the elevator. Tall and muscular, he was dressed in hip-hop gear: an expensive tracksuit, gold jewelry. His eyes were wide, the pupils dilated, and he was manic, hyperactive, gesticulating wildly as he spoke in a nonstop stream.

"I'm looking for Walter in 546. I really need to talk to him. I'm supposed to be staying at his place, and he knows this but I don't know where he is. He was supposed to let me in. I've been looking for him all day and I can't find him." Despite his crazed aspect, I thought I detected a note of cunning in his eyes.

"I don't know him," I said.

"I don't either," Gerald said.

"A short, balding man, with glasses. Room 546. You couldn't miss him. Have you lived here long? You look like you have. You must know him. I've got to find him. It's very important."

We assured him once again that we didn't know Walter.

"If you see Walter, you've got to give him my message. It's very important, please see that he gets my message." He got off on the fifth floor, apparently to wait for Walter. I noticed that somehow, for all that, he had forgotten to say what the message was.

When the door had closed and we were safely underway, I laughed and said, "Well, I guess if I ever meet Walter, I'll give him the message."

"Oh, I know Walter," Gerald said.

"You do?"

"Sure. He's a poet. Room 546, like he said."

"So are you going to give him the message?" I joked.

"Yeah, I'll give him the message: Run!"

———————

Gerald is the composer of the eerie soundtrack for Robert Altman's strange filmic masterpiece *3 Women*. (If you've seen this film you know that the music is more than mere background; it really adds to the mood of dread and foreboding in the movie.) Gerald was born in Tyler, Texas, in 1935 and went to Yale. After that he moved to New York to play the piano and compose music. He had early success with his score for the Paul Taylor Dance Company's *Runes*. Besides his work on Altman's *3 Women,* Gerald also had a role in Altman's 1978 film, *A Wedding.*

I'm not sure if I even knew Gerald's name when the elevator incident took place. If I did, then that was all I knew about him— besides the fact that he was a friendly, pleasant guy, a kindly, white-haired man who always had a smile on his face. Then one day recently, in 2005, Susan and I saw a flyer in the display case in the lobby that said he was giving a concert at the Cornelia Street Café, and we figured we might as well go. Gerald's show was called "The Monologing Composer": Gerald played the piano, accompanying various singers, and between pieces told anecdotes of his early life in Texas and of his later years at the Chelsea Hotel, where he has lived since the late seventies. It was a relaxed, intimate show, designed, the program said, to take classical music out of the concert hall and give it back to the people.

Among other things, we discovered that night that Gerald had been a longtime friend and protégé of the famous composer and legendary Chelsea Hotel resident, Virgil Thomson, up until the older man's death in 1989. Thomson, born in 1896, in Kansas City, Missouri, lived in Paris in the twenties and thirties, hanging out with Cocteau, Stravinsky, Duchamp, Picasso, and James Joyce and composing operas based on the writings of Gertrude Stein, including his most famous piece, *Four Saints in Three Acts.* He wrote the scores to several films, including *The Louisiana Story,* for which he won the Pulitzer in 1949. Thomson was also a well-known music critic, winning the National Book Critic's Circle Award in 1981 for an anthology of his work. Thomson moved into the Chelsea in 1942 and lived there until his death, surely making him close to the record holder in that dubious category.

Thomson was also an accomplished cook, and Gerald, who worked as a chef himself at various restaurants in New York City, is writing a cookbook in which he has compiled Thomson's favorite recipes. That night at the Cornelia Street Café, Gerald told us one recipe, for coq au vin. Here it is, as best I remember, handed down from Virgil to Gerald, to me, and now to you:

1. Cut up the chicken into eighths.
2. Braise chicken with a rendering of beef suet.
3. Add a cup of shallots and a cup of your best burgundy. Simmer until done.
4. Serve with the rest of the burgundy.

Afterward, the audience was buzzing: The recipe sounds so simple and delicious, but what exactly is beef suet? A theater critic sitting at the next table singled us out as southerners by our accents and, thinking we would surely know, followed us out to the street and asked us. Neither Susan nor I had any idea, although we felt pretty confident it was some kind of fat. Later, I looked in the dictionary and found that suet is raw beef or mutton fat, especially the hard fat found around the loins and kidneys. So not just any old fat. Unfortunately, we don't have a kitchen here at the Chelsea, or else I'd cook it and let you know how it turned out. In any event, you'll have to wait for Gerald's book to come out to get the definitive version of the recipe.

Gerald was never able to build on the success he had in the seventies, and this led him to become deeply depressed. Also, at around the time of Thomson's death, Gerald and his longtime partner, Sam Byers, were diagnosed as HIV positive. Sam died of AIDS in 1993, after a protracted illness in which Gerald cared for him. Distraught over the death of his partner, and in declining health himself, Gerald turned to cocaine and stopped composing altogether.

This was what was going on with Gerald when he and I encountered the menacing character in the elevator. Through it all, his sense of humor had remained intact.

When we learned of his troubles—around the time of the Cornelia Street concert—both Susan and I found the story extremely hard to believe. Gerald had always seemed like such a nice guy, and so levelheaded, one of the few genuinely sane people around here. But it's easy to lose it here in the Chelsea around all these borderline cases, not to mention all the people who have already lost it. You just need something to send you over the edge, and for Gerald it was the death of his partner. Gerald ran from his pain, which is easy enough to understand. I ran myself for twenty years, though my drug of choice was alcohol.

Within the past few years, Gerald has got his life back on track, thanks in part to a program called the Estate Project for Artists with AIDS. After not creating any new music for six years, he's been composing by means of the Sibelius computer program, which has given him a big boost creatively. His new CD, *The Music of Gerald Busby*, has just been released on the Innova label. And he recently celebrated his seventieth birthday with a retrospective of his music—though no anecdotes, unfortunately—at Carnegie Hall.

The Gray Man of the Chelsea

An old Chelsea babysitter writes:

Though I never lived at the Chelsea Hotel myself, I
used to babysit for a young couple who lived there
back in the late nineties, when the hotel was just
starting to be gentrified. They were not artists. The man
was an investment banker and the woman owned a
small catering business, and I'm not sure why they
chose the Chelsea. Perhaps because they liked to enjoy
a hedonistic lifestyle (they had an active social life) or
maybe they wanted to be thought of as artistic or
daring. Or maybe just because it was cheap. That's the
only thing I can think of. I was a teenager at the time,
and since they were gone all the time, I babysat for
them nearly every day one summer, and they went out
a lot at night too.

Their little boy was six or seven years old. They
were very protective of the child and tried to keep
him away from the dubious characters that roamed
the halls of the Chelsea, and they were always complaining to Stanley about somebody doing something immoral. Like being a prostitute or a junky and
that was somehow harming their son. In fact, that's

probably why they hired me, because I came from outside the hotel.

Now, what I'm going to say is the God's honest truth, though the couple won't admit it and they called me a liar to my face, but one night they had gone out to a cocktail party and they came home really late with another couple and they were all talking and joking around out in the stairwell. I wanted to leave and I was waiting to get paid. The cocktail party was in the hotel I think, or at least there was some sort of party on one of the lower floors. All I know is it was really loud. They lived on the tenth floor.

The boy, for obvious reasons I don't want to say his name, came out in his pajamas. When we noticed him, we all said, "What are you doing out here? Go back to bed," but he wouldn't. Instead he went to the railing of the stairs and looked up at the skylight. He just kept looking up and finally he said, "Mommy, who is that man up there?" His parents just laughed and said, "Oh, what are you talking about?" But instead of dropping it, the boy became increasingly excited, pointing and screaming: "Mommy, why is that man up there?!" "There's nobody up there, honey," his mother said. "That man! That gray man up there!" "There's nobody up there," his father said sternly. "Get back to bed."

Then the boy got quiet. He kept staring at the sky-light, but he was quiet. I probably should have taken him to bed, but it was late and I really wanted to get paid and go home. "He's just tired," the parents said to their friends, who said their good-byes and got on the elevator and went down. But while we were distracted watching them leave, the boy had somehow managed to climb up on the railing and stand there, I don't know how he did it, balanced on the top rail.

Luckily, they saw him. "Oh my God!" they said. "What are you doing?!" the mother said, and the father grabbed him back down from there before he could jump or fall. The boy started shaking and shivering all over as they both held him, almost having an epileptic fit, and he peed in his pants. The parents were drunk and had been smoking pot I think, but that really sobered them up quick. I didn't even get my money that night but I guess after that I forgot about it and really just wanted to get the hell out of there as fast as possible.

Like I said, they say I'm a liar about this. But what they can't deny is that their son changed after this incident. I can't prove anything but I personally think he was possessed by some kind of spirit that night. He was a really sweet kid before but after that he was either like a zombie or else he would go into a violent rage. They told me to keep sharp objects locked up and not to let him out of my sight and not to go anywhere. They were keeping him locked in his room at night because he would try to sneak out, and one time he turned on all the burners on the gas stove and almost killed them all. When you took him out, you had to hold onto him because he would go for the railing, not rushing for it but pulled to it in a trance. And he was strong too. A couple of times he got away from me and tried to climb up onto the railing, whether to jump or what, I don't know, but I was able to pull him back down and get him into the elevator, thank God. I don't know if he was trying to get to the man or to throw himself over, but it was clear that if he kept doing it he would fall eventually. Darkness was bad, but an overcast day was the worst. He tore his room all up when he went into his violent rages and he graffitied all over the walls in crayons in gibberish or an unknown language.

After a few days of this I wanted to quit, but the parents begged me to stay and said they couldn't get anyone else. These days they would probably say the child had ADD, and they got a doctor and medicated the child and it kept him quiet, but he still couldn't be left alone or he would go out into the hallway and head for the railing. I lasted about two weeks, but it was not worth the money, even though they agreed to pay me double.

Now I've done some research on this issue since then, and this type of possession is never straightforward. (Though I was a babysitter then I went on to get a college education and studied psychology and parapsychology.) The boy was smart and he knew what was happening to him in a way, though, understandably, he would often become confused, and I think this was the source of his violent rages. Sometimes he thought that adults were trying to lead him to the railing or even to throw him over. He would scream and run away and hide in his room. I guess in these instances he was not possessed and maybe he even thought the adults were the Gray Man. When he was like this, then you couldn't get him out the door for anything.

I mention this because of what happened next. I was trying to take him out to the dentist one day. His parents were stupid for making me do this but they insisted because they wanted to pretend that nothing was wrong. I knew better by this time and I kept a tight grip on the boy and kept my body between him and the railing as I steered him toward the elevator. This time, though, he didn't go into a trance like usual and try to make it to the railing. Instead as soon as we got near the railing, he started screaming hysterically and struggling against me. I held on and told him to shut up as I pushed the elevator button. But he bit my hand and got free and ran back to the room and started struggling to open the door, turning the handle and pulling and pushing against it. Of course it was locked, but he started screaming at me and cursing me, calling me a fucking bitch and every other name in the book, telling me to open the door and let him in or he'd kill me. All right, that's it, we're not going anywhere, I thought, and I got the key out of my pocket and opened the door. He burst in, and before I could get in, he grabbed the door and slammed it on me. I got my body in the way and stuck my foot in the door so he couldn't close it all the way, but he was freakishly strong, and I couldn't push it open. He got the chain on somehow and he ran back into the apartment. I couldn't just leave him in there because who knows what he was going to do, so I tried to stick my hand in and get the chain off. When he saw that he ran at the door but I had my foot in it and though it hurt like hell he couldn't close the door. Where he got the scissors I'll never know, but the next thing I know, he stabs me in the hand! I screamed and pulled my hand out and my foot too, and he slammed the door and threw the dead bolt.

So then I was standing there bleeding and I didn't know what to do. I was bleeding profusely and I couldn't even leave to go to the hospital because what if the kid got out and killed himself? Or killed himself in there? I tried calling for him in my confusion, begging him to open the door, but of course that did no good. Finally I banged on all the neighbors' doors, and eventually somebody opened up and gave me a rag to wrap my hand in.

I told the lady to call the mother at work, and she came home and tried to act like it was no big deal and I was the one who was crazy and caused the problem in the first place. I don't think anybody believed her, but still! I was the one who was trying to help! I had to get five stitches in my hand at the hospital.

There was no way I was going back after that, and I told them they should get the child institutionalized. They didn't appreciate that one bit, but there wasn't much they could say after the kid had just stabbed me. The man paid me, overpaid me by several times, trying to pay me off I guess, to buy my silence, and it's true I didn't say anything to anybody for nearly a year after that, and by that time they had already left the Chelsea. And New York, I think. The reason I didn't say anything was not the money but because they made me feel like I was crazy for even mentioning it. I was just seventeen, remember.

They got another babysitter, a girl in her twenties who I knew from the hotel, and the kid drove her crazy. She started taking drugs, maybe she had been taking them before, and eventually she had to get psychiatric help. I think she may have even spent some time in a mental hospital. The couple tried to blame her for their child's condition, saying she was a junky, but she had nothing to do with it, since, like I said, the child was like that before. I feel more sorry for her than for anybody, to tell you the truth. Except for maybe the child. He was supposed to start school in the fall, but they held him back, and I doubt he was ever normal again.

Since then I've often thought of the Gray Man, wondered who he was, perhaps the ghost of someone who committed suicide by throwing himself down the stairwell. Or maybe a more elemental spirit, a sort of evil pied piper of children. When I asked the boy one time who the Gray Man was, he said he was smoke. I don't know whether this makes any sense or not, but this was when the boy was in a good or rational state of mind. The parents and their child disappeared into Middle America and obscurity, trying to put as much distance between themselves and the Chelsea as possible. The boy would be in his early teens now, which is typically when a dormant mental illness manifests. I assume they've had him on medication all this time, but now that he's entering these rebellious years, what if he decides to stop taking it, as often happens? There was a powerful attraction working on him, that I know, pulling him toward that railing and that skylight. And so I have to ask, is this paranormal force still drawing him to the Chelsea? Will he some day return to the scene of his childhood and his lost innocence? And what form will his madness take in adulthood? It seems only time will tell.

Wow, this place is even scarier than I thought. Junkies and schizophrenics are one thing, but elemental spirits are more than I can handle. Almost makes me want to live in the suburbs! And this woman seems pretty authoritative too; after all, she's studied parapsychology. Keep your doors locked tonight!

The Paintah

I was walking through the Chelsea Hotel lobby one day. Stanley Bard was standing up by the desk talking to a younger man with a beard and paint-stained overalls—a common type at the hotel. The man had obviously come to inquire about getting a room. "So what do you do?" Stanley inquired.

"I'm a paintah," the bearded man said, in a heavy Brooklyn accent.

"That's great," Stanley said, visibly excited. Stanley loves the arts. And he is always happiest when given an opportunity to speak of the glory of the hotel. "This is just the place for you," he said. "We have lots of painters living here. Famous painters. Philip Taaffe has a studio here, and Julian Schnabel. Larry Rivers used to live here. You'll get along fine. What kind of stuff do you paint?"

The man gave Stanley a quizzical look. "I paint houses, whadaya think?"

"Oh," Stanley said, obviously disappointed. "Uh, what I meant was, abstract or figurative?" he stammered. "I thought maybe you painted pictures."

"Nah," the guy said. "I said I was a paintah, not an ahtist."

How to Get Yourself Sent Away

A semifamous painter, a surrealist who had studied in Paris in the forties and fifties, Mr. Peyton was gray-haired, stocky, lumbering like an old bear, genial. He was always cheerful, though sometimes slightly addled and forgetful, since he was, after all, in his eighties. He was sociable and always stopped to shoot the breeze, sometimes beneath his own large canvas, which hung prominently in a place of honor in the hotel lobby. One sensed he had had a good life overall. He had never gotten rich but he had been able to make a living with his art. You never heard him complaining.

Mr. Peyton had one of the best apartments in the whole building, on the tenth floor. Filled floor to ceiling with his paintings, it was really a studio—an atelier, I suppose—though Mr. Peyton worked only sporadically now. His rooms opened onto a huge patio on the roof.

I was up on the tenth floor visiting friends one evening, when the fire alarm went off. We all piled out into the hallway to see what was going on, just in time to see smoke streaming from the open door of Mr. Peyton's apartment and rolling out along the ceiling. Mr. Peyton stood there outside his door, frantically fanning at the air.

"What happened?" I asked. "Are you OK?" Everybody on the floor was popping their heads out of their apartments to ask the same questions.

"Don't worry, it's just steam," Mr. Peyton said. "I overflowed the tub."

Of course, nobody believed that for a moment. The hall was filled with smoke, not steam.

"We'd better go downstairs and wait until it clears," I said.

"No, it's nothing," Mr. Peyton said. He refused to go downstairs.

He was right that it wasn't much: Mr. Peyton had placed something in a casserole dish in the oven, then forgot he was cooking and dozed off. The fire had gone out before the firemen even arrived, though they made a big fuss with their sirens and about a dozen of them tromping through the hotel lobby. Better safe than sorry. Most of the residents didn't even notice it anyway, ensconced as they were behind their thick, soundproof walls.

But Mr. Peyton's children got wind of the incident. Now his son came to live with him, to take care of him and to make sure he didn't try to cook anything too ambitious.

A few months later I noticed that I hadn't seen Mr. Peyton lately. Hoping that he wasn't sick, I asked his son what had become of him.

"He's in France," the son said.

"Oh," I said, surprised. "What's he doing there?"

It turned out they had put him into a nursing home there. The time Mr. Peyton had spent in Paris in his youth had apparently qualified him for government benefits, including a free stay in a nursing home. "I checked out several places upstate, and even in New Jersey, but they were all too expensive. They wanted an arm and a leg," the son said. "We won't get to see him that much now, but we decided that this was just the best situation for him overall." Now the son lives in Mr. Peyton's gigantic apartment with his wife and two kids.

And now we tease all the older residents, especially the ones who burn candles: "One slipup and it's France for you!" But after all, I think it was less the fire itself than the story about the tub and the steam that did Mr. Peyton in.

It all sounds rather grim, but I like to think that maybe it didn't turn out so bad for Mr. Peyton after all. France, after all. Rather than New Jersey. Mr. Peyton used to hang out at the Dunkin Donuts on Eighth Avenue, one of the few in the city that had outdoor seating. He told me once that when he sat there he would often find his mind wandering and he would catch himself thinking, just for a moment, that he was back in Paris, sipping his coffee at a café on the Boulevard Saint-Germain.

Donuts Sandwiches:
Jack Kerouac at the Chelsea

Before it closed, Donuts Sandwiches, along with the Chelsea and the McBurney Y, was one of the pillars of the bohemian community of West 23rd Street. At this all-night diner at Eighth Avenue and 23rd you could get a Cheeseburger Deluxe—that's a cheeseburger with lettuce, tomato, a pickle, and French fries—for $2.95 in the mid-nineties. For a dollar, you got two donuts and a coffee. You could even pay with a subway token, if that's all the rehab center gave you for the day.

The cook was a middle-aged man named Jerry, who looked like Jack Kerouac—when Jack Kerouac was a fat drunk. Despite his bulk, if somebody acted up, if a junky cursed him, say, Jerry would grab a baseball bat and hop the horseshoe counter and run the guy out the door.

Every time I came into the diner I would order my coffee black with no sugar.

This always seemed to offend Jerry. "No milk, no sugar?!" he would say every time. "Why don't you want some milk? How 'bout at least some sugar."

"I don't like it like that."

"Why don't you like it?" he would say in his outer-borough accent. "It's good like that. I can't understand it, I can't understand how anybody drinks their coffee like that."

Luckily, he wasn't generally the one who fixed the coffee.

Jerry was talkative and, aside from the thing with the coffee, usually cheerful. Over the years I learned a lot about him: he lived in Queens, he was an expert fisherman, a fine gardener, and he could fix anything around the house. He had a son who was a lawyer, apparently the best in the business, who made five hundred thousand, or sometimes it was a million dollars, a year. Jerry was a Mets fan, permanently disgusted with their performance.

One day, over the Christmas holidays, Jerry's wife died. Though she had had serious medical problems, it still came unexpectedly. For all his talk, I had never heard Jerry mention his wife before, except in passing. Now he discussed her at length:

> I'm just glad it was my wife instead of my mother-in-law. I loved my wife, but my mother-in-law was the one that cooked and took care of the house. I know maybe that sounds funny, but it would have been more of a loss if she had died. My wife was always like a child, she never could clean, never could cook. There at the end she was an invalid, she got really fat. She just laid in bed and drank beer and smoked cigarettes, three packs a day, watching TV and killing herself.
>
> She had diabetes. She should've got out more, it would've helped her circulation, but it was hard for her, it made her tired. She was always in and out of the hospital for something. A blood clot went to her brain and killed her, a stroke, just like that, died in my arms almost.
>
> Now, I'm not saying I'm glad she's dead, but I'm gonna save a lot of money now, I'll tell ya. I figured it up, and I'm gonna save three hundred dollars a week just on beer and cigarettes alone.
>
> My mother-in-law was the one who took care of her. My wife couldn't have made it without her. My old mother-in-law—she's eighty—had to wait on her hand and foot. If my mother-in-law had died she

wouldn't have had anybody, so that's why I say it's a good thing she went first. I know it sounds weird to say that, but that's how I feel.

I did think it was weird—though not so much to feel it as to say it. It was natural to be relieved that someone who was so much of a burden had died, and it was natural also to feel guilt at experiencing that relief. I decided that Jerry, being a talker, had to deal with his feelings verbally.

The real Jack Kerouac never had a Cheeseburger Deluxe in Donuts Sandwiches. Though the diner looked like it had been there forever, Jerry told me that it only dated from the early seventies. (I know that an opera house used to sit on that spot, but that was around the turn of the century, when 23rd Street was the heart of the theater district.) The building, however, probably dates from before the time of Kerouac, so maybe it was a diner in those days too.

The real Jack Kerouac was born in 1922 in Lowell, Massachusetts. Descended from French-Canadian immigrants, his family spoke Quebecois French at home. Jack was a star halfback in high school and won a football scholarship to Columbia. He was injured early in his first season and spent only about a year at Columbia, but it was there that he met Allen Ginsberg and William Burroughs. In the early-to-mid-forties, the three began hanging out in jazz clubs in Harlem and coffee shops in Greenwich Village, and the Beat movement was born. It was around this time, too, that he met Neal Cassady, the man with whom, in 1949, he embarked on the cross-country tour that was to become the basis of his seminal novel *On the Road,* the work that defined his generation and has been an inspiration to disaffected college students for ever afterward.

Legend has it that Jack wrote *On the Road* in 1951 at the Chelsea Hotel in a three-day, Dexedrine-fueled torrent of spontaneous prose. On a roll of toilet paper. Or something like that. (Those Beats sure were mythmakers; the best minds of their generation would be in PR these days.) I'm not quite sure I buy the part about him writing it at the Chelsea. Although some sources say this, other sources say variously that he wrote it at the apartment he shared with his second wife, Joan Haverty, at 454 West 20th Street or at his mother's house in Richmond Hill, Queens. The 20th Street place is close, in the Chelsea neighborhood, so maybe that accounts for the confusion. Or maybe, after all, Jack slipped around the corner to the hotel for three days of (Dexedrine-fueled!) peace and quiet in which to write his masterpiece. He did certainly spend some time in the hotel at around this period of his life, famously having sex with Gore Vidal here. My money is on the Queens location, as Jack, for all his famous wanderings, could never stand to be away from his mother for long.

(On the other hand, that roll of toilet paper—or maybe after all it was teletype paper—does sound suspiciously Chelsea-like.)

On the Road came out in 1957, propelling Jack to instant stardom. Notoriously, he couldn't cope with the fame: fans lauded him, but critics derided him, both for sloppy writing and for advocating a dissolute lifestyle. *On the Road* was such a big success that publishers began bringing out his books at a furious pace before they had been properly edited and before the public had digested his earlier works. They overhyped him and burnt him out, and Jack retreated into alcoholism. This only gave critics more fuel for their attacks.

In the last years of his life, Jack became a shell of his former self, living parasitically off the legend he had created for himself. He retreated to the bosom of his mother, and she sheltered him; they moved around together from town to town, from Lowell, Massachusetts, to Cape Cod, to St. Petersburg, Florida. Fat, bloated, suffering from cirrhosis of the liver, Jack drank a quart of liquor a day, popping speed to write and throwing in Benadryl to sleep. He became increasingly paranoid and belligerent, going out at night to bars and getting falling-down drunk, bragging loudly and starting fights that he could no longer finish, alienating new and old friends alike. A political conservative, he raged against the hippies who idolized him and he supported the war. He was given to spouting homophobic, anti-Semitic, and racist diatribes and once set a cross ablaze in a black neighborhood in Orlando. His writing suffered, of course, and by the end the man who routinely pulled days-long marathon sessions of fevered creation was only able to manage a couple of hours a day. (Actually, that's not bad, considering.) When Jack's mother was incapacitated by a stroke, he married his third wife, Stella Sampas, to care for both his mother and himself. But neither his mother's decline nor the death of his friend Neal Cassady in 1968 seemed to slow Jack's self-destructive juggernaut. In September 1969, Jack and a friend went drinking in a rough black bar in St. Petersburg, and apparently the friend made a pass at the manager, an ex-boxer, or in some way offended him. When Jack stepped in, the manager—who probably didn't much care for Jack in the first place—beat him up badly, breaking two of his ribs. Jack refused to go to the hospital. On October 21 he died of bleeding associated with cirrhosis of the liver, perhaps exacerbated by the beating. He was forty-seven.

Over the days that followed, more about Jerry's wife came to light. Jerry learned that she had opened several secret charge accounts over the years, which she had used to order things over the phone, running up tens of thousands of dollars in credit-card debt. Naturally, this increased his anger at his dead wife even further. There went the three hundred dollars a week he thought he'd be saving.

But a week later, after the funeral, Jerry seemed to soften a bit toward his wife and to regret that he had made her look bad. He started trying to puff her back up.

When my wife was in the hospital, hundreds of people would come by every day. Some days somebody would order twenty pizzas to feed them all, another time somebody bought two hundred dollars of chicken parmigiana subs. For the funeral, all the cops from the neighborhood came and carried her coffin down the street wearing their dress uniforms and white gloves. She was only fifty, you know. Everybody loved her.

After the funeral I threw a big New Year's Eve party. We always used to do it, me and my wife, every year. So this year I turned it into her wake, and everybody from the whole neighborhood showed up. Went on 'till dawn. We went through dozens of kegs.

"Yeah, sounds great," I said. It was a relief to hear him rehabilitate his wife.

"So, enough about me," Jerry said. "What did you do for New Year's?"

Actually, I had been having health problems myself. I had had appendicitis a few months earlier, and somehow my body was never the same after that. I was trying my best to cut down on drinking, a habit I had cultivated over twenty years. I had had to give up smoking even earlier. "Oh, nothing really," I said, trying to put a good face on things. "I just stayed home and read, and went to bed early."

"Really?!" Jerry said. "What, don't you have any friends?"

"No, it's not that," I said, rather defensively. "It's just that it's too much of a fuss. There's all this pressure on you to drink. And then you just feel bad the next day. You're starting the new year off on a bad note."

This was not the right thing to say, apparently. Jerry got mad at me, really angry. Perhaps he felt guilty about having a party and getting drunk when his wife just died. No doubt drinking contributed to her death. For once he had nothing to say. He served my cheeseburger sullenly and didn't say good-bye when I left.

Jerry never was too friendly with me after that. He never made my sandwiches quite right again, and one time he gave me some bad chicken salad that made me throw up. I didn't go back so much after that, at least not while Jerry was working.

Donuts Sandwiches closed at the end of the nineties, the victim of the rising rents that came with the gentrification of the Chelsea area. Its storefront was taken over by an overpriced muffin shop. Jack Kerouac would have nowhere to get a cup of coffee at 3 AM. The McBurney went down too, at about the same time, and now it's a condo building, called, cynically enough, the Y Building. The Chelsea Hotel, filled with the ghosts of the old bohemians, is the lone holdout.

2000

Eccentrics
Famous and Obscure

Dee Dee's Challenge:
Dee Dee Ramone at the Chelsea

Somebody new had moved into the room next door. I had heard him moving his stuff in late the night before but as yet I hadn't met him. He was quiet now, just before noon, apparently asleep.

Some workers began doing renovations on the floor above us: a lot of sawing and tap-tap-tapping with a hammer. After about half an hour of this noise, the guy next door started banging on my wall, screaming, "Shut up! Shut up! Shut up!"

I didn't think he could be talking to me, since all I was doing was sitting there writing. But after a few more minutes of banging on my wall, the guy came out of his room and banged on my door.

I opened the door and there stood Dee Dee Ramone. I had seen him around the hotel, but never like this. He wore only his underwear, his white jockey shorts, and he was covered with tattoos: skulls, pistols, dice, black cats, a scorpion, the numbers 13 and 666—over his arms, chest, and legs.

I was taken aback and stood marveling at his tattoos. Though Dee Dee was small and skinny, skeletal even, with all the tattoos he was still kind of threatening. On top of that he was insanely angry, shaking with rage.

"Is that you making that noise?!" he demanded.

"No, Dee Dee. It's not me," I replied. "I think it's the construction workers upstairs."

Without another word, Dee Dee went back into his room, flung open his window, stuck his head out, and yelled up at the construction workers: "Shut up, you motherfuckers! You do that work later! Shut up!"

One of the workers must have looked down from the window above, because then Dee Dee said, "I see you, motherfucker! I know who you are! I don't wanna hear that hammering again!"

It got real quiet for a moment. And then from above I heard a very deliberate: TAP TAP TAP TAP TAP TAP TAP!

"You motherfucker! I'll kill you!" Dee Dee screamed. "You come down here to the eighth floor! I've got a knife, and I'll be waiting for you in the hallway!"

Sure thing, Dee Dee. Be right down.

PART II: DEE DEE'S PLIGHT

Dee Dee Ramone was born Douglas Colvin in Fort Lee, Virginia, in 1952 and grew up in Germany, an army brat. (The first time he introduced himself to me—a few days after the construction incident—he said his name was Dee Dee, then corrected himself, and said actually he was trying to get people to call him Douglas, since that sounded more adult.) Dee Dee moved with his mother to Queens in the sixties, where he picked up his annoying outer-borough whine. It was also where he met and sniffed glue with other disaffected teens such as Tommy, Joey, and Johnny, with whom he formed the seminal punk band the Ramones in the early seventies. Dee Dee played bass for the group and wrote most of the songs. Among the Ramones' more famous numbers are "I Wanna Be Sedated," "Blitzkrieg Bop," "53rd and 3rd ," based on Dee Dee's experience as a street hustler, and—my personal favorite—"Beat on the Brat."

Famously, the members of the band didn't get along and fought all the time. Dee Dee reputedly was among the fiercest of the combatants and was always quitting and rejoining the band. He split from the group for good in 1989, though he continued to write songs for the Ramones until they disbanded in 1996.

Dee Dee lived in the Chelsea on and off for much of his adult life. He told me on more than one occasion that all he wanted was to be a regular guy, to eat in a diner and ride the subway like everybody else, but people were always bothering him—*stalking him,* he said. "Get me a record contract, Dee Dee," he said, mimicking them. "And I can't even get *myself* a decent record contract!" This was a problem that genuinely bothered Dee Dee. Unfortunately, he bore the curse of being very friendly and outgoing. He just couldn't help himself in this respect. No one had to stalk Dee Dee; he would come right up and befriend you.

A couple of years before he moved into the Chelsea for the last time, Dee Dee married Barbara Zampini, a Ramones groupie from Argentina—a very pretty one, of course. At the time of their marriage she was fifteen years old, beneath the legal age of consent. (Dee Dee himself was in his mid-forties.) Though they had the consent of her parents, Dee Dee had to smuggle Barbara out of Argentina to avoid the wrath of the authorities. He tried to live with her in Belgium for a time, but apparently the authorities there didn't like the arrangement much either and threw them out of the country.

The next stop was the Chelsea. "She's like a kid," Dee Dee told me, his incredulity apparently real. "She lays around in bed all day. Don't be so lazy, I tell her. Why don't you get out and do something? Sometimes I feel like her father."

Part III: Dee Dee's Bad Night

Dee Dee moved around from room to room in the hotel. He was always dissatisfied with whatever room he landed in—there was too much noise, or too much light, or his neighbors were stalking him—and after a few months or a year in one room, he would move to another floor. He told me that one time they had put him in a new room, and no sooner had he moved his few possessions in than he began to feel uneasy. Though he knew he hadn't lived there before, he had a vague feeling of déjà vu. He thought his unease would pass, but as the hours wore on he just couldn't shake it.

Finally, nodding off in bed late that night, it suddenly hit him, and he sat bolt upright with a shock of awareness.

"It was Sid's room!" Dee Dee told me. "I knew him! I lived here when he was here. He was my friend! I partied in that room. I hung out in that room."

But it wasn't really Sid's room, because Dee Dee would have noticed that at once and would've never agreed to move in. As I mentioned earlier, Sid's room no longer exists: Stanley Bard carved it up and distributed its parts among several other rooms. But Dee Dee had got a window. And the play of the shadows in the corner, in the half-light of the moon and the streetlights, had been something that the renovations had failed to alter, something that had remained constant over time.

In a panic, Dee Dee fled the room, refusing to stay there another minute and demanding to be moved to another room immediately. They didn't have any rooms open on such short notice—or perhaps, as Dee Dee thought, they just wanted to torment him—and so Dee Dee ended up drinking coffee in an all-night diner until morning.

"I knew him!" Dee Dee repeated. "I knew them both. They were my friends. I used to visit Sid there, him and Nancy. We sat in that room together and got drunk and played the guitar." Even in the retelling, Dee Dee shuddered and seemed genuinely terrified by the incident. "I told Stanley, how could you do that to me!?"

Dee Dee—he would always be Dee Dee, never Douglas—had a lifelong drug problem, especially with heroin. And it was heroin that finally claimed him at the age of fifty, on June 5, 2002, only a few months after the Ramones had been inducted into the Rock and Roll Hall of Fame.

The Easter Nest

One Easter Sunday morning, Susan and I were walking along the Hudson River. We had started taking long walks as a way of relieving stress: I had just finished one novel and was starting another; and Susan was having a rough time at work. Besides that, we liked the exercise.

Recently they've been cleaning up the waterfront, planting trees and grass, attempting to turn it into one long park, so you can walk or bike all the way around Manhattan Island without having to go out into the city. They've gotten pretty far along on this plan by now, but on this particular morning they were just beginning, and so the waterfront was still pretty rough in spots.

By 11 o'clock we were all the way up in the seventies, near the Trump Towers, which were under construction. Traffic was light and there was no one else around, only the occasional bike rider. We were passing a little patch of scrub brush and weed trees, a place where there was no flood wall and the banks of the shore were lapped by the waves washing up from the river. The little wooded area was filled with garbage that had drifted up amid the debris of twisted steel wreckage and ruined concrete pylons. Over beyond a chain-link fence, there was someone rooting around in a pile of trash that had washed up on the shore. He was pulling at a big mass of rope and seaweed that had tangled around some rusted steel cables. Though I could see that the

135

man was busy, it seemed so odd, so incongruent, that I had to yell down: "Hey, what are you doing down there."

"Oh, good morning," the man said. "I'm searching for driftwood."

"What for?"

He approached the fence. A little man in his fifties, still appearing youthful and thin, with piercing gray eyes, he was dressed in a sort of peasant costume: an old shearling vest, lace-up boots, and an old gray hunting cap with earflaps. "I use it to create art," he said.

"Kind of slim pickins in the city, ain't it?"

"You'd be surprised," he said. He picked up a bundle of sticks from the brush nearby; he had tied them together with an old yellow rope. "I'm working on a special project for today," he said as he untied the bundle. "A nest to use as a centerpiece for an Easter brunch I've been invited to."

The man showed us how several pieces of wood fit together, interlocking, like a puzzle, with the minimum of twisting. He knew how to place them in such a way that they did come together to form a sort of nest, hollow in the center, upturned around the edges.

"That's really nice," Susan said. It did look like it would be an interesting—albeit unsanitary—centerpiece for a table.

"This is approximately what it will look like, but as you can see, I need another piece to go in here—like this." He wove his fingers into the piece to demonstrate. "Who knows, though? It's what I find that determines the actual shape. In the end it may look totally different from this."

"But still," I said, "a nest."

"Yes, of course, still a nest." He glanced around as he spoke, as if eager to get back to his work.

"You're rather far afield," I said.

He looked at me like he didn't know what I was talking about.

"I mean, aren't you running kind of late? That is, if you're gonna get to brunch. It's already eleven."

"Oh, is it that late?! I'd better hurry!" he said. He walked back down to the river to resume his scavenging.

"By the way," I called after him, "what are you going to put in the nest? Eggs?"

He turned back to face me. "Eggs?" he said, as if the thought hadn't crossed him mind. "Well, I suppose you could. And certainly it could be used to hold many other things besides." He appeared to be giving the matter thought. "Things related to Easter," he said. "Yes, certainly, eggs."

I guess I hardly need to tell you the punch line. Though I didn't know the man, I had seen him around before, and that was the reason I spoke to him in the first place. First floor maybe, since he didn't ride the elevator. Of course he was from the Chelsea Hotel.

Charles James's Drafting Table: Charles James at the Chelsea

Sarah is an older lady, scatterbrained, though endearingly so, with a wild mane of curly gray hair. A jewelry designer, she's lived here in the Chelsea since the sixties, when she outfitted the Warhol superstars.

Sarah's large apartment/workshop is filled floor to ceiling with a lifetime's accumulation of dusty junk: tools, boxes of bolts and clasps and beads and sequins, broken-down sewing machines, teetering piles of old magazines, you name it. I've offered several times to help her clean out her apartment, which has become so cluttered that there's not much living space left, but she's collected all this stuff for a reason and, who knows, never can tell when it might come in handy.

But one afternoon she called me and said she did have a few things to throw out, so I came down to her place to help her move them out. Mostly, it just looked like her usual trash, but she had a box or two of papers for me to carry out, and there was a metal cabinet, the drawers filled with ticket stubs and receipts and other scraps of paper that she thought she could live without.

When I had carried all that stuff out to the trash can, Sarah said, "I've been thinking of getting rid of this."

From somewhere in the bowels of her rooms she had dragged out an old drafting table. Of dark wood, the table was worn and beaten but still sturdy and functional, with an ancient, heavy iron mechanism to control its slant.

"Wow!" I said. It was a really good-looking piece of furniture, must have been seventy or eighty years old. But then I caught myself and said. "Yeah, get rid of it. And how about some of these old magazines too."

"Those have my designs in them," Sarah said.

We turned our attention back to the drafting table. "I don't use it anymore," Sarah said. "Never have. But it belonged to Charles James, so I've kept it all these years."

The son of an American mother and an English father, the fashion designer Charles James was born in Sandhurst, England, in 1906. He was expelled for a sexual scandal at his public school, so his parents sent him to Chicago in 1926 to work in an architectural firm, but he didn't much care for that. Instead he opened a hat shop and then moved to New York in 1928, where he quickly won fame in the world of fashion. Known primarily for his evening wear, James looked upon his one-of-a-kind creations as works of art, "sculptures in fabric" that reshaped and remolded the body, often using forms, such as the tulip, inspired by nature. James helped create the "femme fatale" look of the *film noirs,* and his gowns can be seen in countless movies of the forties and fifties. Many of the Barbie doll's early gowns are based on his designs, including one of her most popular, called "Solo in the Spotlight."

James moved to the Chelsea in 1964 after he went bankrupt and his marriage subsequently dissolved. The forties and fifties were the decades of his greatest success, and James came to be seen as old-fashioned in the sixties, with its minimalist aesthetic and the decidedly antifashion pose of the hippies. James refused to change with the times, and hence toward the end of his life he was more respected in the art world than in the fashion world. He died in 1978 at the Chelsea, and in 2001 he was honored by a plaque on the Fashion Walk of Fame on Sixth Avenue in the garment district.

———

"Oh, did James give it to you?" I asked Sarah. "Did you know him?"

"I did know him, but no, he didn't give it to me. I think Viva gave it to me," she said, referring to the Warhol superstar who lived here into the nineties, "but I can't really remember, it was so long ago."

I made to seize the old table.

"I just don't know," Sarah said, vacillating. "It seems a shame to throw it away. Maybe I should just keep it."

"Sarah, you have to get rid of something," I scolded.

The upshot of this was that, in order to make Sarah feel less guilty, and since the piles of junk were threatening to fall over on her and bury her like the Collyer brothers, I agreed to take the table.

(I must admit, too, that I harbored a secret desire to own the table—because of its origins, because it looked cool, and also because, like Sarah, I'm a pack rat at heart and can't bear to throw anything out.)

I thought for sure I was in for trouble. My girlfriend, Susan, and I had had arguments before about my habit of dragging home junk. Susan had a stressful job, which she had to take just so we could have the money to live in New York, and it stressed her out even more to come home and be surrounded by clutter. But maybe, after all, I was kind of hoping she *would* bitch me out, so that would give me an excuse to get rid of the table.

Instead, she had even more enthusiasm than me for the table, especially because of the Charles James connection. "Oh my God! That's really beautiful!" she exclaimed. "But what can we do with it?"

"Well, maybe I can use it for a desk," I said, thinking of replacing the one I had but knowing all the while that that wouldn't work at all. The table was too high and wasn't really meant to lay flat. It was for an artist rather than a writer.

Folded up as far as was possible, the table sat in the middle of our room for a year. Everybody who came to visit thought it was really nice, but nobody actually wanted to own it. Finally, it just got be too much of a hassle to move it whenever we wanted to get into our closet.

Late one night, when I knew Sarah would be in bed, I set the table out by the elevator with a note on it that said: Charles James's Drafting Table: Free To A Good Home, and it was gone within the hour. I was sad to see it go, but glad in a way also because I felt it had gone to someone who needed it—surely it's still in the Chelsea—and maybe, with any luck, someone who could tap into the energy of the old designer in a way I wasn't quite able to.

The Transient Room

The Chelsea is a mix of permanent residents and transients—who could be tourists or businessmen, or prostitutes or junkies—and though that keeps things interesting, sometimes it makes for some pretty dicey situations. For the past year we'd been lucky: first we had Dee Dee Ramone next door, and then the room was rented by a dancer who kept weird hours but was reasonably quiet. But then she found a boyfriend and moved to New Jersey.

About a week after the dancer moved out we heard a commotion in the hallway. Someone was rattling all the doors on our floor, trying them to see if they were open. He rattled ours—but it was locked, thank God. He seemed to get into the dancer's old room, and then things settled down for perhaps two minutes. Then somebody banged on their door and we heard Bart, one of the bellmen, say, in a loud voice, "If I had known it was you, I would have never rented her this room!"

What had happened was that an old junky—I had stuck my head out for a look and seen a thin, toothless, older man—had gotten his slightly younger girlfriend to rent a room for them and then he had tried to sneak in past the front desk. "You were trying to trick me, Tony!" Bart said.

"Ah, no I wasn't," Tony said, in a thick Brooklyn accent.

Bart seemed ready to let Tony and his girlfriend stay. Referring to the bathroom we were to share with them, Bart said, "Be sure to keep this door locked at all times." (We had a note on the door to this effect. This precaution was designed, ironically, to keep out the junkies.) Bart left them in the room and went back downstairs.

"You told me this was gonna be okay," I heard the woman say. They both spoke very loudly, almost yelling.

"It's gonna be okay, baby, just let me handle it," Tony said. "He's letting us stay, you see?"

But Bart was back in a flash. He had talked it over with the night manager. "Sorry bro, nothing personal, but you got to go. You're eighty-sixed from the list, bro. You want a room, you'll have to talk to the owner, Stanley Bard. He's the only one who can rent you a room."

"Stanley's my friend," Tony said. "He'll rent me a room. Just talk to him."

"*You* talk to him," Bart said. "Stanley's in at six in the morning."

Then Tony's true feelings toward Stanley surfaced, as he exclaimed: "That fucking bastard! That bloodsucker!"

"So you gonna make it easy or do I have to call the cops?" Bart asked.

"Yeah, go ahead and call 'em," Tony said. But then he immediately thought better of it and agreed to go. He was probably well known to the police, and who knows what kind of contraband he was holding. "We'll be down in a few minutes," he said, but Bart wouldn't leave them there for even a minute.

"Don't worry, baby," Tony said as they left, "we'll go over to a place I know on East 23rd. It's much better than this dump. They have a weight room and everything, and they're thirty dollars cheaper."

The woman wasn't having any of it. As they walked out to the elevators, she said, "I didn't know they would call the cops on you!"

We were relieved to be rid of them. For a moment there it looked like the return of the bad old days. Sharing a bathroom with junkies is no picnic.

Fifteen minutes later somebody was down on the street, yelling hysterically, "I'm done with you! I'm done with you!" He yelled the same thing, over and over, for about half an hour: "I'm done with you!" Then he moved on down the street, still yelling, and his voice trailed off and finally died away as he rounded the corner.

Later that night I asked the night manager, "Was that Tony yelling in the street?"

"Yeah," he said. "He was yelling in the lobby too. I just wish people would keep that shit upstairs so I didn't have to deal with it."

The Long Black Hairs

Hiroya, who had long, wild, black hair that hung in a tangle in his face, shared a bathroom with us on the eighth floor. Every single day, almost without exception, he would flood the bathroom floor, and every day the maid, Rita, would argue with him about it. I came to believe that Hiroya enjoyed these arguments in some perverse way. He would swear up and down that it hadn't been him, that a junky or some other lowlife had broken into the bathroom and done it.

I was coming down the hall one day when I heard them outside the bathroom, arguing. "Every day there be two inches of water standin' on the floor!" Rita was screaming in her thick Jamaican accent. "Every day I be havin' to mop this floor! Every damn day! I be tired of it! Next time you mop yourself."

"It the homeless," Hiroya said in his broken English.

"I know it not be no homeless!" Rita yelled. "I know it be you, Hiroya! Because the long black hairs be a swimmin'!"

2001

Hollywood Knocks

Chelsea Soundstage:
Sean Penn at the Chelsea

We get lots of film crews at the Chelsea, shooting videos, TV episodes, and even big-budget Hollywood movies. They pull up in their trailers, blocking the street so you can't get across it, and they set up tables on the sidewalk and pile junk in front of the door, so even entering the hotel becomes something of an ordeal. They crowd the lobby and the stairwells and tie up the elevators, holding them on one floor or another while they load them up with equipment. At first it's exciting, but after a while it gets to be a nuisance. (As the neighborhood and the city gentrified, and it became "safer" at the Chelsea, we started to get more and more of these crews.) We have to put up with a lot for the sake of art here at the Chelsea.

But we do get to see the stars. Lately I've run into David Duchovny, Robert De Niro, Julie Delpy, and Randy Quaid. I can't even begin to name all the famous people I've encountered in the elevator. (Arthur Miller was the most illustrious, but then he's a celebrity of a whole other order.)

One day—must've been in 2003, now that I think of it—I was riding the elevator down with a girl who lives on our floor, Carla, a dancer, a pretty, wacky, cheerful girl. There was a big movie shoot going on—though neither of us had any idea what it was for—and

149

we were laughing and joking about all the inconveniences it was causing us. Then, when the ancient elevator finally creaked its way down to the lobby, the door opened and who should be standing there, mere inches from us, but the great Sean Penn himself, surrounded by a mob of his retainers.

———————

Penn, who first came to America's attention as the spaced-out surfer dude Jeff Spicoli in *Fast Times at Ridgemont High,* was born in 1960 in Burbank, California, the son of McCarthy-blacklisted actor Leo Penn. Sean famously, and heroically, married the singer and cultural icon Madonna in 1985, a union that lasted nearly four years. He's been married to his second wife, Robin Wright, for about ten years now, and they have two children. Career acting highlights include: *Bad Boys* (1983), *Colors* (1988), Brian DePalma's *Casualties of War* (1989) and *Carlito's Way* (1993), and *21 Grams* (2003).

———————

I looked at Penn, and he looked back at me. Penn's hair was slicked back in a sort of pompadour, and he had on stage makeup. As often happens when you run into stars, he was shorter than I had imagined. Penn's retinue was blocking the elevator, and I couldn't go anywhere. I didn't know what to say. But Carla has a bubbly personality, and was seldom at a loss for words. It was two days after Penn had been up for an Oscar at the Academy Awards, and Carla said, "Congratulations!"

Penn just glared at her. His bodyguards moved aside slightly to let us squeeze past. As we walked through the lobby, Carla, a bit puzzled by his reaction and concerned that she had offended him, turned to me and said, "He *did* win, didn't he?"

Indeed he did. He won the Best Actor award for *Mystic River* that year, in which he plays a man hell-bent on avenging the murder of his daughter. But apparently, he was not one to rest on his laurels: it was full speed ahead on to the next project for him, and all Chelsea weirdos best stay out of his way.

———————

Sean Penn's former wife, Madonna, by the way, shot her book *Sex* here, in room 822, one of our more beautiful suites, but since then she hasn't been back. Ethan Hawke is here all the time, so who cares?

But for the most part these film crews seem to be made up of kids in their twenties: trust-funders straight out of college, arrogant, thinking the world owes them a living. This is probably the first job most of them have had in their lives. You can tell they all fancy themselves the next Spielberg. (Not the next Bergman or Fellini, in other words; that would be beneath them. If they were little Bergmans or Fellinis they would probably move in.) They think what they're doing is of the utmost importance, even if it's just running to the deli for a cup of coffee for Robert De Niro, and they can be incredibly rude and disrespectful.

But to get back to Sean Penn, the movie he was filming that day, though no one would give us any information at the time, turned out to be *The Interpreter,* which also stars Nicole Kidman. Though I must confess that I haven't seen it, apparently the movie contains a scene in which someone slashes their wrists at the Chelsea. This seems plausible enough, I suppose, since so many people have killed themselves here, though we usually rely on drugs or else throw ourselves down the stairwell if we crave a bit of drama—both if we really want to finish the job.

Anyway, the crew was filming a scene from this movie in front of the hotel. We were all dutifully standing by—residents and passersby alike—because we were told to and also to see whatever star they were filming appear from his trailer. It was taking a long time, but finally they got the cameras rolling. I spotted Sean Penn lurking in the wings, waiting for his cue. (No sign of Nicole.) At

151

about that time, Magda, an elderly lady who lives in the hotel, came walking up on her cane, irritably calling out "Excuse me! Excuse me!" as the crowd parted to let her through.

"Could you please wait a moment?!" a trucker-hatted hipster snapped.

"No, you wait!" Magda said, and walked right through the scene they were filming, taking her own sweet time, I might add. We were all very proud of the old girl that day.

The good news is, the older guys who are actually in charge of these crews are usually polite and respectful, and if you approach them with a problem, they'll usually take your concerns seriously—although you don't see them all that much, and I sometimes feel they are using the young Spielbergs to do their dirty work. The film crews will set up shop right in front of an apartment door, oblivious to the fact that people live in the room and will eventually need to get out. They yell and carry on and run noisy machinery and blow the fuses. Their activities drove the Japanese artist Hiroya crazy, stark raving mad, and since the desk staff knew this—due to his incessant complaining—they made sure to send as many crews as possible to our floor.

One thing that all the crews inevitably do is to set up their lunch buffets on the trash bin. Bizarre, I know. Nearly inconceivable, I realize. But sometimes truth is stranger than fiction. "Don't you know that that's the trash bin?" I asked a sleepy-eyed hipster one time. "There could be roaches crawling out of there, or even mice." He just shrugged his shoulders as if the matter didn't interest him. (I think the general feeling among them—somewhat justified, I must admit—is that all the permanent residents are crazy.) I didn't mention that people throw cat shit and dirty diapers in there too. The only thing I can think of is maybe they've neglected to bring tables and the trash bin is the only flat surface around, which they then turn to in desperation. In any event, this weird practice never fails to crack me up, and I always make sure to take out my trash at least once or twice while a crew is on our floor. "Hey! Hey!"

somebody always yells, "That's our food there!" as I open the lid to deposit my waste, careful not to disturb the steaming platters of delicacies. (Who's crazy now, by the way? The Chelsea insanity is catching.)

The obvious question, which I heard the writer Jordan Atkinson ask a group of the young film hipsters one time, is, "Can't you rent a Hollywood sound stage for this?" They made no response, but for one thing, they get tax breaks for shooting in New York. Besides that, they want the bohemian cachet of the old hotel, and in general it's a fun place to hang out. (They've opted to make "art" that sells, but they still want to think of themselves as starving artists, since that's way cooler than selling out.) It's okay, though: Stanley is charging them out the ass so he can keep the rents of the real artists low. He also likes the attention people pay to the hotel, and maybe it's good advertising, too. And perhaps some of the young hipsters will stay on as guests or even residents and, even as they join us in growing increasingly detached from reality, at least eventually learn not to eat their food out of the trash.

PART II: NAKED MODELS

On a more positive note, many times I've arrived home to find naked models cavorting in the stairwells. So the presence of the film crews has its upside, though I would feel like a lecher if I stood there watching such a spectacle for any length of time. Sometimes, though, it can't be avoided. One time there was a naked girl right in front of my door. There were three guys, one with a camera, standing over the girl, who lay prone in the corner of the corridor. About twenty years old, the girl was quite pretty, with dark brown hair, slim, with a good body. She had on dark makeup to make her look like a vampire, though she was sprinkled in glitter too, and so I didn't know quite what to make of her: a glittery, naked Goth girl. My jaw dropped and I just stood there gawking like an idiot.

"Can I help you?" one of the guys said.

153

"Uh, pardon me," I said. "I need to get into my apartment."

"No problem," he said. One of the other guys helped the girl to her feet and they all three moved aside. When I closed my door I heard them gather back around my door to continue the shoot. Just another day in the Chelsea.

Unlike poor Hiroya, once I get into my apartment, I'm usually able to ignore distractions and just focus on my writing. The walls are thick, after all. But one night in 2001, Hollywood came knocking, and like a fool, I answered the door.

It was a girl in her mid-twenties, blond, with tattoos. "Hey, you want to be part of a movie?" she said, very chipper. "We need to use your room for a couple of hours. We want to shine some spotlights down on the street so we can film an outdoor scene. What do you say?"

I thought about it, very briefly. "No, I don't think I want to do that. I'm busy right now."

"Aw, come on! It'll be fun. We won't bother you at all. We'll just move our crew in here with the spotlights, and you can go about your business."

"I'm really not interested," I said.

"We'd pay you twenty-five dollars."

"No thanks."

She made a face like she couldn't believe my stupidity. I tried to close the door, but she still wanted to talk. "Who's in this room right here," she asked, indicating the room to my right.

"That's Mr. Greene."

"You think he would do it?"

"I seriously doubt it. But I can't really speak for him." I knew there was no way in hell. Mr. Greene was rather reclusive and he hated the film people as much as anybody I knew. I heard him stirring behind his door, listening in.

"What about this other room?" the girl asked, pointing to the door to my left.

"Transients," I said. That's just what we call people who are staying for a few days; guests, in other words. No negative connotation is intended.

But the film girl didn't know that; I got the sense that she was picturing junkies or similar lowlife. She wrinkled her nose in disgust.

"They may very well need the money," I said, playing along. The girl knocked on Mr. Greene's door. I took the opportunity to shut my own door. I could hear her out there banging away for several minutes. Perhaps she had been instructed not to return without an affirmative answer. She never did try the transient room.

After an extended period of silence, I thought she was gone. I had just gotten back to work when I was startled to hear the banging again, this time on my own door. When I opened it there was the girl again. "What will it take to make you change your mind?" she asked.

"I really don't want to do it."

"Everybody has their price."

"I wouldn't do it for any amount of money."

"Oh come on, just name a figure."

"I don't want to."

"Come on. What can it hurt?"

I thought about it. If she was going to keep bothering me I might as well make some money. "All right," I said. "Five hundred dollars."

"That ain't gonna happen!" the girl almost yelled at me.

I closed the door on her. For the next few minutes, I half expected the girl, or perhaps her superior, to return and grudgingly fork over my extortionate price, but apparently they had their limits. They must've got someone to go along with their plan, however, because soon the street outside was lit up like a Christmas tree, and it stayed that way long into the night.

Chelsea Barbershop

There's a tiny old barbershop around the corner from the Chelsea. It must have been there for fifty years and it doesn't look like it's changed much in that time, either. The old brown barber chairs are patched with cloth tape, and the linoleum is worn through where the barbers circle the chairs. On the counter are dusty cardboard displays of plastic combs and Hav-A-Hanks. There's an autographed picture of Rocky Marciano on the wall, though not even Vincent, the sixty-year-old Italian proprietor, remembers him ever coming into the shop.

One day I was in there getting my hair cut, when a hip young man in his twenties, a college student, came walking by the window and did a double take, stopping dead in his tracks. He took an expensive camera out of his shoulder bag and came into the shop, jingling the bell above the door. Everybody stopped what they were doing and looked at him.

Vincent, overweight but with a thick head of curly, salt-and-pepper hair, had the chair closest to the door. "Can I help ya?" he said in his thick Brooklyn accent.

"Would you mind if I took a few shots of the premises?" the young man asked.

"What?!"

"Can I take your picture?"

"Whataya wanna take my picture for?" Vincent asked.

"Because you're picturesque," the young man said.

Vincent rolled his eyes and jerked his thumb toward the door. "Get outta heah!"

Two Thefts:
Ethan Hawke at the Chelsea

I

Maxwell was an old man, probably mid-seventies, with a potbelly and thinning gray hair pulled back from his forehead. Though he was generally disheveled, his clothes unwashed, his shirttail out as he shuffled through the lobby on his way to the deli for a 40-ouncer of beer, sometimes he was more lucid than other times. At such times I would often sit with him in the lobby and flip through some of his photographs, which were always nicely done, professional; Maxwell was well known in the art world, and in the fashion world as well, which is where he made his mark in the sixties and seventies, shooting magazine layouts.

One evening I was walking down the stairs. Maxwell was skulking behind the doorframe, and when he saw me coming, he came out into the elevator lobby. "Come here for a minute," he said, motioning for me to follow him into the hallway. "I have something I need to tell you." He spoke almost in a whisper. "I have to tell somebody."

I had something to do and so I was kind of annoyed. "What is it?" I asked, impatiently.

"They've been gassing me," he said. "And injecting me." He made a motion as if injecting his arm with a needle.

"Who has?" I asked.

"That I don't know."

"Why would they do this?"

"So they can steal my photographs, of course," Maxwell said. "They make a lot of noise going through my things, and they have to be sure that I don't wake up and catch them. Of course they're very careful to put things back the way they found them, so that then I might think that I've just mislaid the photographs. But I've set traps for them, and so I know when something has been disturbed."

Huddled together in the dark corridor, we spoke in conspiratorial tones. I was wary of getting pulled into Maxwell's world of delusion. Still, curious, I played along. "Why would they want your photographs?" I asked almost in a whisper.

"Well, it's very good work. They can't do work that good themselves. That's why they need it. For their careers, you see. To advance their careers."

I nodded my assent. I could see that he was going to have all the angles figured out on this one.

"I wouldn't reveal this to just anyone," he said, leaning in closer and placing a hand on my shoulder. "But I have a feeling that you know about such things."

I didn't say anything, but I was becoming uncomfortable and I wished I could find some pretext to tear myself away.

"I need to put a stop to this theft," Maxwell went on, "which is ongoing, by the way. And I wanted to know what you thought I should do about it."

"Why don't you tell Stanley?" I suggested, facetiously. I was referring, of course, to our illustrious proprietor, Stanley Bard. "Maybe he can look into it."

"Oh, he would be glad they were doing it! He wants to get rid of everyone who's been here for a long time so he can rent out their rooms at a higher rate."

I chuckled. "Now *that* I can believe!"

Maxwell looked at me crossly. "I know you think I'm just

imagining this, but I have proof. Just the other day a young man came up to me in the lobby and said they were going to take my talent away if I didn't start taking photos again."

Though expressed in the language of delusion, it was a fear I understood all too well: if you don't use your talent, it might atrophy; you might wake up one day needing it, and it would be gone. "Aw, come on," I said, to reassure him. "How could they do that?"

"What do you mean? They'll just come up and take it away. I'm an old man. I can't fight them."

I thought his delusion was causing him to make some kind of category mistake. "But your talent is something inside you. They can beat you up but they can't take that away."

"No, no no! I said, my *camera*. "

"Oh. That makes more sense," I said, though I didn't think I had heard him wrong. "Well, it wouldn't be a bad thing, would it? I mean, if you just did as they said and took more photos. You should keep taking them."

"But why should I take more? They'll just steal those too." They were selling his work for millions of dollars, Maxwell said. He was sick of others getting all the money and all the glory. He had seen his own work in magazines, he said, and when he called the editors to ask about it, they refused to talk to him.

"I feel like people steal my ideas all the time," I said, "but I don't worry about it, or I try not to, at least, because I know they don't know what to do with them."

"Well, it *is* shoddy work," Maxwell acknowledged. "They change it all around on the computer. And you're right that they can't capture the experience."

"Well, then, you have nothing to worry about," I said, dismissively. I pushed open the swinging door at this point, and was halfway through, trying to get away.

Maxwell gave me a look that said, yeah right. "What do you think I could do to stop this? It doesn't do any good to call the police. They don't do anything, and in fact I think they may be in on it."

"No, you shouldn't call the police," I said with a sigh.

"You think I'm imagining it all, don't you? I knew you did. It's not going to help for you to tell me that. Maybe I *am* imagining it, but it's real for me."

Just when I had almost made good my escape, something about this remark drew me back in. Certainly I empathized with Maxwell: I saw in him a distorted reflection of my own hopes and dreams, myself in thirty years. I sincerely wanted to help, but I was also in a sense nervously teasing when I said: "What this calls for is a certain amount of cleverness. You may be able to trick these people in some way. Maybe when you go to sleep at night you can set out some crappy work so they'll take that instead of your good work. If they're such hacks as you suggest, they probably won't notice the difference."

Maxwell seemed to take offense. "I don't have any crappy work," he said.

"Oh, no, I didn't mean to suggest that," I said, backpedaling. "What I mean is, maybe you could produce some. Just go out and take a bunch of random shots of really stupid subjects. Then set them in a prominent place like they're important."

"I'm afraid I can't do that," Maxwell said. "It erodes the soul."

"Maybe you could find some pictures in the trash and set them out," I said. "Or maybe get somebody else to shoot them for you."

Maxwell thought about it and then said, "Why can't I just take them to court and let the judge straighten it out. I don't have any money, but surely one of these universities would help me, someone who cares about the true value of art. They don't care about art much in this country anymore, it's true, but I believe they care more in Europe."

Maxwell then launched into a long rant about racism and anti-Semitism, and about how, if I understood him correctly, an outspoken newscaster on the local news had been disappeared and then replaced by a more pliant look-alike. I couldn't bear to listen to him go on like this, and when I got half a chance I made my excuses and said I had to run.

II

When I came home one night not long after the episode with Maxwell in the hallway, there was a big party at Serena's, the club in the basement of the Chelsea. Serena's had only been open for a few weeks, and so it was still a novelty with the hotel residents. Several people from the hotel, including the guys who worked at the front desk, were hanging around outside to see what celebrities had come to the party. They mentioned a couple of names; Juliette Lewis was one, but I can't remember what the others were anymore. When a big white limo pulled up to the curb, they all became really excited—though it turned out to be nobody recognizable.

There was only one person sitting in the lobby, as it seemed everyone else had gone outside to check out the action. Erica Crandle was an older lady, perhaps early sixties, her frizzy black hair streaked with gray and pulled back in a ponytail. She had once been pretty, and you could see the outline of her features, still finely chiseled, through the leathery skin of her face. She had put on weight not evenly but in her belly mostly; her chest and limbs were rail thin, almost skeletal.

I plopped down in the chair next to her and was going to ask her if she'd seen any celebrities, but then I noticed that something about the whole scene seemed to be getting on her nerves. She spoke before I could.

"What is wrong with them? Are they retarded?" she said crossly, wrinkling her long, aristocratic nose. (Erica was often irritable like this—she had that irascible sort of personality that would be annoying if it weren't also sort of charming—at least in small doses.) "Why would they want to see people like that? What could

161

they possibly get out of it?"

"I don't know. Maybe just to tell everybody they saw them," I suggested.

"But who would care? Certainly not me. If they told me, I'd think they were idiots."

"Yeah, I can see your point," I said. "I guess I'm more interested in the club itself. I'd kind of like to go down there and have a drink or something just to see what's going on."

"I wouldn't. It's just a bunch of kids going down there. Why should I care what they do? I have nothing in common with them."

"Still, I *would* like to see what the place looks like. They say it's pretty fancy."

Erica rolled her eyes at me. "Well, here's a clue: it's in the basement. It probably looks like a basement."

That made me laugh. "I wonder if they'd let me in tonight," I said, jokingly.

Erica lit up a cigarette despite the fact that they weren't allowed in the lobby. The way she did it, with her brows knit, indicated defiance of the rules. I realized that she had probably wanted to go outside to smoke but felt that she wouldn't be comfortable due to all the commotion.

As she reached over and flicked her ashes into a Coke can on the table, Maxwell, the old photographer, walked into the lobby. Staggering, visibly drunk, he had apparently been to the party in Serena's. "Well, there's your answer right there," Erica said. "If they'd let him in, they'd let anyone in."

I didn't think that was quite true. Maxwell had probably got an invitation on the strength of his old connections. Either that or he had stumbled down there and they hadn't the heart to turn him away. Maxwell looked at us and slurred some kind of greeting on his way to the elevator.

When he had got safely out of earshot, Erica said, "At his age you'd think the man would have more sense."

She looked to me for some kind of a response, but I didn't say anything.

"To get stinking drunk like that at his age," she went on. "Falling down drunk." She took a draw on her cigarette. "Have a little bit of dignity, I say. And he had a good reputation, too, in his field." She shook her head in dismay. "To throw it all away like that. I think he's burned out his brain on alcohol and is just wallowing in his sorrows."

"Ah, he probably only had a couple," I said.

"A couple too many!"

And then I told her about how Maxwell felt that someone was stealing his ideas—my point being, I guess, that Maxwell was already rather addled.

It surprised me when she came to his defense: "Well, you can't really blame him for that, now can you? He's worked all his life on his art, and now he's old and without much to show for it. He sees these young people doing work similar to his and getting lots of attention for it, and it just doesn't seem fair."

I was struggling to get a handle on her apparent about-face, as Erica went on. "I hardly call that evidence of derangement," she said crossly, "or whatever it is you're trying to claim."

Then I told her about the more embarrassing parts of our conversation—which I had withheld before—about the gassing and injecting, and about people breaking into his room.

But Erica didn't want to hear it. She shook her head and flipped her hand at me dismissively. She must have thought I was making fun of Maxwell. "You can't really talk until you've been there yourself," she said.

Feeling like a jerk, I was about to get up and leave and in fact had half risen from my chair, when the movie star Ethan Hawke walked in the door. He, too, had apparently been to the party. He was dressed in hipster drag, wearing a trucker hat and a red vintage Adidas jacket, and with a dark-haired, heavily tattooed girl on his arm. Our conversation stopped short; I plopped back in my chair and we watched as Ethan and his date walked past us—drunk, cheerful, oblivious to our presence—on their way to the elevator.

"You see that little shit there," Erica said loudly, while he was still within earshot.

"You mean Ethan?" I asked, speaking softly.

"Yes, the one who made that movie. That petty, insipid little movie." She said it bitterly.

"*Chelsea Walls,* you mean?"

She nodded her assent. "That has got to be the absolute worst movie ever made. The cardboard characters, the wooden dialog; a screenplay written, I suspect, by someone not of this earth. The tedious repetition and the pompous droning of the narration! How can you mess up a movie like that? With all the material this hotel has to offer, all the history! It boggles the mind."

She was taking it all too seriously, I thought. But I had run into this attitude before among residents: a possessiveness, an almost pathological identification with the hotel. "Yeah, it wasn't too good," I agreed. "It almost made me want to move," I added, jokingly, trying to lighten the mood.

"Don't go that far," Erica cautioned, dead serious. "It's not worth it."

Ethan Hawke was born in Austin, Texas, in 1970. He started out in show business at an early age, starring alongside River Phoenix in a forgettable kids' movie. When he was a teenager he starred in *Dead Poet's Society* with Robin Williams and later in *Reality Bites* with Winona Ryder. Other notable films include the science fiction film *Gattaca* and the big-money blockbuster *Training Day.* Ethan's greatest critical success came with the Richard Linklater–directed films *Before Sunrise* and *Before Sunset,* in which he costarred with another occasional Chelsea resident, Julie Delpy.

Ethan directed the film *Chelsea Walls,* which concerns a group of loosely connected bohemians who live at the Chelsea Hotel.

Though the grainy digital camera work captures the spirit of the hotel, the dialog is patently absurd. People were actually walking out of the theater at the screening I attended. I was really rooting for Ethan on this one—especially since I love the Chelsea so much—but it turned out to be pretty much an unmitigated disaster.

In addition to his film work, Ethan has also published two novels: *The Hottest State* and *Ash Wednesday*.

In 1998, Ethan married the actress Uma Thurman, his costar in *Gattaca*. They were married for six years—living on 13th Street in the Village—and had two children, a girl, Maya, and a boy, Levon. (Susan and I walked by Uma one time on 13th Street: she was out for a walk with her baby and her maid. Susan found a little baby booty on the sidewalk, a little shearling booty, and Uma sent her maid to retrieve it.) A few years back the couple ran into difficulties and split up, eventually getting a divorce. Some say Ethan was jealous of Uma's success. Rumor also has it that Ethan suspected Uma of having an affair with Quentin Tarantino, her director in the *Kill Bill* movies. In any event, Ethan showed her: he went out and had an affair with a waitress. For Uma, that was apparently the last straw.

After Ethan broke up with Uma, he moved into room 712 at the Chelsea, where he hung out and played guitar and did the bohemian trip with Julie Delpy—not bad for a consolation prize.

Ethan and his date—who was *not* Julie Delpy, by the way—had, I was glad to see, gone up on the elevator by this point. I breathed a sigh of relief. "At least I thought the photography was good," I said, referring, of course, to that of *Chelsea Walls*. "Kind of dark and grainy. Appropriate for the hotel."

Erica wasn't going to give him even that. She shook her head in exasperation and disgust. She said, "You know, don't you, that he interviewed people from the hotel for the movie, to get material."

"No, I didn't know that."

"He couldn't have done it otherwise. He knows *nothing* of this hotel. I'm surprised he didn't talk to you."

I didn't consider it too surprising. I was thinking, well, that's good at least that he did some research.

"He got a lot of that material from me," Erica went on. "You know that scene where the girl is dancing in the stairwell?"

"Uh, yeah." There was a scene in the movie—shot from above to capture the filigreed rails of the famous cast-iron staircase—where a young girl, in a billowing white dress if I remember correctly, twirls ecstatically at the bottom of the stairwell.

"That character is based on me," Erica said.

"Oh really? I didn't know you were a dancer."

This seemed to incense her: "*Everyone* knows I'm a dancer. I danced with Martha Graham and many other important companies. I knew Balanchine and Maria Tallchief."

"Wow," I said.

"Yeah, *wow*," she said, sarcastically.

"So you originated dancing in stairwells," I said, stupidly.

"Of course not!" she said. "People have been dancing in stairwells from time immemorial. I'm just saying that I was the first to dance in the Chelsea stairwell. Or if not the first, then at least I did it. And way back in the sixties too. And that's where he got the idea."

I didn't know quite what to say. "Well, it was a crappy movie anyway."

"I'm talking about the principle of the matter," Erica pointed out. "He used my idea, and do you think he gave me credit? Well, do you?"

I didn't reply.

"Well?"

"No?" I ventured.

"Hell, no!"

We didn't speak for a while. I was about to take the opportunity to leave. There was a commotion outside as some star or other came out and got into a limousine.

Erica used this opportunity to relax and to consider my words. "However," she said, "yes, as you point out, I suppose I should be glad not to be associated with such a piece of trash. If I had known what that movie was going to be like I would never have helped him."

Maxwell and Erica are both a bit, how shall I say it, *eccentric*. There are a lot of people like them wandering these halls. Even if you're not that way when you get here, all the years of laboring in obscurity for the sake of art will do it to you. So it's hard to take their claims seriously. Nevertheless, in a way, they're right. There's rarely any artistic work that's strictly original, and if you're young and attractive and well connected, it would seem fairly easy to get by on derivative work. Then again—and Erica seems to intuit as much—the older artists most likely did the same thing themselves when they were young. But realizing this probably doesn't make it any easier to take.

New York Breakdown

I was coming out of the Whole Foods on Seventh Avenue, around the corner from the Chelsea, when I heard a loud crash. A guy in a blue SUV had rear-ended a cab at the corner of 24th Street. Despite the loud noise, it was clear that neither of the cars had been damaged.

A middle-aged man in a shirt and tie sprang out of the SUV and ran to the window of the cab and started apologizing profusely: "Oh my God I'm so sorry! I'm sorry! I'm sorry, I am *so* sorry!"

The cab driver, who looked Indian, got out to look at the damage. "Oh, don't worry about it," the cab driver said. "It's nothing."

The SUV driver then burst into tears and dropped to his knees, begging forgiveness. He would have embraced the cab driver around the knees, had not the Indian man scampered nimbly out of the way. Instead, the SUV driver started kissing the bumper of the cab and weeping.

There were some Whole Food workers standing nearby, taking a cigarette break. They had seen the whole thing, and now they called out: "Dude, get up! It's nothing, it's no big deal! There's no need to act like that!"

The cab driver, as well, kept repeating that it was nothing, that there was no damage. Still on his knees, the SUV man continued to apologize.

All I could think of was that the SUV guy must have been having a bad day and had finally reached his breaking point. All it took was that one incident to send him over the edge. New York will do that to you. It could have been anything; it just turned out to be that one thing.

The cab driver was helping the man to his feet as I walked away. Having just braved the nightmarish shopping experience of Whole Foods, I thought I could empathize especially well.

Alchemy and the Depths of Human Experience: A Movie Star at the Chelsea

There are several actors living at the Chelsea, most of them pretty minor—character actors or has-beens—and then there's one big movie star. I run into him in the elevator all the time and I always say, "Hi, how are you?" Usually all he does is grunt in reply, "Unngh," if that; certainly he rarely lowers himself actually to speak to me. I would say he's being a dick, but I can see his point of view: everybody's constantly trying to mess with him, when all he wants to do is walk down the street to the deli. He's right to be doubly cautious in the Chelsea, as the place is filled with con artists. All in all, he seems like a perfectly normal, likable sort of guy.

There's another sort of people who don't talk to me much, though for very different reasons: because they're either too shy or too disturbed, too preoccupied with the struggle with their own inner demons. Alice—though I didn't learn her name until much later—was one such person. For a couple of years I would see her moping around the hotel, wrapped in a long, formless, thrift store coat. Shuffling about with her head down, shrunken into herself, she wore an old floppy hat from which her hair, the color and texture of sand paper, stuck out at odd angles. It was hard to get a look at her face.

Anyway, either because he has extremely perverse sexual tendencies or else because he saw the diamond in the rough, the movie star befriended Alice and subsequently seduced her.

Nobody could believe it. It was the hot topic of conversation for several days around the hotel. Understandably, this really lifted Alice's spirits. I had never known her to have any friends, much less boyfriends, and now she had really made a catch. The movie star brought her out of her shell, taking her out to dinner and the theater, and who knows where else. She became more outgoing and started to smile a lot more. Now everybody wanted to be her friend, if for no other reason than to get close to the movie star, and this helped to build up her confidence. She started dressing better and began standing up straight, revealing that she really didn't have a bad body after all. She was only in her twenties, though I had thought she was much older. She had pretty green eyes too, which you couldn't see at all in her previous incarnation. And now they were really sparkling. This was when I finally learned her name and for the first time spoke with her.

Obviously, this could be no more than a dalliance for the movie star, and it proved to be a short one at that. He soon started trying to avoid Alice, and she started stalking him. I was witness to a scene in the lobby: the movie star came walking through with his new fling on his arm, a tall, glamorous, Botoxed European model. Alice was skulking around the corner and she jumped out and confronted him. "Where are you going?" she demanded, with fire in her eyes.

As the model eyed her up and down as if she were dirt, the movie star greeted Alice warmly with a hug and a kiss on the cheek, saying, "How are you, Alice? We're off to the theater."

The movie star grabbed the model around the waist and made to quickly leave, but Alice followed them to the door. "Can't I go with you?" she pleaded.

"Alice, we're on a date," the movie star said.

They left her standing there and went to hail a cab. Alice

watched them get into the cab, then stomped her foot, turned around, and stalked off, scowling and swinging her arms angrily.

I thought this would crush Alice, and since I had gotten to know her lately, I was rather pissed off at the movie star for doing this to her. At least Alice had attained a sort of equilibrium before; I felt that now, at best, she would retreat even deeper into her shell. I expected her to drag her ragged old coat out of the closet and go back to her old moping ways.

But that's not the way it turned out at all. Alice had made friends with all sorts of people at the hotel, and some of these friendships endured. Just by lifting up her head, she had found kindred souls here, people she could relate to. She got a job doing people's laundry, which enabled her to keep busy and also to get out of the hotel and get to know the neighborhood. She seems to have gotten over the movie star.

People often wonder why such a big star would want to live at the Chelsea, since he's got enough money to live anywhere he pleases. I tell them, half jokingly, that he moved to the Chelsea in order to plumb the depths of human experience in service to his art. But the movie star wasn't just slumming, since he brought something valuable with him. Because, let's face it, anybody can seduce a woman, but to totally change her personality is a feat of alchemy.

Then again, in the end, Alice escaped him. She wasn't dependent even on her magician, her Svengali. It was the movie star who transformed her, but the Chelsea that sustained her.

Or maybe the movie star just turned her on to some really good drugs.

Victor Bockris and Patti Smith at the Chelsea Hotel, August 1973. **Victor:** Would you consider yourself to be the greatest poet in New York City? **Patti:** Um, the greatest poet in New York City? Um . . . shit, I can't think of what to say. I don't think I'm a great poet at all. I don't even think I'm a good poet. I just think I write neat stuff. *Copyright Victor Bockris, 1973*

Michael Maher and Dan Courtenay in Dan's Chelsea Guitars,
April, 2007. Courtenay's guitar shop in a storefront of the
Chelsea Hotel is a relic of a bygone era of New York. Australian filmmaker Maher was shooting a documentary on the
gentrification of the Chelsea neighborhood, and of the
Chelsea Hotel itself. To view the documentary, go to
www.abc.net. And for more on the guitar shop, go to
www.chelseanow.com *Photo by Ed Hamilton*

Left: Charles James in his apartment at the Chelsea, 1977. James is showing his
work to a gallery representative in preparation for the "Fashion is Fantasy" art
show at New York's Rizzoli Gallery. Photographer Gregory Kitchen says that the
famous light pink "Kiss Sofa" that James designed was present in the apartment at
the time. *Photo by Gregory Kitchen*

William Burroughs and Andy Warhol having dinner in a room at the Chelsea Hotel, late 1980. Neither Burroughs nor Warhol liked to be interviewed on television because they couldn't control their images. Victor Bockris coordinated this dinner for a BBC documentary as a way to get around that. **Burroughs:** I'd choose a bazooka as my weapon of preference if I was shooting a rhino. But I don't see any reason for killing a rhino or even having a confrontation. **Warhol** (completely out of the blue but painfully sincere): I'm going to miss you if you go off to Kansas. You're not going to go off to Kansas are you? *Copyright Victor Bockris, 1980*

Right: Rene Ricard in his room at the Chelsea Hotel, 1992. In a gesture typical of his generous spirit, Rene delivers elaborate bouquets of flowers to various hotel residents, almost on a daily basis. No one knows quite where he obtains them, but as with many things around the Chelsea, we feel it's best not to ask too many questions. *Copyright Rita Barros*

Ethan Hawke in the Chelsea Hotel during the filming of *Chelsea Walls*, December 1999. Photographer Rita Barros was taking out the trash one morning—clad only in her sleeping t-shirt—when she opened her door to find a full film crew, but no trash bin. "What do I do with this?" she asked, holding her bag of trash. "I'll take care of it," Ethan said. For her trouble, he later let her photograph him. *Copyright Rita Barros*

Underground filmmaker Harry Smith, probably late seventies. In the seventies and eighties, Smith shuttled between various SROs in New York, including the Hotel Breslin and the Chelsea. Smith was an ordained bishop in Aleister Crowley's Ordo Templi Orientis. *Photo Courtesy of Anthology Film Archives, All Rights Reserved*

A still from Harry Smith's magnum opus *#18*, better known as *Mahagonny*, much of which Smith shot at the Chelsea Hotel from 1970–72. (He completed the film in 1980.) The film includes scenes featuring Chelsea Hotel residents such as Allen Ginsberg, Patti Smith, Robert Mapplethorpe, and Jonas Mekas. *Photo Courtesy of Anthology Film Archives, All Rights Reserved*

Stormé DeLarverié in the Chelsea Hotel, 1997. Stormé is the drag king who threw the first punch at the Stonewall Rebellion in Greenwich Village, lighting the spark that set off the gay rights movement. *Copyright Rita Barros*

Arthur Miller, Arnold Weinstein, and Stanley Bard in front of the Chelsea Hotel, October, 1994. Photographer Rita Barros says that Chelsea Hotel proprietor Stanley Bard has been asking her for a print of this photo for years, but she had lost track of it. Now he can have one for the price of this book. *Copyright Rita Barros*

Gregory Corso and Herbert Huncke on the balcony of the
Chelsea Hotel, 1991. Though the two Beat legends lived at the
hotel at the same time in the late eighties and early nineties,
they never became friends. Huncke thought that this was
because Corso suspected him of being a con man. *Copyright
Rita Barros*

Right: Dee Dee Ramone on the balcony of the Chelsea Hotel, September
1993. Bruno Wizard of the punk band the Homosexuals says that in the late
eighties, Dee Dee was trying to kick his drug habit and had holed up in his
room at the hotel for two weeks. On the day that he finally felt confident
enough to venture out, a woman threw herself from the ninth floor of the
hotel and, as Dee Dee stepped through the front door, landed on the pavement
almost at his feet. In the photo, he stands almost directly above the spot where
she landed. *Copyright Rita Barros*

Above: The painter Hiroya, holding a pair of women's shoes, in front of the Chelsea Hotel. In 2001, Hiroya came running up to me in the hallway: "Fashion people say I steal shoes! They say they want five hundred dollars or they sue me! What I do?" I advised him to return the shoes. It wasn't until I was looking for photos for this book that I found out why he needed the shoes: as a prop for his own photo shoot. He's posing with one of his Bunny paintings, as well. *Photo by www.lindatroeller.com*

Right: Photographer Mia Hanson with poet and mystic Ira Cohen at the Chelsea Hotel, February 2007. I took this photo at a Valentine's Day party held in memory of Vali Myers, the Australian painter and witch who lived at the Chelsea off and on in the seventies, eighties, and nineties, and died in 2003. The photo is shot in Vali's elaborately painted old room. To read the story of the party, go to www.chelseanow.com. *Photo by Ed Hamilton*

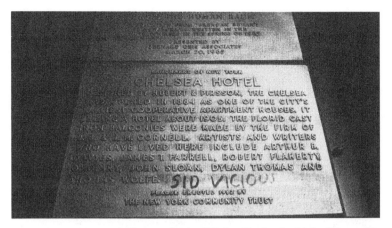

Plaque on façade of Chelsea Hotel, early eighties. For years following Nancy Spungen's murder in 1978 and Sid's subsequent suicide in 1979, reverent punk fans added this inscription to the plaque, refreshing it diligently every time it was scrubbed off.
Photo by Claudio Edinger

Artist Paul Richard, no doubt just back from one of his shows at
the Gagosian, displays a self-portrait, 2006. *Copyright Julia Calfee*

The front desk of the Chelsea Hotel, 2004. Though it looks like this guy is planning an art project of some sort, the branches he is holding are actually just Christmas decorations for the lobby. *Copyright Julia Calfee*

Left: Kyle Taylor in part of Thomas Wolfe's old suite of rooms at the Chelsea Hotel, 2003. Kyle is selling off his stuff in preparation for moving out. Since his departure, Kyle has designed a fragrance, called "Kyle 831," which attempts to capture the seedy essence of the hotel. *Copyright Julia Calfee*

Stanley Bard on his final day as manager of the Chelsea Hotel, June 18, 2007. With him is his right-hand man, Jerry Weinstein. **Stanley:** Over the years people here have created some really beautiful, meaningful things, and they just needed that little extra bit of help to be able to do it. I've always tried to do what I can. *Photo by Ed Hamilton*

A Different Kind
of Currency

The Downtown Hipster:
Hiroya, Part II

In many ways, Hiroya was an innocent, almost an idiot savant. He thought that if he just got out there and made his work known, it was inevitable that people would recognize his genius. In a way he was right, although the main achievement of all his networking lay in attracting the attention of certain washed-up members of the Downtown art crowd. In this way he fell into a scene with people who were much tougher and more cynical than he was, people who saw that he had talent, was entertaining, and—especially, I believe—had a pipeline to money through his family back in Japan. All kinds of moderately famous people began coming around to visit him—he was quick to brag about it—and included him in their schemes, inviting him to gallery openings and parties.

One was Dee Dee Ramone. It's probably best not to identify the others. Unfortunately for Hiroya, Dee Dee and many of these other unsavory characters were drug addicts.

Hiroya started hanging out with these junkies, going with them to all the parties and clubs. It wasn't long before Hiroya, too, was using drugs. (At least it got him off the liquor.) Inevitably, it changed him. He would sleep all day and stay out all night. He could no longer sustain his work habits; he piddled away on the same canvases for months and sometimes stopped painting altogether for weeks at a time.

Hiroya had been overweight when he moved into the Chelsea, and he became seriously fat when he decided to hit the bottle. But then, almost overnight, he dropped fifty pounds and became really skinny. It was amazing how quickly he lost the weight. Before I knew the cause of his weight loss I told him that he looked good. "You must be working out or something," I said. He gave me a sad, weary look as if I had no idea.

The art world remade Hiroya in its own ironic image: his clothes, his philosophy, and even, ultimately, the style of his own art. His new friends convinced him to get rid of his old paint-spattered overalls. They took Hiroya to the tailor and had him fitted with a black Armani suit. Though he looked every bit the part of the hip, Downtown artist, this new attire didn't suit his lifestyle. Hiroya needed to be an untamed wild man, able to whip out a brush and fling paint around at any time. Soon, despite all the care he took, he had paint all over his new suit.

"You gotta paint in your overalls, Hiroya," I told him.

"I know, I know," he said with eyes downcast, as if I was scolding him.

But what would happen was that somebody would ask him for a demonstration, or an inspiration would strike him, and he couldn't be bothered to change clothes. People asked him why he had been so stupid as to paint in a suit worth several thousand dollars, and he didn't have much of an answer. Luckily, he had the money to buy another one; in this way he went through several Armani suits in rapid succession.

They put words in his mouth: "Art should be for the people." How else to explain Hiroya's embarrassing penchant for going around putting those silly Bunny paintings in all the shops? But Hiroya didn't care about that; it was all to get his name out there, all about self-promotion. They wanted to make it sound less mercenary, but from Hiroya's mouth the words only ended up sounding false. What they couldn't take about Hiroya was his sincerity. They wanted it to be a joke, an ironic wink-and-a-nod of self-promotion.

I was in the hall one time when a Downtown art critic came to see his work. Hiroya was at his best, dragging out all of his canvases, bustling all around, babbling on about the groundbreaking character of his work. As we were viewing the paintings, the critic whispered to me: "I love his act! It's so obnoxious! He's so annoying that he's positively charming!"

Eventually, the art-world hipsters even forced Hiroya to change his painting style. They thought they could tweak it, make it more saleable. They tried to stick him with a more painstaking, intricate style, a style for which he was ill suited. Soon he lost confidence in his own work. He couldn't finish a canvas, when he had been so productive before. After a while I was embarrassed for him and stopped asking to see his new work, because I knew he would show me the same old unfinished canvases I had seen a million times before. He spent less and less time in his room painting and more time in the lobby bothering people. Increasingly, too, he spent more and more time away from the Chelsea, on the street, finding drugs. He dried up creatively.

So what did the art-world hipsters do for Hiroya? Well, for one thing, they were able to arrange interviews and pictorial spreads for him in several magazines. One of these occasions was how they got him to start wearing a suit. It was an article about what artists wear, artist's fashion, in *Vogue Italia*. Of course, he couldn't wear his overalls for this: that wouldn't sell any clothes. He bought his first Armani suit for the photo shoot, and then, since everybody told him how good he looked and praised him to the high heavens, he was easily persuaded to switch to this look permanently.

They used the magazine articles to create a mythology for Hiroya; I remember one particularly ridiculous article that claimed that he slept in a coffin. (They apparently got the idea from Sarah Bernhardt, who really did sleep in a coffin when she lived at the Chelsea—or maybe that was all hype too.) In all the times I was in his room, I never saw any evidence of this. I asked him about it once, about whether he ever slept in a coffin like they said, and he became embarrassed and was kind of evasive. He said, "Oh, sometimes. No more."

The art-world people got Hiroya into a group show at the Gershwin Hotel, which is sort of a knockoff of the Chelsea, a bohemian theme hotel for slumming hipsters. Hiroya put up a huge yellow banner on the side of the hotel in his graffiti style, proclaiming: Yellow Is The New Black. Besides the trite slogan, it was an impressive work and it hung there for several months, even long after the show had closed. Though they never did get him a real gallery show, they introduced him to rich people who liked his work and potentially might buy it. Hiroya was proud of these acquaintances and put up a sort of shrine to them on his door: pictures of himself standing with famous designers, artists, actors, and musicians.

If he hadn't been so dysfunctional to begin with and, by this point, so incapacitated by drugs, Hiroya might have been able to parlay this exposure into a real success. However, when people showed a willingness actually to fork over some money, Hiroya would tell them to go to hell if he didn't like them.

Three Chelsea Elevator Stories

I: Knoxville

Slightly hung over, I was going out to the deli one morning to get coffee and muffins. The elevator was packed with fat midwestern tourists and one tall, thin Japanese hipster girl talking loudly into her cell phone. I got on, and as I turned to face the front, the Japanese girl screamed in my ear: "OH, NO!!!"

What happened?! I thought. Something with the elevator? Did *I* do something? It took a moment for it to register that she was simply talking on her phone. "Why did you scream like that?" I asked, shaken, but she ignored me.

A moment later she screamed again: "Oh my God! Push 4 for me!" This time she *was* talking to me. I pushed 4. She went on talking into the phone: "I'm going to the *Saturday Night Live* after-party tonight!" There was a pause, then: "Johnny Knoxville is my close personal friend!"

Perhaps this impressed the Midwesterners, I don't know. I found myself hoping that Johnny Knoxville and his buddies would hold her down and shave her head. The fourth floor came, the door opened, I looked at her with raised eyebrow, but she didn't get out. She rode down to the lobby and got off with the rest of us.

II: On the Nod

Coming back from the deli, a bag of muffins in one hand and a tray of coffees in the other, I rounded the corner to the elevator just as it was opening. There was a man in a black leather jacket in the back corner of the elevator, head down, slumping forward, on the nod. Without thinking, I stepped into the elevator, and as soon as I was fully inside, he fell right into me. "Shit!" he yelled, loudly. Luckily, he caught himself just as he hit me; I couldn't have caught him because my arms were full. "Oh, sorry," he mumbled.

The desk clerk had seen what had happened and he called out, "Hey, what's going on in there?! Everything all right in there?!"

"Yeah, it's okay," I said. I hit the button for my floor and up we went. The guy in the leather jacket had apparently slept through his floor the first time he went up, and had ridden back down to the lobby. Now he remembered what he was doing and hit his button: 4.

"Sorry, man," he apologized again, seeing the coffee slopped out on my jacket. "I just forgot what I was doing. I'm really forgetful sometimes. I just woke up and I haven't had my coffee yet."

"Yeah, I hear ya," I said. "I know what you mean."

"It was one of those senior moments," he said, laughing. He was probably in his mid-thirties. "It could happen to anybody," he said as he got off.

Yeah, anybody who shoots heroin.

III: True

Much later in the day, after Susan and I had returned from a walk in the Village, we got on the elevator with a large black man wearing a porkpie hat and carrying a saxophone case. He said, "I've seen some *unusual* things in my stay at this hotel."

"Tell me about it!" I said, laughing.

"We've lived here for seven years," my girlfriend said. "So I think we've about seen it all."

"Well, I don't know if I'd go that far," I said.

The man looked at us disapprovingly, as if we were criticizing or mocking him. "To thine own self be true," he intoned solemnly.

We didn't say anything. He kept looking at us, at me in particular, and seemed to want a response of some kind. Finally, as we were getting off the elevator, he said, "That's true, isn't it? Isn't that true?"

"I suppose it is," I said.

A Second Chance

Stanley Bard says that getting into the Chelsea is harder than getting into an Ivy League college. He says he does extensive research on each potential resident. And while I've no doubt that this is true, even at the best of schools the registrar sometimes loses your transcript.

A man in his late thirties was moving into the hotel. He wore his gray hair cropped short and was slightly overweight. He seemed respectable enough—in the Chelsea sense, that is: he wasn't wearing a suit or anything. He had his van parked out by the curb, and in between carrying in boxes, he stopped up at the desk to say hi to the manager, a tall Italian man named Harvey.

"I used to live here before, back in the eighties," our new neighbor said. "Stanley says he doesn't remember. You remember me, don't you Harvey?"

"Yeah, I remember you," Harvey said, though he didn't sound too convincing, and I thought maybe he just said it to make the guy feel better.

"I lived here for almost a year, and Stanley doesn't even remember me!"

"We get a lot of people passing through here, you know," Harvey said. "And sometimes it's hard to keep them all straight."

"I was worried about that, whether he'd remember me."

"Well, he let you in anyway, so he must've liked you."

"Back then I was a drug-addled eighteen-year-old," the new-comer said. "Partied all night. Totally irresponsible. Never even paid my rent. Maybe I paid it once. Stanley kicked me out himself." Harvey didn't say anything. He looked on impassively.

"But now it's cool," the new guy said. "Blank slate, you know. Now it's all good."

A Time to Every Purpose

Hiroya was hanging out in the lobby as usual, wearing his painted Armani suit and aggressively accosting and annoying tourists. I said hello to him as I came in the door and walked by him to the elevator. The elevator was already there, so I got right on, but before the door could close, Hiroya decided he had to tell me something. He ran after me and stuck his hand in the elevator just as it was about to close, and stood there in the door jabbering away excitedly. "What?!" I said. "What is it?!" But due to his poor English, I couldn't understand a word he was saying.

It was then I noticed that Magda was standing behind him, trying to get on the elevator. A dancer in her prime, Magda was now a prim, white-haired old lady in an immaculate green suit. I saw her trying to get on, but I couldn't get a word in edgewise.

But it didn't matter. Magda was not one to be intimidated by anybody, that's for sure. "Excuse me!" she said loudly. "I'm trying to get on the elevator. Do you mind?"

Hiroya jumped aside immediately. "Oh, sorry! Sorry!"

As soon as the door shut and we were on our way up, the old lady asked, "What in the world did he want from you?" It seemed clear from her tone of voice that she despised Hiroya.

Wanting to distance myself from him, I said, "I have no idea." It was the truth, after all.

"Hmmm. He probably wanted to show you his paintings."

"Yeah, that's probably it," I said. At this point I didn't dare admit that he lived on my floor and that I had already bought two of his paintings.

Then all at once Magda seemed to soften toward Hiroya—a fellow artist after all. "Well, he's new around here," she said.

It's an unspoken rule that you don't bother the other residents with too much self-promotion. Everybody here has their own artistic irons in the fire.

"I'm new around here too," I said.

"Well, at least you don't go hawking your wares in the lobby!"

I laughed. "No, not yet I haven't."

"I suppose there's still plenty of time," Magda said, rolling her eyes.

Maybe. I never did find out what Hiroya was so excited about that day. Perhaps he had sold a painting or accosted a celebrity who had come through the lobby. It was probably nothing, but whatever it was, he would take it with him to the grave.

The Whopper

When our next-door neighbor was about to move out, Susan and I had some trepidation about who would move in to replace her. She hadn't been staying there much recently but had been letting another girl use her room: Juanita, a girl in her mid-twenties who worked on and off as an artist's model, a brown-eyed, raven-haired beauty.

One afternoon Susan and I ran into Juanita in the halls, and she proudly proclaimed, "I'm going to be your new neighbor!"

"Oh, that's great," I said, wondering immediately where she had obtained the money.

"I told Stanley I don't have any money now," she went on, "but I have a Larry Rivers painting in the room worth thirty-five to fifty thousand dollars. I told him, 'when I sell the painting I can give you the rent for several months, or a year, whatever you like.' And he said that was fine."

"Wow!" I said. "Fifty thousand dollars!"

"Well, estimates differ," Juanita said. "But it's worth a lot of money. I asked Stanley, 'Don't you want to see the painting?' And he said, 'no, I trust you.'"

Didn't sound like him, but I didn't say anything.

"Isn't that weird that he'd let me move in without any deposit or anything?"

Yeah, pretty weird.

"The guys at the desk said Stanley just reads people. Isn't that funny? He doesn't need any references. He doesn't need to do any background checks. He can tell if you're a good person just by talking with you for a while. My mother was a poet and my father was a sculptor. They knew Brendan Behan. He even wrote them a letter. I showed it to Stanley, and he read it. He agreed that it was worth something, though of course not as much as the painting."

"What's in the letter?" I asked.

"Oh, it describes how Brendan had trouble getting toilet paper and getting his drain unclogged and other basic services when he was living at the hotel. It's typewritten, but you can tell it's by Brendan by the scathingly satirical tone."

Neither I nor Susan believed any of this about the painting or the letter; that's why we didn't ask to see them. But we figured probably Stanley just liked her—she was a pretty girl, after all—and so was doing her a favor and letting her move in, hoping she could make enough money through modeling or other means to pay the rent.

Then, late one night near the end of the month, we heard a racket outside our door. When I looked out to see what was going on, I saw that Juanita and her boyfriend were moving out her furniture—or anyway, somebody's furniture—and I asked her if she needed any help. She acted kind of nervous and didn't seem to want me around. The piece they were moving at that moment was an old, rickety writing desk; she asked me if I knew anything about antiques, and when I said no, she dismissed me with a wave of her hand.

A couple of days later, I asked a girl who knew Juanita, and she said, "There's no way in hell Stanley would rent a room to her. He never wants to see her again in his life."

There are any number of con men and pathological liars wandering these halls, but most of their lies aren't so easily disproved. Juanita seemed to desperately need to believe her wild story, and to need others to believe it. She also might have been hinting around that we should give her a recommendation. "I really feel like I belong here," she had told us at one point. Most likely, she was right.

No Change at the El Quijote

We were eating at the El Quijote one night, Susan and I. I wasn't drinking—which would have relaxed me, but I was trying to quit—and I was distracted, worrying about something or other. Perhaps we had had an argument. We ate without saying much. At the end of the meal I looked at the check, counted out the money, including the tip, and, as the waiter was nowhere to be seen, handed it to the busboy. "No change," I said.

The busboy, a short, stocky young Latino man, looked puzzled, but he took the check and went away. But after a few moments, he came back, still holding the check, and asked: "Did you say no change, or keep the change?"

"No change," I repeated, annoyed, "Keep the change." When he had gone, I said, "What's his problem? Didn't I make myself clear?"

"Maybe he just didn't understand you," Susan said. "I don't think he speaks real good English."

"Well he works in a restaurant, so he should be able to understand things like no change. It isn't like it's his first night. I've seen him here before."

We puzzled over it a while in silence, as I finished my iced tea.

Finally, Susan suggested: "Do you think maybe he thinks that's what you say to a homeless man?"

"What do you mean?"

"I mean, when he asks for money."

"No way!" I said. "That's what I always say when I want the waiter to keep the change."

"Maybe it was the way you said it. You *were* kind of brusque."

I rejected this notion out of hand. But then on our way out, we had to pass by the kitchen. Somebody in there seemed to have told a really good joke, because there was an uproar coming from within. In between the raucous laughter and the loud Spanish banter, we heard interjections of English language phrases such as:

"No change!"

"No change, motherfucker!"

"Get a job, bum!"

Chelsea Style:
Arthur Miller at the Chelsea

What is the Chelsea Hotel style? My girlfriend and I have been discussing this question lately and failing miserably to come up with a definitive answer. Some of our residents look like they just stepped out of a fashion magazine, while others wear black leather and tattoo themselves heavily. One woman has blue hair, and another guy wears a rumpled suit and manages—whether by design or accident—to look exactly like Dylan Thomas. Some dress up, some dress like slobs. And some people, like me, just wear T-shirts and khakis like we've worn since college. Though it may be true, it seems strangely unsatisfactory, a cop-out, in fact, to say it's just whatever you want to wear. There must be some unifying theme.

Keeping this in mind, I was out in the hall looking through some magazines that somebody had thrown out, when, looking up, I saw a man walk past me and go into the Madonna *Sex* room with a roll of toilet paper looped onto his belt. I did a double take: what the hell? I thought my eyes must be deceiving me.

While I was standing there wondering about it, the man came back out of the room. He was a young hipster cat, with sideburns and a trucker hat, stovepipe jeans, and, sure enough, strapped onto his hip by a black, silver-studded belt, the toilet paper. A fashion accessory? I had to find out, and so I followed him out to the elevators. "Looks like you come prepared," I said, indicating the roll.

"Hell yeah, dude," the hipster said. "I been to this hotel before."

In an article in *Granta*, the literary magazine, Arthur Miller relates a similar tale. He tells about coming back to the Chelsea after many years' absence to visit his old friend Arnold Weinstein, with whom he was collaborating on the musical version of one of his plays. He tells of how Arnold's huge apartment was full to overflowing with junk, as if, Miller says, Arnold was preparing to make a massive donation to the Salvation Army. He says that while he was there, the huge Jamaican maid came strolling in the door with four rolls of toilet paper held aloft in triumph—two on the fingers of each hand—and loudly announced, "I haven't forgotten you, Arnold!"

The playwright Arthur Miller really needs no introduction, but I'll give us one anyway for consistency's sake. Born in 1915 in Harlem, the son of a working-class clothing manufacturer, Miller worked in a car-parts warehouse to earn enough money to pay his way through the University of Michigan. He became famous early for such masterworks of the theater as *Death of a Salesman* and *The Crucible* and even more famous when he married his second wife, Marilyn Monroe, in 1956. He was indicted for contempt for his refusal to name names in the McCarthy hearings.

Miller lived in the Chelsea throughout the sixties, moving here after his separation from Marilyn in 1960 (they divorced in 1961). Hounded by the press, he wanted a quiet place where he could do his work in peace, and the Chelsea fit the bill. While here, he hung out with such luminaries as the science fiction writer Arthur C. Clarke and the composer Virgil Thomson.

Arnold Weinstein was somewhat younger and much less well-known than Arthur Miller. Born in 1927 in New York to English parents, Arnold grew up in Harlem and the Bronx. Unlike Miller, who sat out the war because of a football injury, Arnold served on a Navy destroyer in World War II. After the war he went to Harvard and received a Rhodes scholarship and a Fulbright. Later he taught at Yale.

Arnold, a playwright and librettist, showed early promise in the theater with an off-Broadway production of his play *Red Eye of Love,* about an all-meat department store. That early near-success was as good as it would get for Arnold, who seems to have achieved his greatest fame as a drinker and party guest. Arnold was good at making friends; he was clever and witty, a fun guy to have around. Though he worked with a lot of well-known people over the years—Miller, Philip Glass, William Bolcom—he seems not to have collaborated in their most famous works and in any event not to have collaborated in anything that made any money. Still, he became known and respected in his field—even if he never did have that hit that would have put him over the top.

Arnold lived in a large suite of rooms at the Chelsea for over three decades and was apparently the proud tenant of the building's last remaining rent-controlled apartment. It was a good thing he had that sort of protection, because he never made much of a living from his writings and toward the end, even with the miniscule rent he was paying, he had to resort to selling off his books to pay his medical bills.

I didn't know Arnold all that well, just from running into him around the hotel, in the lobby or on the elevators. A gray-haired, round-bellied, affable old man, usually more or less disheveled as he shuffled through the halls, Arnold nonetheless had a sharp, sarcastic sense of humor.

One day Arnold came up to Susan and me in the lobby and handed us a flyer: a company in Philadelphia was producing a revival of one of his old musicals. He was excited, hopeful, as if success was just around the corner, and he wanted us to share in his excitement. But we're not that interested in musicals, and tickets were expensive—I think they were $100—and of course it was in Philadelphia. We treated it kind of lightly: "Philadelphia, eh?" I said. "Oh sure, we'll be there."

My jocular tone had hurt Arnold's feelings. "No, it's really good," Arnold said. "You really have to go." And he kept on insisting. He thought it should be just as important to us as it was to him, and he didn't seem to understand why we couldn't just get on a bus and ride out there for the evening. His cheerful good humor concealed a more vulnerable side.

Sometimes, toward the end, Arnold seemed kind of addled, seemingly not recognizing me when I said hello, and maybe that was because of his drinking—it was liver cancer that finally claimed him—or maybe just because he was, after all, in his late seventies.

———

Since I love and seek out all things related to the Chelsea, I had to be the first to get a hold of Arthur Miller's *Granta* article. I had heard about it well in advance of its publication and had ordered it straight from the publishers. When I got it, I read it right off; I must say it's one of the best things ever written about the Chelsea. It really captures the spirit of the place.

As luck would have it, I ran into Arnold in the lobby of the Chelsea soon after that. He was very excited when I told him about the article, his chest swelling with pride.

"Oh, yes, Miller's a very good friend of mine," Arnold said. "We're working together on the musical version of his play *A View from the Bridge*. Do you know it?" he asked.

I shook my head, no.

"I've known Arthur for a number of years," Arnold went on. "We go way back, back to the sixties, although this is the first time

I've ever formally collaborated with him. He's a very great play-wright, of course, one of the greatest in American theater. In *world* theater I should say."

"Oh yeah," I said. "Of course."

"I heard he was writing that article and that I would be men-tioned in it. Yes, I'm very eager to see it. It was a good story, I hope."

"Well . . ." I said. I laughingly told him about the article. "He talked about what a junk hole you lived in," I said, and repeated the crack about the Salvation Army. It was the same for many of us at the Chelsea. I, too, lived in a room piled high with junk.

Arnold chuckled a little bit at this, though I don't think he found it too funny and perhaps understood its intent better than I at this point.

Then I delivered the punch line about the maid delivering the toilet paper. "He said you were really grateful, Arnold!" I said.

When I saw the look of shock and disappointment on Arnold's face I immediately felt ashamed, almost as if I had been the one who had written the article. Arnold hung his head and hunched his back and shoulders, and his whole being seemed to deflate. I realized at once that it was easy for me, a man of forty, to make light of such things: I wasn't necessarily going to die in my junk hole.

"Uh, but it was funny," I stammered. "A real funny article." I said I would lend him the journal, and in fact I offered to run up and get it right then, but Arnold declined solemnly, saying Miller had promised to send him a copy and he figured he would read it soon enough.

If he ever did read Miller's article, and, voracious reader that he was, I feel certain he must have eventually, Arnold would have been even more disappointed. The article isn't about messiness per se, and certainly not about toilet paper. The incident with the toilet paper is brought up to show that there are certain unfathomable mysteries and a certain inscrutable illogic that remain constant at the Chelsea over the decades. But Miller is really just using the incident as a sort of metaphor. The issue of *Granta* in which the article appears is titled *Bad Company:* as the editor writes in the introduction, it's an issue that purports to examine the lives of those less fortunate. Miller's own article is called "The Chelsea Affect," which, in addition to the suggestion of a style, of something put on or affected, seems also intended to connote mental illness, as in the "flat affect" of the schizophrenic. Miller writes about all the eccentric and down-and-out people he met in the Chelsea back in his own time of residence: the great fashion designer Charles James wandering befuddled through the halls in his pajamas; the Irish writer Brendan Behan drooling vomit from his mouth as he talks; the deranged Warhol shooter, Valerie Solanas; and an unnamed "minister" in threadbare clothes who's only happy on rainy days because he believes more people die in bad weather, thus giving rise to more funerals at which he might possibly officiate. The implication for Arnold is clear: he represents the continuation of this line.

One morning I woke up early and, on my way to the bathroom, saw that the door of the neighboring apartment was standing wide open. The former tenant, Mr. Greene, had recently moved out, leaving a lot of his stuff behind, including a large library of books, which were stacked and strewn all around the room on shelves, tables, chairs, and the floor. Arnold was in there. Stanley Bard had drug him out of bed and let him into the room so he could go through the books before the workers came and cleared the place out. Mumbling to himself as if he'd just arisen after a night of hard drinking, Arnold wore a dirty T-shirt over his ample belly and a pair of old, baggy, drooping sweatpants. Talk about Chelsea style!

Back in the day, the old men used to prowl the halls in bathrobes, but lately I guess the look has been updated.

An infamous trash-picker myself, probably dressed only a notch or two above Arnold, I was eager to lend a hand in rooting through the piles of books and other junk. Arnold was in his own little world and scarcely acknowledged my presence, glancing up only now and again to comment on some arcane volume he had extracted from the piles. But as he uncovered book after book of interest, he became increasingly excited. "I never knew this guy was so interested in the theater," Arnold said. The two men had been approximately the same age but had never really talked to one another. "To think we had something in common all these years. I only knew him just to say hi on the elevator. He wasn't really a talkative fellow, was he? Do you know what line of work he was in?"

"I think he was some kind of a sound technician," I said.

"Why would he leave all these valuable books?"

"I don't know. He moved back to Greece. Maybe it was too much trouble to lug them all back there." In fact, as I was later to learn, Mr. Greene had been diagnosed with cancer and had died only a few months after arriving back in his homeland.

At one point I moved aside a pile of books and several bags of trash from a chest of drawers. In one large drawer I found a mother lode of old playbills, hundreds of them. I called Arnold over and he went through them all, exclaiming in delight when he found one from some obscure play he remembered from the old days. I got the sense he was looking for a playbill from one of his old plays as he went through the whole huge pile, but if he found it, he never let on. He was content to regale me with tales of the old luminaries of the theater, scarcely bothered by the fact that I had never heard of any of the people he was talking about.

Later, as happy as can be with the obscure treasures he had unearthed, Arnold commandeered the bellman's luggage cart, and I helped him to load it up to wheel it to and from the elevator and unload the boxes into his already overstocked apartment on the floor below.

Though he was a decade older, Arthur Miller predeceased Arnold by only a few months. When Miller died, they dimmed the lights on Broadway. Susan and I happened to be passing through Times Square at the time and found it quite a moving experience. On the other hand, I got the feeling that the bulk of the people there, the throngs of tourists who had come to see the plays, didn't know what the hell was going on and probably felt only a vague sense of confusion. When Arnold died, they didn't dim the lights but they had a memorial service for him in the Walter Kerr Theater, and the place was filled with scores of his old friends from the theater and from the Chelsea, come to pay tribute to a man they had all known and loved. His longtime friend and collaborator William Bolcom played the piano, and several singers and actors sang his songs and recited lines of dialogue from his plays. The songs were upbeat and cheerful, and nobody seemed to mind that they weren't quite catchy enough for Broadway.

Arnold had a sense of humor about his own limited success, joking that he was the president of ITOF, the International Theater of Failure. But you can't really call him a failure. Certainly Arnold never made much money—the measure of success in the "real" world—but it's a good question as to how much he really needed, living in such a place as the Chelsea (Miller calls it a "fictional" place) where another form of currency holds sway.

Shirley and the Angel
of 23rd Street

Shirley Kelly, with her exquisitely coiffed blond hair and painstakingly applied makeup, always dressed to the nines to sit behind the desk and answer the phone, was something of an institution around here. Though she recently left us, hopefully for greener pastures, she's difficult to forget. I remember a conversation I had with her in April of 2002.

That was when the Japanese guy who dressed like an angel lived here. When I came into the hotel that day, he was sitting in one of the lobby chairs, dressed in a long white gown with white wings and a halo. He was talking to a conservatively dressed, middle-aged Japanese woman.

Shirley was sitting in her chair behind the desk, and I greeted her as I walked up.

"Between that angel and Jimbo and the blond woman who runs around here, it's getting to be like a nuthouse," Shirley said.

The blond woman she was referring to was a woman with Tourette's syndrome—I always just called her Blondie—who used to live in the Chelsea. Jimbo was a desk clerk with whom Shirley argued constantly.

"Is this the first time you noticed that?" I asked, chuckling.

As was her way, Shirley paid my remark no heed. "That's his wife he's sitting out there talking to, if you can believe that," she said. "Or at least she used to be. I guess she pays for all this."

"All this luxury?"

"Which makes her crazier than he is!" Shirley went on. "He's a transvestite, but he used to be married." "I guess that's before he died and went to heaven," I said. "Hey, maybe this hotel is heaven!"

"Oh, you're not supposed to notice his wings," Shirley said, sarcastically. "Oh no! Just act like they're not there. Well, I'm sorry, but it's kind of obvious. It's not like he's up on a cloud or something."

2003

Ghosts and
Other Abominations

The Ultra-Famous Incredibly Chic Chelsea Hotel Bar

There's a club in the basement of the Chelsea. Most everybody who lives in the hotel would rather have a laundry room, or something practical, but instead we've got a trendy nightclub where hardly any of us ever venture. (But I did see Monica Lewinsky go in there one time!) I went in Serena's once just to see what it looks like, and—surprise!—it looks exactly like a basement, with low ceilings and exposed pipes. But besides that, it's nicely decorated, in red and black like a lot of clubs these days. I have to admit they did good job with it, under the circumstances.

The club was started by Serena Bass, who actually lived here for a time (maybe she still does) in order to cash in on the hipster cachet of the Chelsea. Serena herself no longer owns the club, however. She sold it, hopefully for big bucks.

One night recently, a thin, pretty, young blond woman in high heels and a dress, burst through the front door of the hotel and came running frantically up to the desk. "Please don't send hotel guests to my club!" the woman screamed hysterically. She was apparently the hostess at Serena's.

"People come downstairs and ask where the bar in the Chelsea Hotel is," the desk clerk said, matter-of-factly, "and so I give them directions to Serena's."

"Oh, my God! Please don't do that anymore!" the woman said. "There's a guy from the hotel out there now trying to get into my club! And he's already been drinking! And he's wearing a sweatshirt!"

I was standing there waiting for the elevator, and, hearing this crazy rant, I burst out laughing, and the hostess turned and glared at me. "Sorry," I said.

The hostess turned back toward the desk. "What am I supposed to do with this guy?" she said, a bit more calmly.

The desk clerk shrugged his shoulders.

"Not our problem!" Shirley, the switchboard operator, piped up from her corner.

I think the staff likes to play tricks on people. Or maybe they just get tired of explaining that there really is no Chelsea Hotel Bar. In certain guidebooks—apparently written by people who've never visited the hotel, they say things like, "Be sure to stop by the Chelsea Hotel Bar, where Dylan Thomas and William Burroughs hoisted beers." If they mean anything, they mean the El Quijote, which was once, eighty or ninety years ago, the hotel dining room. The El Q has more in common with the hotel, and anybody who wants to hoist beers with bohemians would be better off there. But sometimes I guess it's good for a laugh to send a grungy-looking tourist or two down to Serena's.

Another Satisfied Customer

A middle-aged woman and her two teenage daughters had checked into the room next door to us at the Chelsea Hotel. The woman, blond, Midwestern, overweight, was cheerful and seemed open-minded—good qualities to have around this place. Speaking to her in the hallway outside her room, I had to draw her out a little bit to get her to talk about her impression of the hotel. After I'd got to know her a little bit, I asked, "So how do you like this place?"

"It's kind of idiosyncratic, isn't it," she said, tentatively.

"I'll say! Although 'insane' is more the word that comes to mind."

"Well, that's not exactly what I meant," the woman said. "The people here have certainly been very nice. I was referring more to the physical state of the hotel."

"Yeah, it's kind of run down."

"Mmm-hmm. They showed me another room before I took this one, but for one reason or another it was unacceptable."

"Surely it couldn't have been any worse than this one," I said.

The woman looked at me askance. "Well, I hate to say anything, since you live here."

"Oh come on, tell me," I prodded her.

She kept her voice low. "They didn't see it," she whispered, indicating her daughters in the room behind her. "It was a nice room, nicer than this one, clean, and it had its own bathroom, which was a definite plus."

"That's for sure," I said. The room she was in now shared a bathroom with our room and two others.

"But there were condoms scattered on the bed."

"Oh no!" I exclaimed.

"No, listen, let me finish. I didn't mind that. They were unopened. And my first thought was: Oh, that's so sad, the poor people didn't even get to have sex. But isn't that nice of the maid to leave them for the next guest."

"Yeah, that is," I said.

"And then I looked on the floor on the other side of the bed and saw the USED ones!"

I cracked up laughing, and the woman, too, was unable to stifle her laughter. Hearing us, one of her daughters called out, "Mom, what are you doing out there?!"

We chuckled a bit more quietly. I asked, "Now was it Stanley who showed you this room?" I was rather hoping that it *had* been our illustrious proprietor.

"Oh no, it was just one of the bellmen."

"And did he see the condoms?"

"Yeah. He didn't bat an eye," the woman replied. "He just shrugged his shoulders and brought me up to this room."

Offenses against God and Man in Serena's

Serena's, in the basement of the Chelsea, makes lots of noise at night, and sometimes you can hardly get into the hotel for all the hipsters waiting in line for the club. But the thing that ticked me off most was the time the hostess had the nerve to come into the hotel and say she didn't want any Chelsea people coming into her club. (Bohemians are only cool in theory, you see.)

So one morning, when I saw that the place had been shut down, my first thought was, Good riddance. (It's since opened back up, so be sure to visit!) There were a couple of guys I knew sitting in the lobby, old guys, in their sixties. "What the hell happened," I asked them.

"They were shut down for liquor violations," one of them, Taylor, a painter, told me.

"What's that mean, underage drinking?" I asked.

"Probably," Taylor said.

"Pedophilia," Vincent said. I think he's a painter too.

"What the hell are you talking about?" Taylor asked.

"They get those young chicks for those old guys in there," Vincent said.

Vincent was letting his imagination run wild. There was no way he had ever been in Serena's, though maybe, after all, he had been considering it. I laughed and said, "Let's spread that rumor around."

Chelsea Séance:
Thomas Wolfe at the Chelsea

PART I: THOMAS WOLFE

Thomas Wolfe, one of my literary heroes, was a southerner, just like me. Like me, he came to New York to escape the stifling conformism of a small southern town, in his case, Asheville, North Carolina. Unlike me, he lived somewhere else when he first came to New York. But he ultimately found his way to the Chelsea Hotel, and he lived there in his final years, pretty much up until the time he died, getting drunk with the poet Edgar Lee Masters, and writing *You Can't Go Home Again* and *The Web and the Rock,* the final two installments in the vast, relentlessly autobiographical saga that was his life's work.

Wolfe was six-foot eight. The Chelsea, with its high ceilings and door frames, must have seemed tailor-made for his bulk. As he describes himself in his novels, he's somewhat disproportionate, his legs and arms too big for his trunk, his back slightly hunched. He thought he was unattractive to women.

He only had one real girlfriend in his life, a woman named Aline Bernstein, an amateur costume designer for the theater, and a patron of the arts—and a married woman a decade Wolfe's senior. Theirs was a stormy, on-again, off-again affair. They had to meet in secret, and the Chelsea was one of their trysting places.

By all accounts, Wolfe was a troubled man. He was tortured over the fact that his girlfriend was married, the fact that she was much older than him, the fact that—at least before his novels were published—it was her rich husband's money that kept him out of a Bowery flophouse, and the fact that he had been published due to her influence. He was able to live with these things, but just barely, and only because he used his writing to work through his problems. In Room 829 he brooded darkly and stormed and raved drunkenly, throwing Aline out the door and swearing never again to have anything to do with her—only to repent when she returned the next day or the next month, perhaps bringing him food as a peace offering. They were on the outs in 1939, perhaps for good, when Thomas, unwisely venturing out of the Chelsea to give a reading, died in Maryland of tuberculosis at the age of 38.

The novelist Susan Swan is also interested in Thomas Wolfe. He's one of her literary heroes as well. She's written several novels, but the book she's most famous for is *The Wives of Bath*—a tale of secret corridors and hidden desires, not unlike those you'll find at the Chelsea—and that's the one my girlfriend and I knew her from. One day we heard that she was staying in the hotel—she had lived here back in the eighties—and we wanted to meet her. We didn't think it would do just to go knock on her door or wait for her in the lobby, since that might freak her out too much. We didn't know what she looked like or what room she was in anyway. But we heard she was giving a reading at a bookstore in Soho, so we figured we'd go down there and introduce ourselves.

Susan Swan is tall with long blond hair and cuts an imposing figure. She was dressed all in black, which I guess was fine in Toronto, where she lives now, but was maybe not so good an idea for New York in the summertime. It was only June, but the weather was scorching hot, and everyone was drenched with sweat. Luckily, they had the air conditioner going, or else sitting through a reading would have been intolerable. Susan read well, with poise and confidence (even though she admitted later that she had been nervous) from her latest project, a historical novel about Casanova.

After the reading we went up to Susan and introduced ourselves, and found that she was staying on our floor. She said she had come to the hotel because she was interested in writing about Thomas Wolfe. When she told Stanley Bard that, he had immediately put her in what he called the Thomas Wolfe suite. When Susan heard that we had never seen the room, she invited us over for drinks.

Though we knew Wolfe had lived on the eighth floor, we had never known his exact room number, despite having lived on the floor for several years. I suppose we could have asked, but actually I kind of liked it that way, not knowing. When we first moved to the Chelsea I read several of his novels, as well as a biography. I read about the large suite of rooms through which the writer had wandered, and fancied that we were perhaps living in one of them. On the other hand, I read that his toilet sat on a sort of platform overlooking the rest of the bathroom—Wolfe called it the Throne—and the toilet in our shared bathroom did too. Sitting on the throne I fancied I had inherited from him, I reflected upon Thomas Wolfe and his prodigious output.

The doorway of room 829 opens into a long, curved hallway, so that you can't immediately see into the room itself. The end of the hallway lets out into a huge, high-ceilinged, cavernous room with three large windows, two facing north and one west. There's a large fireplace with a mantle atop it on the west wall. Not a suite at all. When Thomas Wolfe had been there the room had no doubt been connected to a couple of other rooms, but now it only had a bathroom and a kitchen attached. The big room was sparsely furnished—its outstanding feature was the polished wood floor—with a bed, a large table that served as a desk, and a small round table surrounded by a few chairs. Despite the natural, cavelike cool of the Chelsea, it was hot in the room. We sat around the small table, drank wine, ate cheese and crackers, and watched the sun set over the gallery district and the Hudson River to the west.

"I imagine he had his desk and his typewriter right over there," Susan said. "That's the best place, I believe." She indicated the place where the large table was situated, facing the window, looking west. She said she had pulled the table over there herself. "Can't you just see him sitting there now, pounding away on his machine? I can."

We looked at the spot, glowing with the last rays of the sun.

"How do you know him?" Susan asked.

"I read him when I was in college," my girlfriend (in this chapter we'll just call her "my girlfriend to avoid confusion) said.

"Oh, they taught him?"

"No, I read him on my own."

"Of course, as he is no longer taught in American universities," Susan said.

"He's not at all popular these days," I said.

"No, he's really gone out of fashion," Susan agreed. "Most young people have never even heard of him. When I mention his name in my classes, my students generally think I'm talking about *Tom* Wolfe, the gonzo journalist."

"Maybe it has something to do with that controversy," I suggested. "With Wolfe's editor, what's his name?"

"Maxwell Perkins," my girlfriend said.

Recently, scholars who had been looking through Wolfe's manuscripts argued that it was Perkins who had shaped the novels—cutting and summarizing where they got out of control—from what they saw as a formless mess of unrestrained literary outpourings. Though I could see what they were saying, I thought they were coming from too modern an understanding of the novel and thus missed the point. I felt that it was the process that mattered, both in the writing and the reading, rather than the end result. You have to really love reading for its own sake, in all its slow, quiet satisfaction, to enjoy Wolfe. The summaries intruded and I feel cheated when I run into one just when Wolfe is on a roll. What I admire in Wolfe is the ease with which he seems to harness his inner demons and pour them out onto the page. Perhaps Wolfe's formless ease was puzzling, I reflected, or even threatening, to modern sensibilities.

We were all of the opinion that Wolfe deserved the lion's share of the credit. Not long ago they had brought out an unedited version of *Look Homeward Angel*, Susan told us, and she said it held up pretty well.

We uncorked another bottle of wine. "I have personal reasons for being fond of Wolfe as well," Susan said. She said that Thomas Wolfe reminded her of her father. Both were large men, she said, and both were emotionally distant. Like Wolfe, her father, a country doctor, tended to put his career ahead of his family. Both men seemed more at ease in their work than in their personal relationships. "How about the two of you?" Susan asked. "What were your fathers like?"

"My father died when I was little, so I never really knew him," my girlfriend said.

"So then, perhaps you don't have that same sort of father fixation," Susan reflected. "Or, maybe you still do. Perhaps to an even greater degree."

"I think *I* do," I said. "My father is like that too. He's a big man. And he's certainly emotionally distant. We've never really talked."

"Mine was never there either," Susan said.

"Oh, mine was there," I said. "He was there every night to play ball with me. He was really good in that respect, and I guess that's how we related, through sports. But as far as writing went, he was no help in that regard. He doesn't read much, and so doesn't respect the craft of writing. At best he's indifferent. At worst, he belittles my literary endeavors."

We sat for a while in silence. I went to take a piss and saw what must have been the *real* Throne Room. It was a much larger bathroom than ours, and the toilet did seem to command the room from atop its dais.

"I wonder if you'd do me a favor," Susan said when I got back. "For the project I'm working on I need to hear a man read Wolfe. As a southerner, you're perfect."

Squinting to make out the small print in the dim light of the room, I read passages from *Look Homeward Angel* and *You Can't Go Home Again.*

As I laid down the book, Susan thanked me for the reading. We sat some more, sipping our wine in silence.

"I'm really feeling Wolfe's presence in this room," Susan said after a time. "I felt it last night too, my first night in the hotel. I had a dream about Thomas Wolfe. Wolfe was in this room, although it was also my father. He appeared to a young girl on her wedding night; she was dressed in her wedding gown. The girl was contemplating suicide, ready to throw herself down the stairwell. She thought Wolfe was there to force her to commit suicide, but he was really there to help her, if only she could have understood."

My girlfriend asked the obvious question: "So did she jump?"

"That I don't know," Susan said, and paused. "Actually, I think not.

"But the point is that Wolfe's energy is very strong here. I really feel that there are still traces of his presence. With someone with such a strong personality, such a presence, there usually are. Traces of that energy, that vital force, can remain after death in the things he touched, the floor he walked, the rooms he inhabited." She glanced around the room expectantly.

"If we're all concentrating together and if our energy is strong, we may get through to what is left of him," Susan continued. "That is, if there are any traces, and I believe there are. This is a potent place, psychically. It has a real aura emanating from it. I dreamed of Wolfe last night because I needed to see him. This place seems to focus that sort of energy."

We nodded, if not our assent, then at least to say we followed what she was saying. I drained my wineglass. "A lot of people who live here feel the same way," I said.

"Hey," Susan said. "Since we're all together, thinking about and remembering Thomas Wolfe, and we're all fond of him, what would you say to trying a little experiment? I think it would help me to get into the proper frame of mind for writing."

I was skeptical, but hey, what could it hurt?

"It may help *you* too," Susan told me, "as a writer."

We cleared the table of our drinks and food. Susan set a candle on the table in a simple holder, together with a small bowl. We turned out all the lights. Our only light was the single flame in the middle of the low table in front of us.

We joined hands. "You should concentrate on Wolfe as you yourself see him," Susan said. "Your own personal conception of him, the way you yourself think he looks, his bearing, his attitude, his demeanor." We each conjured up our own vision of the writer as we gazed into the light.

After two or three minutes, Susan took out a notepad and tore a sheet of paper into three sections. She said we should write our wishes on them. "It should probably be a literary wish," she said, "or at least something related to Thomas Wolfe." Susan and my girlfriend promptly wrote theirs on the slips and folded them up.

It took me longer. I must admit I found the whole thing a little bit silly. I did finally write a wish, though—and after all, I could have just left the slip blank—so maybe on some level I wanted to believe.

We held our wishes to the candle's flame, and placed them all together in the bowl to burn. The paper in the bowl flared up brightly, illumining our faces and casting shadows about the room, then died down and glowed for a moment, then went out, leaving only ashes. The burning slips had filled the air with smoke. But the table didn't knock, there were no disembodied voices, no myste-rious breezes. The air was hot and still, and the candle didn't flicker at all. After a while we turned on the lights and blew out the candle. I was drunk and tired, sure to feel bad in the morning. My girlfriend and I said good-bye to Susan and went back down the hall to our own room.

Part II: The Blackout

I forgot about Thomas Wolfe for a while and moved on to other writers, even as my own writing took off and I went through a period of fevered creativity. I was struggling with my own demons, which came mainly in a bottle. As the summer wore on, it got even hotter. In late August the heat was sweltering. Susan Swan had planned to come back to the hotel later in the summer for a visit, but she decided against it; she was used to living in Toronto and she just couldn't bear suffering in that room with no air conditioner.

I was sitting in my own room sweating and writing on my computer when the power went out. At first I thought it was just a blown fuse as usual, the result of somebody trying to run a hair dryer or a toaster—or, God forbid, an air conditioner—on the ancient electrical wiring of the hotel. Sluggishly, I got to my feet and went out into the hall, ready to yell at whoever had committed the offense. (They knew better!) But when I got out there, I saw that all the lights were off, not just the ones on our circuit. Soon it became clear that we were in the midst of a citywide blackout.

When my girlfriend came home from work, we walked down into the Village to see what was going on and to see if we could get anything to eat. Sixth Avenue was chaotic, with people running this way and that on various errands. But the struggle to find flashlight batteries was mitigated by all the free ice cream you could eat, as stores cleared out their freezers. The only places still serving food were the pizza parlors, because they had wood-burning ovens. We had a couple of slices and walked around until it got dark.

Walking through the winding streets of the Village in the pitch-black night was surreal, as if we had been transported back to an actual medieval village. Shadowy figures lurked in candlelit bars drinking warm beer on MacDougal Street. We almost walked into several people: you stumbled about almost blindly and couldn't tell they were there until you were right up on them. There was something fascinating and yet terrifying about the experience. We felt that some of these people were surely up to no good, lying in wait to mug someone, waiting for the streets to clear so they could start looting the boutiques. Even out on Eighth Avenue it was nearly pitch-black; there were no traffic lights and vehicles ran about anarchically. It was a wonder no one was run down. It really brought home to you the power of light—how much we all depend upon it, especially in New York.

Back at the Chelsea, things were equally surreal. The permanent residents were, for the most part, taking it all in stride, the dark night of their own souls presenting a much more daunting challenge. But there were tourists staying with us, and, as no planes were flying and busses were sporadic, businessmen desperate for a place to stay. They were all assembled—in a state of confusion and trepidation—in the lobby, which was dimly lit by a few candles placed here and there. The overwhelmed staff had pressed several of the younger residents into service, giving them candles to guide the weary and exasperated guests to their rooms.

It was too hot even to try to drink the warm beer I'd brought home from the deli. It would only make me sick the next day, anyway. Trying to read by candlelight made us sleepy, and so we went to bed early. I awoke in the early morning hours and lay there in bed wide awake, restless, unable to get back to sleep. I got up to take a piss, groping my way across the room in the dark and stumbling out into the corridor. In the impenetrable blackness of the bathroom, pissing blindly in the general direction of the toilet, I knew I'd found the right place only when I heard the sound of water.

Stepping back into the corridor, I felt a vague uneasiness mixed with a certain curiosity. There was very little light in our corridor, so I stepped out into the main hall. There had been a candle or two burning earlier, but these had gone out. The hall was lit only by the moonlight from the one window. The old moldings of the ceiling cast eerie shadows. It was absolutely silent, absolutely still.

But then I noticed something strange: there was another source of light, faint at first, coming from a corridor off the main hall. I walked onward to investigate. When I turned into the corridor I found that someone had left their door ajar, and a white light—which now seemed piercing, obviously electric—was coming through the crack in the door. Somebody had their power back on, that was what I thought. How the hell had they managed that? There was a whole block over on Ninth Avenue that never lost its power: perhaps it was a similar phenomenon.

I wanted to ask the occupant. Stealthily, I approached the door. I knocked loudly, and called out, "Hello in there, anybody home?" But I got no answer. As I pushed open the door, the light seemed to grow increasingly brighter. There was a long, curved hallway leading into the room. I knocked on the wall and tried to make as much noise as possible as I rounded the curve. "Hello," I called out again. I got all the way into the room, which was huge, without furniture, bare except for the wooden floor.

Around the corner to my right, a large, hulking man sat on a stool. His broad back curved over a drafting table where an array of papers was spread out before him. He seemed to be working on some sort of outline. The one light came from a curved floor or desk lamp—I wasn't sure which—a hooded lamp that shone on the papers. The man was wearing a starched white shirt, and the papers were white, which added to the brilliance of the scene.

He was poring over the papers intently, pencil in hand, and he didn't glance up. His dark hair hung down in tangles over his broad forehead: I could see only a glimpse of his face.

Why hadn't he heard me? I wondered. The desire to ask about the light left me. I didn't dare speak to him. What struck me was his concentration, his intensity, how he didn't look up from the page. I stood there for several moments. Then I backed out of the room, back down the curved hall, then out into the corridor—closing the door so as to leave only a crack as before—and into the main hallway.

And I ran right into someone. Shit. My heart jumped up into my throat. It was a tiny gray-haired woman, hunched over, dressed in dark clothes. "You *could* look where you're going," she mumbled.

"Oh, Edith!" I exclaimed. "What are you doing here?" Edith was a fixture of the hotel, having lived here for thirty years or more. She habitually prowled the halls, collecting anything of value that she could find.

"I could very well ask you the same thing," she replied, rather crossly.

Though relieved, I was still nervous. My heart was still pounding in my chest.

"Maybe you can help me," Edith said. "I've always gotten along well with my neighbor, even though he's much younger than I." (She named someone I knew vaguely from around the hotel.) "But now suddenly he won't talk to me anymore. He has a drug problem and he goes away every so often for treatment. He goes—I don't know—to the mental hospital, I suppose. He's come back recently from just such a stay."

What a thing to start talking about, I thought. But it was typical of Edith to rope you into this sort of conversation, and it was typical Chelsea fare.

"He's supposed to stay five weeks and he only stays four, so he doesn't ever get it fully out of his system," she said.

I noticed that we were standing directly beneath a large abstract painting—engulfed in shadow—about which we'd had a disagreement a couple of years ago: I liked it; Edith thought it was crap. Edith was a painter, or had been, and so no doubt knew more about it than me.

"When I look at him now," Edith said, "his eyes are filled with such hatred. I truly believe he's possessed by some sort of demon."

"Yes, sometimes it can be like the drug possesses you," I said, distractedly.

"I'm not talking about it as a metaphor," she said.

Good God, I can't get into this now, I thought—in the middle of the night, in a pitch-black hallway, after I'd just had an unsettling experience. I cut her short. "I have to go to bed, Edith."

"Oh, excuse me," Edith said, sarcastically. "I'm sorry to have detained you."

"Good night," I said, and turned to go.

But then I thought of something and turned back. "Edith, what is that light down the corridor there."

Edith peeked around the corner. "There's no light down there," she said.

I looked and she was right. The light was out—though I hadn't noticed it go off—and the corridor was dark. The door appeared to be closed. Back in the hallway, I noticed that the candles had been relit.

The old hotel, with its crumbling gothic architecture, is a famous abode of ghosts. Everyone who has lived here for any length of time has a ghost story, and no book about the Chelsea would be complete without one.

I'm reasonably sure I wasn't dreaming. It was much more real than a dream, and, though she's not the most reliable witness in the world, Edith says she remembers seeing me that night. My exchange with her in the hall, though surreal, seems vivid enough.

But there are certain things that don't add up. For instance, why would Wolfe be sitting at a drafting table? And surely he wrote on a typewriter. And, though I guess it's less of a quibble, the desk seemed to be situated in an odd place, rather than the more logical location that Susan Swan had chosen.

Perhaps, after all, it was all in my mind. But does that make it less real? There are different levels of reality, certainly, and the truth is that we never touch the world directly save through the intercession of the mind. The drafting table looked suspiciously like a table I had owned a few years earlier—one that had belonged to Charles James, the famous fashion designer—a table that I had thrown out and often regretted doing so.

Which brings me to my wish, the one I wrote down on the slip of paper that night with Susan and my girlfriend in Wolfe's old room. Though it wouldn't do to come right out and tell it, suffice it to say that there was something in Wolfe's attitude of intense concentration that gave me at least part of the answer I was looking for.

The Bad Coffee

My girlfriend Susan likes her coffee with cream, no sugar. So that's what I tell them in the deli every morning when I go to get the muffins and coffee. But you have to watch these guys, because if you turn your back on them for a moment they'll shovel about six spoonfuls of sugar into the cup, and then you'll really be screwed. It's a moral thing with them: you *ought* to have sugar in your coffee, whether you like it or not.

That's what happened one morning. I was hung over and I must have been distracted. I think I started playing with the little gray deli cat. So when I get back to the room my girlfriend takes one sip of the coffee and declares that she can't drink it.

"All right, goddamn it," I said, annoyed. "Give it here." I grabbed the cup and put the lid back on it. "I'll take it back."

"Don't worry," she said. "Go ahead and eat your breakfast. I'll get it myself." She got up and made to leave.

"Take this with you," I said, proffering the cup, "or else they'll try to make you pay again."

"No, I don't want the hassle. Their coffee sucks, anyway. I'll just get it somewhere else."

"Well, what do you want me to do with this?"

"Just throw it out."

I did just that. I took the full cup of coffee out to the trash bin, opened the lid, and dropped it down in the can. It landed straight up, without spilling, in the bottom of the empty bag that lined the can.

I went back in and sat down and had a bite or two of my muffin. About a minute later, I hear this god-awful racket from out in the hall: "SHIT! AH, FUCK!" Then somebody slammed down the lid of the trash bin. A second or two later somebody opened the bathroom door and a moment after that slammed it shut.

What was that all about? I wondered. I didn't put two and two together. Like I said, I was hung over, slightly slow that morning. Just an unrelated bit of Chelsea lunacy, I thought, nothing out of the ordinary. Susan got back with an acceptable cup of coffee, and we finished our breakfast.

Then I went to use the bathroom, and when I opened the door I was startled to see that someone had sprayed the place with a milky brown liquid. It was all over everything: the walls, the sink, the toilet, the mirror, even some on the ceiling. A real mess, still wet and dripping. Obviously somebody had got the bad coffee out of the trash, and, standing in the doorway of the bathroom, slung it boldly, creatively, in a wide, sweeping arc. The Jackson Pollock of bathroom slobs. It was hard to believe there was that much coffee in that little deli cup.

What on earth!? Who could have done it? I immediately suspected the trash man. Who else would have got that coffee out of there? Remembering the noises I had heard, I figured he had burned his hand and, pissed off, had chosen to display his anger in a manner suitable to the art-infested realm of the Chelsea.

So why didn't I feel guilty? Because I figured it was his own damn fault. He only needs to empty the trash two or three times a day, but instead he empties it twenty times or more. He goes around and grabs every little scrap of paper out of all the trash bins on every floor. A half an hour later he's back again, whether anybody has thrown anything in the trash or not. If he had just waited an appropriate interval until there was liable to be something more in the trash, it wouldn't have happened. The coffee would have cooled, there would have been stuff piled on top of it, and he never would have burned his hand.

Puzzling, also, was the choice of venue. Why the bathroom? I wondered. Why not the hallway—that was the obvious choice—or, if creativity was at a premium, the supply closet or the elevator? I decided that it must have been directed at me. He must've seen me come in with the coffee. This was more than mere paranoia. Everybody knew I was the crazy bathroom person for this floor (every floor had one), the guy who would lurk around the corner to see who was stealing the toilet paper, the guy who would make sure the lock was changed regularly so no junkies got in. Apparently, this was a revenge sloshing and a warning to me to avoid such offenses in the future.

It pissed me off a little, both the part about messing up the bathroom and the warning part. "I'm gonna ask that trash man about this," I said.

"Just drop it," Susan said. "It's no big deal. It's not worth it to get involved in somebody's crazy games. That's how this place sucks you in, and the next thing you know, you're nuts too."

"I'm not getting involved in anything. I'm just curious, that's all." I felt like I had to confront him.

I threw out the deli bag with the remains of our muffins and coffee, knowing the trash man would be around shortly to collect them. When I heard him slam down the lid, I ran out there.

Hugo, the trash man, was a middle-aged Russian or Eastern-European man, his face haggard, bloated from drinking, his coal-black, balding hair slicked back with grease.

"Hey Hugo," I said, "was that you who slung coffee all over the bathroom?

He gave me a dirty look. "I don't know what you're talking about." He was probably hung over too, just like me.

"Well, I don't care. It's not me who has to clean it up. But I'm telling Rita it was you!" I said, half-jokingly. Rita was the maid; she would scream at Hugo and bitch him out.

"You go on," he said, with real hatred. "You tell her that."

I tried a different tack. "Hey, I'm sorry I threw that coffee in the trash. I just wasn't thinking."

"I burned my hand! You must be crazy! Who would do that, throw a full cup of coffee in the trash!?"

"Why don't you just wait?"

"Wait for what?"

"For there to be enough trash to make a load. You don't have to take out every single piece of trash as soon as anybody throws it away. Wait a couple of hours and then load up your trash cart. The rest of the time you could just be sitting around, taking it easy."

Hugo sighed. "They'd just find something else for me to do."

Locked up in this magical fortress of bohemian madness, I had forgotten the simple lessons of manual labor. It was a rare instance of relative sanity around this place.

The Vortex of Psychosis

The lobby of the Chelsea Hotel is the vortex of the building's fabled madness. I rarely spend much time there, since, well, my tender psyche can't withstand the heavy spiritual and paranormal onslaught. But one night I was feeling particularly reckless, and so I had a seat in the middle of the crowded lobby to wait while Susan was getting ready upstairs.

None of the regular lobby-sitters—those bold psychonauts who daily venture into uncharted reaches of the collective unconscious of the hotel—were in attendance. Instead, it was just a bunch of tourists sitting around. But what tourists they were. A man sitting in a chair behind me announced loudly, "I'm writing a book called *Women Who Read and the Men Who Are Homicidal Maniacs and Kill Them!* "

What?! I couldn't resist it; I turned around in my chair to see who had made such an asinine remark. It was a sixty-year-old man, his eyelids and jowls sagging, bald on top, with long, stringy, gray hair on the sides. He glared at me, as if to say: What the hell you lookin' at?

I turned back around in my seat, feeling a bit uncomfortable. A small, tidy, red-haired man sitting next to me was talking to a large woman and he immediately said to her, "I have lived in *two* societies where the dogs and cats run wild."

Not one such society, mind you, but *two*. The italics were his. He was speaking rather pedantically.

"If they were cornered," he went on, "they would kill you."

"Even the cats!?" I exclaimed, chuckling.

"Excuse me?" he said.

"Oh, nothing," I replied.

My head exploding with visions of rabid cats shredding my skin, I decided to go stand outside, where the metaphysical air was sure to be a bit fresher. Before long, Susan came out, and we walked together down the street. We were going out to dinner but we had to stop in the deli first to get something, a pack of gum, I think.

An elderly man who had lived in the Chelsea for years was in front of us in line, fumbling with his change. One of the deli men from the back came charging up to him and shook an open bag of Oreos in his face. "Why did you open this bag and eat a cookie and then put it back!?!" he demanded.

"I only ate ONE!" the old man replied indignantly.

Of course, the cookies were not individually wrapped, so the deli man couldn't have resold them. It looked like they were going to argue for a while, so I jumped in front of the old man and paid, and we left the store.

Now, I know you're probably thinking that there must've been a shortage of Zoloft at the Duane Reade Pharmacy or a brownout at the shock treatment facility. I couldn't tell you whether there was a full moon that night because the sky was overcast. But full moon or not, I can assure you that it was business as usual at the Chelsea.

2004

Tricksters and Inadvertent Performers

The Stage

I: LOBBY MASCOTS

Stanley Bard, our justly esteemed proprietor, always sees to it that his guests are well entertained. In particular, he provides us with an unbroken series of inadvertent performance artists, appearing daily on that grand old stage known as the Chelsea Hotel lobby.

The first during my residence was Hiroya. In his red overalls and later in his paint-spattered suit, the fat, then suddenly thin Hiroya was a self-promoter par excellence, in fact almost to the point of mania or psychosis. Toward the end he became such a pain that the desk people began to call him Annoy-ya.

After Hiroya's untimely demise, we were treated for a time to the otherworldly stylings of the Angel, another Japanese man you have met, who dressed in drag with feathered wings on his back. He was usually attired all in white, but sometimes he would appear as a sinful red angel or even as a black angel of death. But no matter what color he wore, he was essentially a seedy angel. Though at times he would wear a splendid long gown, topping it off with a bejeweled tiara, at other times, in keeping with the faded grandeur of the hotel, he allowed his costumes to deteriorate, the lace to get torn and dirty, the feathers of his wings to molt, like an angel fallen to earth. When it was hot, the Angel would sometimes just wear his frilly panties with a pair of wings on his back—maybe he got the idea from Victoria's Secret—and I think that was what finally ran him afoul of management and got him kicked out.

Then there was the long run of Blondie, a disheveled woman with Tourette's syndrome who would stand out on the street in front of the hotel and make weird guttural noises and who would generally flee if you approached her—several times she ran out into the street to escape me—though sometimes she would hold her ground and hiss at you like a snake. She refused to go into her room—demons lurking in there, apparently—and would sleep in the lobby or in the hallways. Periodically, Blondie would disappear for a week or two, apparently to get treatment, and then come back looking more bedraggled than ever. Her sojourns abroad increased in frequency and duration, and then one day she returned no more.

We seemed to be heading downhill with that third one, I must admit—though some of the crueler bohemians among us got their jollies by chasing after poor Blondie and running her up the stairs—but lately things are looking up, especially now that we have the Umpire in residence.

II: THE UMPIRE

The Umpire is a middle-aged woman who hangs out in the Chelsea lobby and apparently can't control her gestures. (Maybe she has Tourette's too. Unfortunately, I'm not a psychiatrist.) When you walk through the lobby, she'll let you know what she thinks of you through a series of hand signals: thumbs-down, up-yours, the finger, the cuckoo sign, holding her nose: P-U. She's really more like a third-base coach giving the batter a series of signals, but somebody once called her the Umpire, and the name stuck. Though she usually expresses a rather negative opinion of people, sometimes the Umpire will actually give the safe sign, or the thumbs up, or even the okay sign.

One day three tourists came into the lobby, three young

women in pastels: two blonds, slightly heavy, and one brunette, thinner. They were staying at the hotel and had gone out for the day, but one of the women had lost her sunglasses, and now they had come back looking for them. They looked around briefly near the chairs where they had been sitting earlier in the day.

But it wasn't long before they noticed that the Umpire was sitting across the room wearing a pair of sunglasses that looked suspiciously like the ones that had been lost. (They may very well have belonged to the Umpire, I can't say for sure, but the tourist women thought otherwise.) The women huddled, exchanging nervous glances, whispering among themselves. They were intimidated by the Umpire and were afraid to ask her about the sunglasses, because whenever they would look in her direction, she would give them the finger or make some other obscene gesture. Finally, they decided to tell the manager.

The Umpire had stood up and walked toward the desk to wait for the elevator, so the manager didn't have to go far. He came out from behind the desk and asked her, "Are those your glasses?"

The Umpire nodded up and down in reply.

"You didn't find those glasses sitting here in the lobby?"

She shook her head back and forth.

The manager threw up his hands. "Well, if she says they're hers, there's not much I can do."

As often happens, the elevator was taking a long time to arrive. The three women, slightly dazed, stood there waiting for it with the Umpire.

Finally, one of the women, the brunette, the one whose glasses had been stolen, couldn't take it anymore. "Why are we going back up to the room to look for the sunglasses?!" she said. "We know where they are! She's wearing them!"

The other women tried to shush her and calm her down. I think by now they had begun to realize that the Umpire was rather off.

The brunette refused to be mollified. "What? I'm just supposed to do nothing while she steals my glasses and then gives me the finger? I'm just supposed to just lie down and take it? I don't think so!" And she launched into her own series of gestures, imitating the Umpire: "Same to you! Up yours too! How you like them apples?"

The Umpire shrugged her shoulders, unfazed. She gave them a final flurry of signs, threw in a leg shimmy for good measure, and then, as the elevator had by now arrived, stepped on and left the women standing there in the lobby.

III: A THREAT

It was inevitable that the Umpire should eventually run afoul of Magda. A ballet dancer in the forties and fifties, now elderly, Magda was a tough old broad who never took any shit from anyone and was in fact famous for engaging in shouting matches with Stanley Bard.

I was sitting there in the lobby when Magda came walking through, dressed jazz-age cool, her hair in a snow-white bun. Though she wasn't frail, she walked with a cane, perhaps for defensive purposes. As soon as she caught sight of Magda, the Umpire began running through her usual repertoire of signs, unambiguously disparaging this time.

Most people just ignore the Umpire or else, if they're feeling cruel, they make a series of their own gestures back at her. Magda, on the other hand, advanced right up to where she was standing and said, "Something bothering you, honey?"

Though showing, I thought, some distress, the Umpire continued alternately to hold her nose and give the old heave-ho.

"You got something to say to me?" Magda asked.

The reply was another series of hand signals.

I cringed, half expecting Magda to assault the Umpire with her cane. Instead, showing remarkable restraint, she marched up to the front desk, and said, "You better keep that woman away from me, or I'm gonna kill her."

"Ah, come on, Magda," the manager said, in his Brooklyn accent. "Give her a break. She's crazy."

The Umpire had followed, either unafraid or, more likely, compelled by her madness, and now stood nearby, making her signals behind Magda's back.

"I know damn-well that bitch is crazy," Magda said. "I'm gonna kill her crazy ass."

Disparate (Albeit Strangely Complementary) Reactions to the Hotel

I

Two junkies were walking by the Chelsea Hotel one February evening—a skinny man with a drawn, skeletal face and a fat woman with no teeth—both bundled up against the extreme cold, the man pushing a shopping cart loaded with scavenged junk. Suddenly the man let go of his cart and darted up to the side of the building, bringing his face close and squinting to see the print on one of the bronze plaques that hung there. "It used to say 'Sid Vicious' on here!" he proclaimed, spitting out the words with disgust.

II

Three teenage girls, two of them tiny and thin and one, a couple of years older, heavier, more punked out with blue hair and multiple ear piercings, were ambling by the hotel, ill prepared for the cold in only thin jackets. One of the younger girls glanced over and saw the sign. "Look! It's the Chelsea Hotel!" she cried out, excitedly. "Oh, the *Chelsea* Hotel!" the older one exclaimed sarcastically. "The *Chel-sea* Hotel!" She proceeded to drop to her knees—clad in ripped fishnet stockings—and then to prostrate herself fully, arms outstretched toward the building in an attitude of mock worship.

All Hopped Up and Ready to Go

A clean-cut middle-aged man in a polo shirt and neatly pressed khakis sat in the Chelsea lobby one evening. He looked like a Frenchman—though maybe that had something to do with the bottle of wine he was swigging from.

An old rocker in a T-shirt and tight, ripped jeans burst through the doors. Tall and thin with spiky gray hair, his face had the gaunt, drawn look of a heroin addict. He was wearing huge headphones and dancing and bopping around to the tune in his head.

To my amazement he bopped straight up to the Frenchman and tapped him on the shoulders: "Hey, you ready to go? What are you doing? Come on!"

The Frenchman rose wearily from his chair. He must have been the rocker's handler. He followed the rocker onto the elevator. I got on too.

The rocker never stopped dancing. As we went up, he was hopping and bopping all around so much that he was really shaking the old elevator. Between the second and third floors he snatched the headphones off his head and proffered them to the Frenchman, saying, "Hey man, listen to this!"

"I'm really tired," the Frenchman said. He did indeed have a French accent.

The rocker shrugged, put his headphones back on, and continued rocking and bopping.

"Do you know who died here?" the Frenchman asked the rocker, loudly, so as to be heard over the music. "I'll bet you don't even know that do you?" He turned to me: "Can you tell him who died here?"

"Everybody knows that Sid killed Nancy here," I said.

"You hear that?" the Frenchman said. "You didn't even know that, did you?" Somehow I got the sense that they had known Sid and Nancy, or at least run in the same circles.

The rocker didn't pay him the least attention. He kept on rocking, and when their floor came, he hopped off the elevator and bopped on down the hall.

Eastern (European) Philosopher

There was a new guy staying next door in the transient room. "I hear him out there," Susan said. "Open the door and see what he looks like." It was late at night, and she had just settled into bed. I didn't feel like talking to anybody, since I was tired and ready for bed too, so I waited until I didn't hear anything outside before I went to take a piss.

The guy was still out there, hanging out in the hallway. Short, thin, with gray, close-cropped hair, he eyed me up and down as I stepped out of my door. "Are you something?" he inquired.

"Uh, well, I'm a writer," I said.

"I'm a writer myself, of a sort. I do ontology. I'm from Tennessee."

He was an older man and halfway distinguished looking, so I thought he meant he was a professor there. "You must be in the philosophy department," I said.

He clearly didn't know what I was talking about, but decided he didn't mind being taken for an academic. "Uh, yeah. I just got back from Hungary. I decided I needed to familiarize myself with Western philosophy before I immersed myself in the Eastern variety. But you know what, once I started studying, I found out that they were the same thing."

It seemed like an oversimplification to me, but I didn't feel like getting into it at the moment.

"You live here, don't you?" the philosopher inquired.

"Yeah, nine years." Since he was curious, I opened the door and showed him my room. Susan hid her head under the covers.

"Not bad," he said.

"Thank you," I said, closing the door. I still had to use the restroom, and I headed in that direction.

"Can I live here?" the man asked hopefully.

In the old days, no problem, I thought; he would have fit right in. "Well, I don't know," I said. "You'll have to talk to Stanley Bard. It's pretty expensive these days."

"I saw a bag lady in the hall. She can't be paying much, if anything."

"Well, you're probably right about that. But she's been here thirty years."

"I'm going down to the Spanish bar next door for a drink," he said. He seemed to be inviting me to come along.

"The El Quijote," I said. "Say hello to Santi for me."

The philosopher left a Hungarian bill on the bathroom sink when he checked out. A tip for the maids? Or was it meant for me: proof that he had indeed visited Hungary—and studied ontology—in case I doubted his word! I left the bill tacked to his door in case he came back looking for it.

Glass Houses

There was a bum raving in front of the hotel: "These fuckin' rich people are living in glass houses! Can't be throwin' no fuckin' stones! You see what I'm saying!? One more terrorist attack and they'll be out of here! Out of this fuckin' city! Runnin' scared! Glass houses, I tell you! There's one over on the West Side Highway! And another on the Lower East Side! They even got one going up on the Bowery!!!"

Indeed, many new luxury residential buildings, glass from ground to roof, were being built around the city. It was funny how the man's metaphor suddenly became literal, as if he hadn't quite understood it in the first place or as if his brain was not firing on all its cylinders. On the other hand, what with all the poor people being priced out of their homes in the recent real-estate boom, it seemed also strangely apropos.

World of Dream: Hiroya, Part III

It all went by very quickly. Hiroya burnt out in a little less than two years from the time he attracted the attention of the art world. In the end, he didn't have what it took to be what they required of him. The new style he had adopted in response to their criticism proved unsustainable. He tried to go back to his old style, but this failure—and the drugs—had knocked something out of him. He despaired of having the talent or the staying power to succeed in New York. He started falling apart: I heard him behind the closed doors of his room, weeping and blubbering to himself in Japanese. It wasn't long until this happened again, and from there the episodes increased in frequency. This was at about the time when he stopped working altogether. He lost interest even in giving his art shows in the hallway and he stopped making the pretense of dragging out the two canvases he had been working on for a year.

Concurrent to his artistic collapse, Hiroya was abandoned by his Downtown friends, Dee Dee and the rest. Once they had remade him, they decided he wasn't all that original anymore. They decided that he wasn't going to be that easy to mold, so they cut him loose. They found that he wasn't like them, that he wasn't like any other self-promoter they'd run into, but was in fact completely serious. Or to put it another way, his phoniness ran through and through: he was phonier than they could ever hope to be. In any event, Hiroya couldn't quite understand this, because he thought they were his friends, and that increased his feelings of alienation and hastened his decline.

When he saw his shot at success slipping away, Hiroya tried to reassert his identity in the only way he knew how—through art. If his suits were going to be slopped with paint anyway, he decided to transform them, spattering them with symbols in his wild graffiti style. The art-world hipsters said that he had remade himself into a work of art, but that wasn't quite true, that was just another example of them putting words into his mouth, of stuffing him into a category in the same way they had stuffed him into a suit. The suit painting was just another token of Hiroya's defeat: he couldn't transform a suit into the antithesis of a suit. Whether he painted it or not, in a suit he was smaller, not himself anymore. Instead of a great, blustering trickster, now he was merely a skinny, manic, slightly creepy, Downtown New York weirdo.

One day, pretty much out of the blue, Hiroya told me he was going away to Europe, Paris in particular, to study painting and to try his luck there. He had actually talked about this before, and other painters in the hotel had, over the years, urged him to make the trip, but I never got the sense that he was seriously considering such a move. He said that after 9/11 the city had become too much for him, the energy had become negative, and he needed a break. People were scared, he said, less likely to invest in art, but maybe the climate would be different in Europe. He said he was only subletting his room and that he would be back. He said that he knew the Chelsea would always be his home but he just needed a little time away from New York.

Now, of course, everybody always says this when they leave. It's hard to give up the Chelsea, and New York, and the dream. But somehow, with Hiroya it seemed different: I believed him; I believed he would return. He just had so much energy, so much drive—which is what I always envied about him—that the thought of him giving up never even really occurred to me. He

241

had convinced me, I suppose, of his brilliance, and I fully expected him to become a rich and famous artist. I had as much trouble as he did in admitting the obvious: that the city, and the drugs, and the art world had worn him down.

Hiroya didn't go to Paris. Instead, he checked into a drug rehab center out on Long Island. Although I didn't learn this until some time later, it quickly became apparent that he hadn't gone to Europe, since he stopped in at the hotel with some frequency. At first I was surprised to see him: "Oh, Hiroya, I thought you were in Paris!"

"No, no. London," he said.

"London?" I said. First I'd heard of London.

"Yes, but must keep in touch with New York," Hiroya said. "And Chelsea." He seemed kind of embarrassed, so after the first couple of times I didn't ask him anymore. (By then I'd heard the rumor of the rehab center anyway.)

Usually, when he returned for his visits, I'd run into Hiroya right outside the hotel under the awning, and I didn't think anything of it. But one time I was talking to him in the lobby, and one of the staff people, Gary, came up and told him to leave. Hiroya tried to ignore him, to go on talking to me.

"I know you understand English," Gary said. "You don't live here anymore. Get out."

"I talk to him," Hiroya said, indicating me.

"You're not here to see him."

"I wait for Cynthia," Hiroya said, naming an artist who lived in the Chelsea.

"Cynthia's not here," Gary said. "I already told you that. There's the door. Now get out."

Hiroya did as he was told, leaving quickly. I was too dumbfounded to speak, having never seen Hiroya treated quite so rudely. I knew he annoyed the staff but I figured if he was subletting his place then he at least had some business around the hotel. And technically, he would have still lived here, right?

But it turned out Hiroya hadn't sublet his apartment after all. I think perhaps he hadn't understood the concept: that you rent your apartment out yourself, collect the rent from your tenant, and then pay the landlord. (Conducting such a business arrangement, as I should have known, would have been beyond Hiroya's powers.) Apparently what had happened was that he had just given up his apartment with the understanding that he would be allowed to move back into it at a later time. And of course anyone familiar with his situation could have told him: fat chance. The staff would have said anything to get rid of him.

After a time, Hiroya stopped coming around the hotel. The next time we saw him, Susan and I, was some months later at an art fair in Tompkins Square Park in the East Village. He was skinnier than ever—his shirt too big for him, his pants sagging, hiked up by a belt—and he seemed shrunken, diminished. His new work, a large canvas tacked up to the fence around the park, appeared trivial alongside all the other canvases, and didn't stand out from the rest. Without the seedy grandeur of the Chelsea as a backdrop, Hiroya's art, like his person, lacked credibility and confidence.

None of Hiroya's art-world friends were around. He had come to the park by himself and he asked us to watch his stuff while he went to use the restroom in the Odessa Diner across the street. When he got back, we talked with him for a while as he worked on his canvas. He had pretty much the same act going, but his heart wasn't into it. He still told people who looked at his work that he was a great painter, though now without much conviction. Though he tried to be as cheerful and manic as before, he seemed deeply depressed. His work had stagnated too. It was the same stuff he had been doing several years ago, only lacking in energy.

But at least he had gotten away from the intricate style that his art-world friends had thrust upon him, and surely it was a good sign that he was at least working again. He confirmed the rumor about the drug-rehab program: he said that he was living in a halfway house on Long Island and had made the trip into the city by train for the day. "But better now," he said, trying to smile. "Moving back to Chelsea soon."

"I'm glad to hear that," I said, though by this point I really didn't believe it.

"We miss you at the Chelsea," Susan said. "It's not the same without you."

"Thank you," Hiroya said. "Very strange when not at Chelsea. Not the same."

"No," I agreed with him.

"I live in world of dream," Hiroya said, with an air of sadness and resignation.

Not long after that, Hiroya showed up at the hotel one Saturday afternoon. He seemed to be in high spirits, greeting everyone who walked through the door. We didn't talk to him for long, just to say hi. He said once again that he was moving back into the Chelsea. And though I still didn't quite believe him, I noticed that the staff at least seemed to be letting him stay in the lobby, so he must've had some business there. I figured he was probably waiting to talk to Stanley Bard—who had always been supportive of his art—to try to persuade our proprietor to go against the wishes of the rest of the staff and let him back into the hotel.

Hiroya talked to a lot of people that day. Almost everyone who lives at the hotel remembers seeing him. And nearly everyone who was friendly with him spoke to him at least briefly.

Susan and I heard the rumor the next day, a Sunday afternoon, as we were returning from brunch: failing to get a room at the Chelsea, Hiroya had checked into the Gershwin Hotel—the scene of his earlier group show—and committed suicide sometime late Saturday night or early Sunday morning. Subsequent reports confirmed that he had ODed on drugs, though whether or not it was accidental or deliberate is still open to debate. Most people who knew him, myself and Susan included, think it was deliberate. His body was discovered by a maid.

In light of what happened, our meeting with Hiroya on the previous day seemed eerily prescient. Had he come back to the Chelsea to begin a new chapter in his life or to say his good-byes? Was he so cheerful because he really thought he could just check back in, or was it because he had finally made his grim decision and knew his suffering was at an end? In any event, he was cheerful because, one way or the other, he believed he was coming home. I only wish he could have gotten back into the Chelsea, if only for the night. It must have been a very lonely death in that strange hotel. Hiroya was in his early thirties when he moved into the Chelsea and when he died he was thirty-seven.

Con Games

The Transformative Power of Dirt

It was a sunny Saturday morning in June 2005. I had begun getting out and interacting more with people that year, rather than just sitting in my room writing and drinking. Susan and I had started *Living with Legends,* our Chelsea Hotel blog, in April, and we made a lot of new friends and contacts through that enterprise. I was giving a reading of my fiction later that day at the Ear Inn, and I was walking around distracted, worrying about how I would do. Readings always stressed me out, which was why I had generally avoided them in the past.

I was walking by the building next door to the Chelsea, when all of a sudden something hit me in the face. Or rather, several small things, felt like a load of dirt. I looked up. There was a stained glass window propped open on the second floor. I didn't see anybody, but I yelled anyway, crossly: "Hey buddy, don't throw stuff out the window!"

A little Latino man—looked like the janitor—popped his head and shoulders up, dustpan in hand, and said, stupidly, "I didn't throw anything out the window!"

Yeah, right, I thought. "Well, good! Don't!" I said.

It had pissed me off, and I still needed to vent some of that anger. So when I got to the door of the Chelsea, I told the few people standing there, "Some guy just threw something out the window and hit me! Can you believe that?"

One of the people standing there was Jordan Atkinson, an old writer. Jordan had had a novel published in the seventies, but nothing had come of it. Now he was bitter, always walking around with a chip on his shoulder. He kept his head shaved, but sometimes he got lazy, and today you could see the gray hair growing in on his scalp and face. He was a drunk, fat and unhealthy, his cheeks sagging, pale. He was hung over that day, in a bad mood, you could tell—just looking for a fight.

"Where?!" he demanded.

"Next door. The synagogue." Jordan was the wrong person to tell, and I immediately regretted it.

"No! Those bastards! I can't believe it!"

"Uh, it looked like the janitor," I said quickly, not wanting to start him on any sort of anti-Semitic tirade.

"Son of a bitch! Well, he can't get away with this!"

Jordan slung open the door and strode through the lobby. I followed behind him.

The manager, Harvey, had been standing there a moment earlier, but when he saw Jordan heading his way, he turned and ducked into the back room. The bellman, Dennis, a brawny Irishman, was left manning the desk.

"Dennis, we need you to kick someone's ass," Jordan said as he approached the desk. He explained what had happened, indicating me as the wronged party.

I stood there like an idiot, not saying anything; I would have just as soon dropped the matter.

"It could've been anyone," Jordan said. "Someone could've been killed! They can't have some asshole like that working there. You gotta go over there and straighten this out."

Dennis stared at him, expressionless.

"Aren't you gonna do anything?!" Jordan demanded.

I guess Dennis was used to tirades such as this from Jordan. He completely ignored him and looked at me instead. "What do you want me to do for you?" he asked.

"Ah, don't worry about it," I said, nervously. "It's no big deal."

Shaking his head in disgust, Jordan stalked off toward the elevator, which had just arrived. I followed, since I was going that way too.

"I can't believe you don't want to do anything about it," Jordan said as we rode up. "You're just gonna let the guy get away with that shit?"

I felt vaguely ashamed of myself. "I didn't want to cost the guy his job or anything," I said.

Jordan rolled his eyes. "Didn't you at least say something?"

"Uh, yeah," I said, thinking quickly. "I said, 'Don't throw shit out the window, you fucking asshole!'"

Jordan didn't say anything, but he snickered, and actually cracked a smile, a rarity for him. I was glad to see he approved.

It had taken a load off my shoulders too. For those brief few minutes I had been able to get outside of myself. I didn't worry anymore, enjoyed the day, went to the bar where it was nice and cool inside—bars are always nicest in the afternoon—and the reading went off without a hitch.

How to Paint Yourself into the Chelsea

One day, Bradley, a young painter with long, wavy blond hair tucked under a beat-up red trucker hat, installed himself before an easel in the hotel lobby. On a round canvas, he began to sketch out the outlines of the lobby: the seating area with its couches and chairs to the left, the magazine stands to the right, beyond these the check-in desk with the mailboxes behind it and the slant of the staircase above. Then he began to paint, filling in the bright yellow of the walls, the gleaming white marble of the floor, and then, in intricate detail, to reproduce, in miniature, the various paintings—the Philip Taaffe, the Larry Rivers, the Joe Andoe—that hung from the walls. He came back day after day, working for several hours each day. His work was painstaking, with an eye to detail.

People are constantly trying various scams to get into the Chelsea: representing themselves as great artists, or saying that they are going to write a book or do a photo essay about the Chelsea, or maybe that they are going to do some renovation work around the hotel for free. Most will attempt to flatter or bribe the owner Stanley Bard in some way—he's the only one who can let you in—though others, lacking creativity, simply barricade themselves in the rooms they've rented temporarily and refuse to come out.

So Bradley's aim was immediately apparent to all: he intended to paint his way into the Chelsea. And I must admit, it did seem like a pretty good way to ingratiate oneself with Stanley, as he does indeed pride himself on being a patron of the arts. Better than writing him a poem, that's for sure. To paraphrase the Beat poet Gregory Corso, another old Chelsea resident: the painter can trade a canvas for the rent, but the poet always has to pay.

After a week, I thought it looked like the painting was nearing completion, but then Bradley decided to people the canvas with the various bohemian denizens of the Chelsea. He painted in the familiar lobby sitters, each in their favorite chairs: Darrell the poet; Michael the painter, his trusty cell phone in hand; Vincent, with his pug, Rudolf, in his lap; and good old Stormé, the drag king and Stonewall veteran, smiling broadly, in uncommonly high spirits. Behind the desk he stationed Stanley, generous and welcoming, alongside his right-hand man, Jerry the manager, ready to give you the best room in the house at a moment's notice and a reasonable price.

At this point I was able to form a definite opinion of the undertaking. The round canvas was undeniably a mistake: too cutesy and affected. The Artistic Kiss of Death. Hard to recover from that. Still, given that handicap, I thought Bradley had made a gallant attempt. He had done a good job from the standpoint of realism: there was nothing obviously distorted in or omitted from the picture. His most glaring mistake was one of emphasis: the colors were too bright and sunny and failed to capture the gloom of the old hotel I know and love. The people too, were a bit too cheerful for New York. Everything, from the shape to the colors, to the characters, contributed to form an overly rosy—or perhaps sunny—vision of hotel life. There was nothing of the dark side of the Chelsea, nothing of failure or frustrated ambition, nothing of bitterness or simmering rage, nothing of madness. (He should have painted the Umpire—that famously eccentric lobby-sitter—standing right there in the middle of it all, defiantly giving the world the finger.) What Bradley had painted was essentially a cartoon Chelsea.

Well, I thought, it's not finished yet. Maybe he'll mute the colors. Or maybe he's counting on the canvas accumulating grime over the years until it more fully captures the moldering essence of the Chelsea.

A week went by. The painting seemed finished, but Bradley was reluctant to leave his post in the lobby. Perhaps Stanley had yet to offer him an affordable room. And then, apparently to extend his stay, Bradley began to paint another little circle in the bottom right hand corner of the canvas. As he filled in the circle, it became apparent that he was painting another miniature version of the lobby. Soon he had the mini-painting standing on its own mini-easel, and then he began to paint himself, the back of his head—the long hair, the trucker hat, a quarter of his face—sitting before the mini-painting on the mini-easel. Bradley was literally *painting himself into the Chelsea*. Within the mini-painting he painted an even smaller painting on a smaller easel, and so on, ad infinitum.

This utterly destroyed the last vestige of the painting's integrity. But with that vestige went something else—call it the painting's pretentiousness. I saw now that Bradley had captured the true essence of the Chelsea: a sublime artistic statement had emerged epiphenomenally from the base dross of the paint and canvas, as a soul emerges from a body. The denizens of the lobby no longer appeared simply cheerful but rather more like they had overindulged in Zoloft—the medication concealing the true pain festering beneath the surface. And the patina that I had hoped would accumulate with age had also manifested more quickly than I would have thought possible, the yellow taking on the aspect of aged parchment, the gloom and discoloration growing and spreading outward, almost as if the process of oxidation itself had been expedited by the degenerative air of the Chelsea. Bradley had sat in the Chelsea lobby long enough for the building's energy to touch him, and his mind had become sufficiently warped to produce a work of real power.

So is Bradley a true artist or a con artist? And does he merit a place in the Chelsea? Well, I'm not the one who gets to choose. Stanley will no doubt be pleased by what is, on the surface at least, a glowing rendition of the Chelsea. And although he won't be impressed by a street artist's chicanery, he knows better than anyone that most successful artists do tend to have a touch of the charlatan about them. I predict that cold, hard cash will be the deciding factor.

Juanita's Baby

There are a lot of dreamers and big talkers here at the Chelsea Hotel, and sometimes it's hard to distinguish them from the actual con men.

There was a grungy diner on Eighth Aveue around the corner from the Chelsea. It's long since gone, but when it was there I used to stop in now and then for lunch. One day, toward the end of the diner's run, I stopped in to get a sandwich. I hadn't been in the place for some time, and as soon as I walked through the door, I felt vaguely uneasy, as if something were amiss. As I sat down at the counter and ordered a BLT and an iced tea, I still couldn't put my finger on it.

Then I noticed that Juanita, a girl who lived at the Chelsea, was sitting a few seats down from me at the counter, drinking a cup of coffee. Juanita seemed to notice me at about the same time. Leaning back to look around the other customers, she waved to me and gushed, "It's my baby!"

What on earth could she be talking about? I wondered.

Noticing my puzzled look, Juanita pointed up and said, "The ceiling."

"Oh yeah," I said, glancing up at the ceiling, though still not quite comprehending what she was getting at.

But at least I had discovered the source of my unease. Since the last time I had been there, the diner had installed a new ceiling. It was a metal ceiling: shiny, silvery. It was textured, corrugated, decorated with raised squares of floral designs. A tin ceiling. It was dazzling, and I wondered why it had taken me this long to spot it.

"I've never had anyone use my design before!" Juanita went on. "Isn't it wonderful."

"You designed the ceiling?" I asked, in disbelief.

Juanita was a pretty girl in her mid-twenties with dark skin and coal-dark hair, and a round, cute nose. She had some Indian blood, she said sometimes, but, like a lot of things she said, you soon learned to take it with a grain of salt. She came from a working-class home in Florida, fleeing a bad situation—though sometimes the story changed and she came from the Midwest. Juanita worked as an artist's model. She had been hanging around the Chelsea for about a year, and though she didn't have a permanent room, she had been living with a couple of men at the Chelsea—artists, of course. In between men, she crashed with female friends, a number of whom shuttled back and forth between two or three small rooms in the hotel.

Now I found that Juanita, too, like about 90 percent of the people at the Chelsea, had artistic pretensions. It was a kind of street cred at the Chelsea: you had to be involved in creative work of some kind. Before, Juanita had always maintained that being an artist's model was a type of art in itself. But I guess that line was wearing rather thin.

We were basically shouting back and forth across the diner. Juanita got up and came over to where I was sitting with my iced tea, which had just arrived. She touched my shoulder, motioning for me to get up. "Let me show it to you," she said.

Juanita led me through the diner, instructing me to examine the ceiling from various perspectives. Essentially, it was the same throughout. "Of course I've studied design," she said, "but I'm really just starting out in the business. I always knew I could do it, though. I just needed the chance."

"It's great," I said, though I had mixed feelings.

"Everyone always said I had talent," Juanita went on.

"Of course."

"It's got that really old Chelsea feel. Just like the hotel. Don't you think?"

I wasn't sure. The Chelsea is a mix of the grand and the seedy— and somehow the mix is uncannily perfect. The diner was certainly seedy, but I didn't know what to think about the ceiling. Grand, however, was not the word for it.

"It's an old-fashioned corrugated tin ceiling, though most of them you see are not really tin."

"Most are painted," I said. "Usually white, or maybe yellow."

"They're tearing them out all over the city when they gut the buildings. It's a shame, really. They're so beautiful."

"Yeah," I said. I really did agree with her there.

"It adds a touch of class, don't you think?"

Not really, I thought. It made the place seem like a boxcar, or a trailer. Or not even that. It was hard to put my finger on, but I guess I'd have to say it had more of an outer space vibe. Weird and disorienting, otherworldly. "Uh, yeah," I said.

"It's much better, don't you think?"

"To tell you the truth, I don't remember it before."

"Before it was just that horrible polystyrene stuff, weathered and yellowed with age. It really was a fright."

"Oh, well, in that case, I'm sure this is much better," I said.

"They've needed to redo the place for quite some time, I'm sure you'll agree."

"I don't know," I said. "I kind of like things to be old and worn."

Juanita ignored this remark. "They just wanted to do the same thing over again, just replace the tiles with newer ones, but I convinced them that wasn't the way to go."

"Well, it *is* just a diner."

"But this is much more elegant, don't you think?"

I gave up. "Oh yeah," I said. "Definitely."

PART II: WHO THE HELL REALLY DESIGNED THE CEILING

I think we were annoying the customers. The manager and the waiters were looking at us like we were crazy. I began to notice that there was something else incongruous about the ceiling. Though the tin itself was bright enough, the tiny bulbs embedded in it didn't cast much light on the tables, which were sunk in shadow. This was especially true the farther you went back into the diner, away from the small storefront that contained the only window.

We went back up to the counter. My BLT had arrived, so I sat back down and began to eat. Juanita's coffee had been taken away and somebody else was in her seat, but she didn't seem to mind. She went up to the register and started talking to the manager: "For the floor you need either a dark wood, or that bright orangey stuff. I don't suppose you've thought about changing the booths, have you? It would be nice to reupholster them, say, in a dark green. It's too dark in here now though. Perhaps you need a color that will lighten things up. The pink has got to go, however."

The manager, an older man, Greek, didn't seem to be paying too much attention to her.

"I suppose the bathroom can wait," Juanita said, "Although— my God!"

Finally, she got bored, paid for her coffee, and left the diner.

The bread of my sandwich was dried out, the lettuce limp, the mayonnaise runny. The bacon tasted like it had been sitting out since yesterday. I looked at the ceiling once again, scanned the room: it wasn't to my taste, certainly, but it was in a sense a bizarre tour de force of gaudiness and bad taste, deserving of a certain respect. I began to appreciate it as a really, really cruel joke on the diner, producing not at all the light and airy feel that I suppose was promised, but rather one of the darkest oppression. It was so bad it was good, so god-awful that it bordered on the sublime. Guaranteed to reduce business to the barest trickle. I chuckled to myself as I chewed. Despite the typically bad food—that much, at least, hadn't changed with the décor—I decided I would have to stop in more often.

I had of course initially rejected Juanita's story as pure fabrication, but now the notion flashed through my mind that she may have actually done it, actually designed the ceiling. After all, it was a work of absurdist art worthy only of a Chelseaite. I glanced up at the manager. Maybe she had fooled him, I speculated, talked him into it, seduced him with her charm. That was her real talent: she was a charmer, with her smile and her big dark eyes.

But no, he was a businessman, right? He wasn't going to throw away his money on some foolish scheme just because a pretty girl talked him up. Or maybe he would have, who knows? But he certainly hadn't seemed to be paying much attention to her when she was trying to talk to him just a minute ago.

I'd known the manager, Alex, for a few years. He wasn't real talkative, and when he did talk he was rather rude and gruff. But that was just his way, and he didn't mean anything by it. When I went up to the register to pay my check, I asked him, "Did she really design this ceiling?"

Alex gave me a wry look, as if to say, don't be an idiot. He was right, I thought. Why had I even bothered to ask? I didn't think he was going to say anything more. But then his tone kind of changed. It was strange how his mood shifted, lightened. "Do you like it?" he asked hopefully.

"Well," I said, "it's a bit different. It'll take some getting used to."

This wasn't the answer he'd been hoping for. The diner had been losing money, and he knew he needed to do something to attract customers. "It's too dark," he sighed. "I know. Her friend was supposed to do it. It was his idea."

I wonder who that could be? I thought.

I must have looked puzzled, because he said, "You know, her friend. Ralph from the Chelsea. He was supposed to do it. You know Ralph?"

I drew a blank. "No," I said.

"From the fifth floor, Room 568."

I shook my head, no. I had no idea.

"He said he would do it," Alex went on. "He was the one who designed it. I tried and tried to get him to do the work, but he never would do it. So finally I had to get someone else."

"Well, at least you got somebody to do it."

"Yeah, but he didn't do it right. You see, it's too dark in here. You can't see anything."

"Maybe you could just change the bulbs," I suggested.

Alex sighed. "Can't change the bulbs. The guy put in the wrong fixtures. That's the highest wattage you can have in there, otherwise you start a fire. It will have to be redone, with all new fixtures."

I didn't know what to tell him. It sucked that he was going to have to waste even more money on such an ill-advised project.

"You don't know Ralph?" Alex asked.

"No."

"I haven't seen him in a while. I know you must know him. You live in the same building. A bald guy, short, stocky."

"I'm sure I do know him," I said, to reassure Alex.

"If you see him, tell him I want to talk to him."

"Sure thing," I said.

I left the diner, walked up Eighth Avenue, turned the corner on 23rd and walked east. Who the hell could that be, I wondered. Ralph? On the fifth floor?

Then it hit me. It was Felton Hearst, the poet—or rather, part-time poet, and full-time con man. Felton did a lot of things, but I knew he worked sometimes as a sales rep for a wholesale hardware supply firm. Though I hadn't known he and Juanita were friends, recently I'd seen the two of them talking, scheming apparently, but had rushed on by, not really wanting to get mixed up with either of them.

Yeah, it had to be him. Oh my God, I thought, I hope Alex didn't give him any money.

Though they did eventually fix the lighting in the diner, the new ceiling turned out not to be the ticket. They never redid the floor or the booths, and certainly not the bathroom. Done in by the rising rents that accompanied the gentrification of the area, their last-ditch attempt at upscaling having failed, the diner soon went out of business. (I guess improving the food never occurred to anyone.) The ceiling is gone now: they ripped it out with the rest of the diner furnishings.

The Unfairness of It All: Movado Part II

In my first year at the Chelsea I wrote a story called "Movado," about a guy who tried to sell me a fake Movado watch when I was helping a friend move some furniture into the hotel. It was published in *Pif* magazine, and then I promptly forgot about it. Ten years later, a guy from Washington, DC—my old friend José Padua—read the story and wanted to make it into a short film. Since he was from out of town, Susan and I volunteered to pick up a fake Movado to use as a prop in the movie.

Canal Street was the obvious place to begin. We went down there on a Saturday afternoon, when the hustle and bustle of the street life was at its worst, the throng of tourists pressing in upon the shopkeepers and hustlers selling scarves and costume jewelry and DVDs recorded straight from the big screen.

The first place we stopped was a tiny little shop crammed full of fake Gucci and Kate Spade purses. They didn't have any watches sitting out, but at the mention of the magic word *Movado* a young Chinese girl rushed us toward the back of the store. I didn't see any watches back there either, but then the girl swung open a hidden door in the shelves and ushered us into a secret back room.

"Don't go back there," Susan whispered nervously.

"What's the matter?" I asked.

"You could be knifed or robbed."

"Yeah, and they'll sell you into white slavery," I scoffed.

I wasn't going to miss out on a chance like this. I'd always heard there was a network of secret tunnels running beneath Canal Street, linking all these shady establishments, concealing hidden sweatshops and gambling dens and making for a quick escape when the heat was on.

Disappointingly, we didn't go down any tunnels, just into a small back room. An old Chinese man lifted a cloth from a display case, revealing the hidden cache of Movados, along with a bunch of other crappy rip-offs of watches such as Rolexes and I don't know what all else. In fact, he didn't have a real good selection of Movados, only about three or four, and I wouldn't have worn any of them, even if they had been real.

Still, the watch wasn't for me to wear. "How much?" I asked.

"Twenty-five dollars," the grim-faced man said.

"That seems like an awful lot," I said.

"For a Movado!? No one has ever complained before."

That seemed implausible. The guy eventually came down to sixteen dollars, but it still seemed a bit steep.

We looked in the next little shop, but they didn't have any Movados. Rolexes seemed to be what everybody wanted.

Out on the street, a large African man—he was at least six-five—came up to us. He had apparently been watching us and had seen that we were looking for watches. "Here, you need a watch?" he said. He showed us a fake Rolex he was wearing.

"A Movado," I said.

"Rolex is better than Movado," he said.

"No, we only want Movado," Susan said.

"I'm telling you, Rolex is much better!"

We started to walk away.

"Wait a minute! Wait a minute!" He grabbed me by the arm. "You want Movado, I got your Movado. Come with me. Step over here for a minute." He directed us over toward a side street.

I was a bit hesitant—the man was kind of intimidating—but there were plenty of people around even on the side street, so we went with him. Furtively glancing back and forth, he pulled a watch case out of the thigh pocket of his cargo pants and opened it to reveal a blue-faced Movado.

I'd never seen a blue one before. "How much?" I asked.

"Eighty-five dollars."

"They're selling them for sixteen dollars inside," I said.

"Those watches are fake!" the man declared indignantly. "You don't want a fake one, do you?"

"Hell, I don't care."

"All right! All right!" he exclaimed. "But I'm losing money on this deal!"

The blue Movado looked pretty cool, and it had a case, which was a nice touch, so I figured it was worth it. Plus, I was afraid the man would kill me if I didn't buy it at this point.

I took out a twenty and tried to hand it to him.

"I said *sixty* dollars!" the guy yelled in my face.

In that case, I decided to risk death. "Oh, okay," I said. "No thanks, then."

Hopping mad, the man snatched the watch back. "Mine is real!" he exclaimed. "It's not fair!"

We turned and walked quickly away from him.

"It's just not fair!" he yelled after us.

I don't know if he was referring to my own refusal to be ripped off or to the business practices of the Chinese who were undercutting him. But it turns out it wasn't so hard to find fake Movados after all. We eventually bought one from a guy who had a table set up right on the street. No secret rooms or anything. It wasn't a blue one, but it looked almost as good. We paid ten dollars, and though we probably could have got it for less, by that point we were sick of dealing with the Canal Street scene, which gets old pretty fast.

And come to think of it, I guess I could have saved myself even more trouble if I had just bought one ten years ago, since obviously, despite my resistance, I was destined from the beginning of time to own a fake Movado.

Dormitory of the Deranged*

Recently, someone came and took a picture of my artwork and posted it on the Web—the *World Wide* Web. In a transom in the hallway—where there was once a stained-glass window—I have mounted two pink plastic ducks, shampoo bottles that can also be used as coin banks once the shampoo runs out. I found them in the garbage, and this is my art. I'm a garbage artist, a practitioner of a little-known genre of fine art that generally goes unappreciated, even persecuted, in this philistine world of ours, even here in the Chelsea Hotel, where you'd think people would know better. Garbage art is related to found art, but it's a more specific subgenre: found-in-the-garbage art.

I can give you a few other notable examples. For instance, one time I found a duck mask in the trash. This was apparently thrown out by a rich yuppie family who lived in the hotel with their two small children. (Yes, there *are* parents foolhardy enough to try to raise their kids in this godforsaken alternate reality.) The mask was red and yellow and composed of some kind of heavy rubbery material rather than the cheap plastic that most Halloween masks are made out of, and that's what attracted me to it.

(It's just a coincidence, I think, that it was a duck, though of course this species may indeed hold a deeper psychosexual meaning to my unconscious mind. It's a mystery for coming generations of art scholars to unravel.)

It may not have even been a duck, come to think of it, but rather some other sort of bird, maybe a hawk, as it had a hooked beak—but it still looked more like a duck than anything, so I'm going with that. I climbed up on a chair and stuck it high up on a little knob that jutted out from the wall, slightly above and to the right of the family's door. It would be like a totem watching over our hallway, stern and foreboding, ever vigilant—and yet cartoonish and therefore strangely apropos, expressive of the playful, tricksterish spirit of Chelsea art as I conceive it.

It looked great up there, and I figured the yuppies would appreciate the fact that their cast-off toy had been put to good use in the service of art. (It was thrown out in a whole stack of perfectly good toys, by the way.) The mask remained up for a couple of weeks, and then someone climbed up and ripped it down roughly, perhaps leaping from their perch to do so, leaving behind a small scrap of yellow duck flesh that remains to this day.

PART II: THE DYSFUNCTIONAL SINK

Another time there was a design show in the Chelsea, with small companies selling furniture and wallpaper and bedspreads and what have you, setting up shop in various rooms throughout the hotel. One of the companies rented the room next to mine and set up a huge sink in the little corridor outside my door, right between my room and the bathroom. The sink, a hulking, solid affair, consisted of a slab of black granite set atop a granite pedestal that stood upon a rectangular base topped with gravel. The funny thing about this sink was that it had no basin. The water came out of a tall, curved spout and ran across the flat granite slab, then down the outside of the pedestal into a drain set into the base. That, anyway, was the concept. The sink wasn't connected to a water supply, so you just had to imagine. There

267

were a couple of salesmen hanging out who had been trained to help you to imagine.

I kind of liked the sink, since, despite its size, it was sleek and minimalist, and I struck up a conversation with one of the salesmen, a big blond guy named Olaf. "It costs fifteen thousand dollars," Olaf said. Olaf was very proud of the sink. He spoke with a German accent, though he said he was from Switzerland.

"Wow," I said, "that's a lot of money. But I guess it's worth it if you've got a fancy restaurant or something."

"Ja, it makes big impression."

"But one thing I was wondering is, won't the water slop out all over the floor when you try to wash your hands in it?"

Olaf rolled his eyes and said condescendingly, "You must not wash your hands in it. It's for the aesthetic experience: watching the water cascade over the sides. You should just use it to get a drink, or to let a small amount of water trickle over your finger-tips."

Though Olaf was nice enough, I decided that the sink was ridiculous.

Furthermore, it annoyed all the residents: a gigantic sink sitting right in the middle of everything. With the base it sat upon, the sink was nearly as wide as the little corridor, and you had to squeeze past it every time you wanted to go to the bathroom. Even so, it was merely a symbol for the real annoyance, which was the crowd of people streaming through the halls day and night to see this and other exhibits around the hotel. Olaf was giving away free beer from a cooler, and that made his room especially popular. Potential "customers"—in actuality mainly young hipsters who just wanted to tour the hotel—spilled into the hall, clustering around the sink, drinking and talking. John from Beyond, a guy from the other wing of our floor, a poet, somewhat of a crank, was driven to distraction and taped up a sign saying: Please Be Respectful Of The Rights Of The Permanent Residents. (John didn't even live near the sink, and I'm sure I got blamed for the sign, since the next day Olaf was especially friendly and gave me a free T-shirt.) Carla, a girl from down the hall, had to squeeze past the revelers in her bathrobe every time she wanted to take a shower, enduring off-color remarks. And at one point, when the noise became especially bad, my next-door neighbor, Nancy, a dancer who slept during the day, popped out of her room and screamed at them hysterically: "Get the fuck away from my door you fucking assholes!"

Anyway, to get back to the theme of garbage art: after a week the designer packed up and moved out. In a pile of fliers and other materials that Olaf had thrown out into the hallway beside the trash bin, I discovered a big mounted poster depicting the sink and detailing its many virtues. To commemorate the design show and also to remind us of the finer things in life to which we might aspire, I taped up the poster in our bathroom: a high-end, luxury sink to contrast with our retro-chic, fifties flophouse fixtures. Where the artistic element came in was in the juxtaposition, of course. A Chelsea Hotel bathroom seemed to be where the fancy yet dysfunctional sink naturally belonged, serving humans of its own kind, and I was quite pleased with myself. It stayed up a few days, and then someone took it down and threw it into the trash bin.

Well, people can't just wantonly desecrate my art, now can they? It was lucky that I found it before the trash man showed up. I got the poster out of the trash and taped it back up in the bathroom, and it stayed up maybe one more day. This time, someone tore it into tiny pieces and stuffed them into the bathroom trash can.

PART III: THE ELVIS ALTAR

Out in the hall beside the trash bin—eternal wellspring of my artistic urge—I found a big, white, wooden pedestal, maybe three feet high, like the kind of thing they would set a sculpture on in a museum. I think it even had a number on it, so you could check the price of the sculpture to see how badly you couldn't afford it.

I knew instinctively that I should hold onto this, though I caught a lot of grief from Susan, who accused me, predictably enough, of junking up our already cluttered apartment. Luckily, later that week I found a bunch of those big hurricane candles in the recycling bin, the ones with pictures of religious icons on them. Though I didn't at once grasp the totality of the piece, I knew they somehow belonged with the pedestal.

It was a good thing I remembered the Elvis poster. On one of the lower floors, someone had mounted a framed poster of Elvis from the Vegas period, doing one of his famous dance moves. Why this was there, in the midst of all the original paintings, I have no idea. We seem to have had a slackening of artistic standards at the hotel lately—my own work is testament to this truth—and apparently one of our deranged dorm denizens reveres Elvis to a fanatical degree. But I guess I can see that: he is the King, after all.

I have an idea who the culprit is. There's this guy with long black hair who goes around in jeans and a black leather jacket, an old rocker. I have never spoken with him, as he keeps odd hours, but one time an elderly lady told me he drove her crazy with a twenty-four-hour marathon of Elvis music on the twentieth anniversary of Elvis's death. "Jailhouse Rock," "I'm All Shook Up," "I Want to Be Your Teddy Bear," "Blue Suede Shoes": the nightmare begins to take form. Though the lady who told me about the infamous "Heartbreak Hotel" music marathon is notoriously prone to exaggeration, I figure anyway it's got to be the same guy.

I lugged the pedestal down the few flights of stairs and placed it in front of the Elvis poster, then ran back up and got three candles. These I arranged atop the pedestal in a fitting memorial to the man who sang "In the Ghetto." It was my most ambitious work to date, and I was quite pleased with myself. Though the effect would certainly have been heightened had I lit the candles, it seemed like it would have been dangerous to go off and leave them burning in the hallway.

But after all, perhaps I should have lit them, as that might have warned off the infidels, for my Elvis altar (though not the Elvis poster!) was ripped down and carted away before the night was through, and by the morning not a trace of it remained. (They didn't even bother to check the price in the catalog. It was going cheap, too, I can assure you of that.) I believe art should be for everyone, and I'm sure that accounts for some of the hostility toward my work. The snobs and elites of the art world—who would strangle the soul of true art—are just not ready for this kind of challenge to their illegitimate hegemony.

The bastards. Everybody always puts up their art on the walls of the Chelsea—most of it good, but some quite atrocious—so I figured, why shouldn't I put mine up too? I expected my medium, garbage art, to be respected here, if nowhere else. But genius is just not appreciated in this world, not even, apparently, in the Chelsea Hotel. Maybe they think I'm making fun of the vaunted creative spirit of the Chelsea—which I am, but so what? Pretension should be mocked. Let's not take our art or ourselves so seriously. My "art" is an ironic commentary on the art we find throughout the hotel —and perhaps also some sort of critique of our throwaway society, now that I think about it.

But let's not think *too* hard about it. In reality, I just drag things out of the trash for the hell of it, because I have nothing better to do. On the other hand, this may not be that far off from the reason why many people, including probably many great artists, create art.

But now, to get back to the pink ducks: finally, one of my creations has been allowed to stand. At first someone kept knocking them down, but I doggedly kept putting them back up. This went on for more than a week. Originally I had the ducks turned to face one another atop the transom, but finally I turned them in the same direction, and this apparently satisfied my critic's aesthetic standards, for the vandalism stopped, and they've been up for about a year now. It feels good to finally have the fruits of my labors recognized—though I'm sure my poor little ducks will be knocked down and stuffed deep into the bowels of the trash from whence they came as soon as anybody from the hotel reads this.

*Finally, a note on the title of this piece: "Dormitory of the Deranged" is a quote (or rather a misquote, since what she actually wrote was "dormitory of the dispossessed," and I remembered it incorrectly) from a piece that Sarah Vowell wrote about the hotel when she stayed here a few years ago. I just love the phrase and so I couldn't help using it. My title is like my art, and obviously my art, like all great art, has complex motives, one of them perhaps being to push people's buttons. Once again, I just can't help myself, you see. I knew that all these pieces would tick somebody off, and I guess I get a kick out of seeing people act out. It's sort of like dog baiting or like tying two cats' tails together. This is crazy, I know, but I just wanted you to know that I, too, can slip over the edge into madness with the best of the Chelsea's deranged denizens.

As an addendum—or should I say, "finally, once again"?—you may have noticed that my ramblings in this piece represent a departure from my usual minimalist style. (Or, if this is the only piece you've read, perhaps you haven't noticed.) What's happening is, I'm being *postmodern,* which, in case you don't know, is a synonym for self-indulgent. (Having an asterisk in the title of the piece that refers not to a footnote but to something in the text, against standard usage, is another thing that should tip you off.) I would probably be more successful if I wrote this way all the time instead of making fun of it, but that's another thing I can't control. When I revise this piece, I will no doubt just keep the parts that tell a story and toss out the other junk—or rather, the garbage (my art)—which means you'll never get to see the rest of this.

Expert Advice on Combating Terrorism

There's been scaffolding up around the Chelsea for several months now, seriously detracting from the building's unique gothic splendor. The workers put it up in the early summer, went away for the rest of the summer—it was probably too hot to work—then came back and worked for about two weeks in October. They haven't done anything since then (I'm writing this in mid-August 2006), although the scaffolding remains up. When the workers were here, they stood on a hanging scaffolding outside my window and yelled back and forth to one another for eight hours a day, when they weren't scraping or sanding with a machine.

There were two workers stationed outside my window (though there were others elsewhere on the building), a New Jersey guy and a Russian. They hadn't met each other before this job, and so on the first day they bonded. "My last rap was a misdemeanor, but they kept me in for six months," the Jersey guy said.

"My last was a felony," the Russian said, as if it were no big deal. "And they only gave me three."

It was comforting to know that if anything went missing, I would at least have someone to blame.

The two workers had to strip and paint the woodwork and paint the windowsills—chores that made perfect sense. But they also had to strip the tar off the gutter—gouging and chipping away at it with their putty knives and then buffing it with a circular sander to reveal the gleaming copper—and then refinish it, all of which made no sense at all, since it had just been refinished earlier that year. The point, apparently, was to change the color from black to gray, maybe to match the paint. The Jersey guy, who was the most talkative, shared my confusion: "Why the hell are we doing this? Why are we making it gray? It'll be black again in a month anyway!"

I couldn't do much work with these guys yelling back and forth all day, so I had to resort to transcribing their conversation to kill time. About 90 percent of what they said was bullshit—the Jersey guy had a lot to say about sports and drinking—but once in a while they got onto an interesting topic. At around this time terrorists had just bombed the subway in London, and the cops had started searching people in the subway here.

"They said on TV, if you see somebody who looks suspicious in the subway, let us know," the Russian said, chuckling.

"Fuck, everybody looks suspicious in the subway," the Jersey guy said.

"They're not going to stop it, nothing can stop it."

"Hell no!" the Jersey guy said. "If I'm a cop and I see some Arab guy with a backpack, I'm not gonna say, open that up. What am I, a fucking idiot? He'll blow us both up. Just keep going buddy, blow some other place up. I wanna get home to my wife and my kids."

"I'd search some old lady, instead," the Russian said.

"Yeah! So the Arab blows some people up, and your boss comes up and says, 'Hey, why didn't you stop that guy?' 'Oh sorry chief, I must've missed him.' What are they gonna do, fire your ass? Better than being dead. 'Sorry chief, I'll do better next time.'"

On this one subject I feel like these guys may have had the proper mind-set to provide us with some insight. They were at least half right about the gutter, by the way: it's not quite black yet, but it does look pretty goddamn scummy. The black sealant was better because it hid the dirt.

The Christmas Con: Ben Lucien Burman at the Chelsea

Susan and I were on our way to see the composer Gerald Busby's seventieth-birthday celebration at Carnegie Hall. (Gerald is the guy who wrote the music for Robert Altman's film *3 Women*.) On the way down in the Chelsea Hotel elevator, another couple got on at the seventh floor. They were a little bit older than us, in their fifties: the man had a flowing mane of steel-gray hair styled into a pompadour, while the woman had her long, straight hair dyed black with bright-red highlights. We knew their names, Peter and Carrie, and we knew that Peter was a furniture designer and Carrie an artist, but we had never really spoken to them much over the years. In the elevator we just exchanged pleasantries.

We walked through the lobby—past the Christmas tree where somebody had hung a photograph of Bob Dylan, another old Chelsea resident. Dylan appeared to be sitting in the lobby—though it was hard to tell since it wasn't a very good photo: there was a lot of glare coming from the reflection of the flashbulb in the window behind him.

Stepping out into the chaotic weekend party scene of 23rd Street, we noticed that Peter and Carrie seemed to be going the same way as us. I asked if they were going to the Gerald Busby thing.

"Yes, we are," Peter said.

"Riding the subway?"

"We were going to," Peter said, "But since we're all together, maybe we can share a cab. It won't be any more than the subway then."

"Subway's only a dollar today," I said. It was a special deal for the holidays.

"Oh, come on."

"Yeah, it'll be okay," Susan said.

"All right," I gave in. "I guess it's only a few dollars more."

But then, once we had hailed the cab, settled into it, and gotten under way, Peter, who had sat in the front, turned around and said, "You know, I forgot to bring any money." He said it cheerfully, without any trace of embarrassment. "Honey, did you bring any money?"

"You know I didn't," Carrie said gravely.

"Hmmm. Don't worry about it," I said.

Carrie seemed a little bit embarrassed. She said, "This must seem like a real con we're running."

"I always thought you two seemed relatively sane," I said. "But now I can see why you're living at the Chelsea." I was implying, jokingly of course, that they were insane like everyone else at the Chelsea, for, I don't know, sauntering out into the mean streets without any money—la dee da! —and without a care in the world.

But Carrie didn't quite get it: "Yeah, we conned our way into the Chelsea," she said crossly.

The cab ride cost ten dollars. "You know we're never gonna see that money again," I said as soon as we had gotten away from them.

"Maybe not, but just because they'll forget it," Susan maintained. "They didn't do it on purpose."

"I know that," I said. "Or maybe not. Sometimes con men are real slick like that, you know? They act like they're scatterbrained just to put you at ease so they can take you in."

"For five dollars!?" Susan exclaimed.

The moment the concert ended, I grabbed Susan and said,

"Let's get the hell out of here before somebody makes us pay for another cab."

When we got back to 23rd Street, we saw that Peter had beaten us back. He was standing in front of the hotel—which was mobbed with hipsters waiting to get into Serena's, the club in the basement. "Here's your five dollars," Peter said as we walked up.

"Oh, thanks," I said, taking the bill. "But you know what? I was really hoping you wouldn't give it back, since that would've made a way better story."

"I'll take it back if you like," Peter said, laughing.

"We'll keep it," Susan said. "It'll come in handy, since Stanley just raised our rent."

This had just happened the day before—talk about ruining the Christmas holiday!—and the increase had been a whopping 36 percent. We were still reeling from the whole thing, disoriented, wondering where we were going to come up with the money, not knowing what to think. In our ten years at the Chelsea, Stanley had never raised our rent before. But now he could get much more for the room, he said. The board of directors was breathing down his neck, he told us, they didn't care about writers and artists; they wanted him to rent to anybody off the street who could pay.

"Oh, he did, did he?! You can't let him get away with it!" Peter exclaimed. "Let me buy you a drink," he said. "I have something I want to tell you."

Peter wanted us to go into El Quijote with him, but I wasn't drinking anymore and so, sadly, had to decline. Instead, the three of us went into the hotel and sat down in the lobby.

"Let me guess," Peter said once we had settled into out chairs. "One day Stanley yelled at you as you were going through the lobby, then dragged you into his office and sprang this increase on you out of the blue."

He had that right: that was pretty much how it had happened.

"Everyone who's been here for any length of time has had the same thing happen to them," Peter said. He said that that was Stanley's pattern: that he would leave you alone for a while, let you get attached to the place, then one day he would spring on you without notice and raise your rent through the roof.

"Well, I guess he could have been raising it all along," I said. "He hasn't raised our rent in ten years. We would probably be paying a lot more by now if he'd been raising it every year." (Actually, as we found out later, due to rent-stabilization laws he couldn't have been raising it very much, if at all.)

"He's not being a nice guy. You should get that thought right out of your head. It's just that he hasn't thought of you in a while," Peter said. "But one day he sees you and that jogs his memory, and he says to the manager, 'Hey Harvey, who is that guy? What's he do? How much rent is he paying?' And then Harvey tells him and his mind starts to working; he starts thinking about how much more money he can get out of you."

Peter seemed like a figure from another era, a gentlemanly, well-mannered type. He was a cheerful, easygoing guy with big, red, happy cheeks. That must have been how he avoided being driven insane by this place: he just let it roll off his back. He had a kind of old-world charm, like an English lord. I found him convincing and at the same time reassuring:

> That's exactly what happened to us. When we moved in, we were paying a lot more than market value. It wasn't a very desirable neighborhood. But I didn't care since I liked the place and I was working on Wall Street then and had plenty of money. Over the years it turned into a pretty good deal.
>
> Then one day, without any warning whatsoever, I was walking through the lobby and Stanley called me into his office and gave us an enormous increase. I said I couldn't pay that much, but you can't negotiate with him. He's completely irrational. He wants his money

and that's all there is to it. If you don't like it you can just pack up and get out.

I couldn't accept that, so I called a lawyer, and he told me that what it comes down to is rent stabilization. Any apartment in a rent-controlled building that rented for less than $88 a week in 1969 was rent stabilized under the new law passed that year. Now of course Stanley's not going to tell you whether your apartment is rent stabilized or not. There's an agency you can contact, but their information is based on what the landlords report, so you can bet that's not going to be too reliable either.

Peter asked around the hotel, and from one of the older residents he found out that the previous tenant in his apartment had been an obscure writer named Ben Lucien Burman. Peter couldn't find out much about him, but one time he was in the Players Club for some function or other and saw a picture of Burman on the wall receiving an award. He asked the people who worked there, and though no one knew anything about Burman's time at the Chelsea, they told him that Burman's papers were stored at Tulane University in New Orleans.

In reviews of his work, Ben Lucien Burman is often compared to Mark Twain. This has nothing to do with the fact that they both lived at the Chelsea but is rather a reference to both men's homespun humor and their obsession with the Mississippi. Though Burman's work now seems neglected, he's not as obscure as all that: his books have sold sixteen million copies and been translated into eleven languages. He was able to make a pretty good living from his writing.

Like Susan and I, Burman was a native of the Bluegrass State. He was born in Covington, Kentucky, in 1895. He fought in World War I, came back to the states and graduated from Harvard in 1920, and then continued his education working on steamboats on the Mississippi River. Deciding to become a writer, Burman moved to New York and published his first story in 1924. He was paid $500 for the story, a sum that seems nearly unimaginable these days.

In addition to short stories and novels, Burman wrote *Reader's Digest* articles with such sensationalistic titles as: "Witchcraft—Mexican Style," "The Weirdness of Death Valley," and "King of the Pygmies." When World War II came around, Burman worked as a war correspondent in Europe, receiving the French Legion of Honor for an exposé he wrote about the Pétain regime in Vichy France.

Burman is best known for his series of novels chronicling the adventures of a community of anthropomorphic animals—with names such as Doc Raccoon and Judge Blacksnake—in the mythical town of Catfish Bend, Louisiana. (I like to think that this is how Burman retained his sanity: by retreating from the mad chaos of the Chelsea into a more genteel world of traditional values, simple pleasures, and talking animals.) Aimed at young adults, several of these novels became best-sellers. Burman continued writing these animal tales right up until the end of his life, concluding the series with his tour de force, *The Strange Invasion of Catfish Bend,* in which Judge Blacksnake is possessed by a space alien and goes about infecting the entire community with both his radioactive venom and his unorthodox brand of justice. (Actually, I'm joking: it's just about an invasion of fire ants.)

Several of Burman's novels were made into movies. Will Rogers starred in the film version of Burman's second novel, *Steamboat Round the Bend,* and John Ford directed, although, unfortunately, this was not one of the animal novels. *Heaven on Earth* (apparently a retitled version of Burman's first novel, *Mississippi*) is the only Burman novel still in print: it was reissued in 2005.

Burman spent his early years in New York living in rooming houses and SROs in Greenwich Village. When he sold his first story, he didn't even have enough money for a ride uptown to get the check. His future wife, Alice Cady Stanton, had to cash in some stamps to come up with the bus fare. They were married soon afterward, and traded in the romance of Village bohemia for what was at that time the comparative luxury of the Chelsea. Alice was an artist and soon enough she was illustrating her husband's books, and together the Burmans took the publishing industry by storm.

When Ben and Alice moved into the Chelsea in the thirties, the building was still pretty nice, but in the fifties the management ripped out all the ornate fixtures and transformed the hotel into what was basically a flophouse. The period of its greatest artistic flowering, with the Beats and the Warhol people, coincided with the hotel's physical decline, a decline that would continue through the sixties and the seventies. The Burmans stayed put through these dark days, growing old in the Chelsea, even as many of the more respectable tenants moved out.

The neighborhood went downhill too. To hear tales of 23rd Street in the seventies, it was pretty much a no-man's-land. There were few stores on the street, no restaurants, and certainly no trendy clubs. In the last years that Burman was there, the neighborhood had deteriorated to such a degree that he—himself a frail old man by this point—feared to let his guests go out on the street to hail a cab for themselves. The last straw was when Alice was mugged around the corner from the hotel on 22nd Street. After thirty-eight years in the Chelsea, the Burmans finally moved out in 1974. Alice died in 1977, and Ben followed her in 1984, passing away in his comfy chair at his beloved Players Club, at the age of eighty-eight.

Literature is not high on the list of priorities in Kentucky—not even literature of the talking animal variety—and so no college in Burman's home state wanted his archives. (On the bright side, they did give him a highway marker in Covington.) That's how Burman's papers ended up at Tulane, where his stories were prized for their realistic portrayal of Mississippi River life.

———————

Peter said that he and his wife figured it was worth the trip down to New Orleans to visit the Ben Lucien Burman collection. "They had forty-one feet of his papers," Peter said. "Drafts and manuscripts of everything he had ever written, all his articles and stories and novels. But more importantly, we found out that he was one of those people who never throw anything away. He had saved all his leases—all the way back to the thirties—all his rent receipts and cancelled checks, everything. A perfect record of his tenancy. That was how we established that the room was rent stabilized. We just made copies of all those papers. We took our case to court and won. Now he can't raise our rent more than 5 percent a year."

Peter gave us the name and phone number of his lawyer. "You can't let this go unchallenged," he said. "The lawyer is as much for your peace of mind as anything. Before I hired a lawyer, it had got so I dreaded walking through the lobby, since I knew at any time Stanley might call me into his office for a dressing down. Now I don't have to worry about it. I just say, talk to my lawyer. He absolutely hates that. The first time I told him that, Stanley said, 'I hate your lawyer.' And I laughed and said, 'Then why are you giving him such a good living?' It was a very satisfying moment, believe me."

At around that point I noticed that the Bob Dylan photograph was already gone from the Christmas tree: someone had stolen it while we were at the concert. Though this was no real surprise— after all, this is New York, and the Chelsea to boot—I was amazed at how quickly it had happened.

"This lawyer is not cheap," Peter said. "He asks for a big retainer, right up front. But then again, you'd just be paying that to Stanley anyway, so you have to figure out who you'd rather pay. And if you go with the lawyer, you'll save money in the long run."

I did think about that, whom I wanted the money to go to, and

I wasn't sure. For all his faults, Stanley was the one who had made possible the wondrous dynamic of this place that we all loved. (Even as this thought went through my mind, I realized how naïve it sounded.) "I think it *would* be a good idea at least to talk to a lawyer," I said. "That way we can find out what our rights are, if nothing else."

Susan seemed to be thinking along the same lines as me. She said, "I think Stanley's rent policy is like the rest of the hotel: kind of idiosyncratic and weird. He said he wanted some of his good tenants to volunteer for a rent increase, so the hotel could continue as before!"

We all laughed at that, because it was so absurd. Of course, there had been no question of refusing to "volunteer."

"Don't let his act fool you," Peter said. "Stanley is *not* a kindly old man. That's all an act. He's manipulative and calculating."

I chuckled at that. I thought Peter was exaggerating a bit, since I believed that on some level Stanley did actually care about the Chelsea's residents. But Stanley is a complex character; I could see Peter's point, and I didn't see any reason to contradict him. Both Susan and I were glad we had talked to Peter. His words had lifted some of the burden we had been carrying around, helped us to see that we weren't alone in our predicament, and, most important, helped us to laugh about it. Peter stood up and put on his hat, suddenly eager to make his escape. I supposed that his drink at El Quijote was by now long overdue. I wouldn't be having one myself, but the need for it had passed, and I wished Peter a good one.

Seemingly out of character with his genteel persona, Ben Lucien Burman once said that if he had to kill a man, he'd do it artistically. "You have to keep your sense of humor," he said. That was the Chelsea talking there, for sure.

Two Tales of Urban Moxie

I: OLD LADY ON A WALKER

A decrepit, bent-over old lady in a green dress and a pillbox hat was trying to make it across Seventh Avenue at 23rd Street. Of course, she moved very slowly, and the light changed before she could get all the way across, and so she was stuck about halfway out in the street as cars whizzed around her. Still, eyes set straight ahead, she struggled determinedly on, step by step toward the curb.

A bread truck roared around the corner and headed straight for her. It looked like he was going to plow her down, but instead he slammed on his brakes, stopping mere feet from her and laying on his horn.

The old lady started, then stopped dead in her tracks, straightened herself up, and turned to face the trucker. "Fuck you!" she said, and gave him the finger.

II: OLD MAN AND A MOTORCYCLE

A bit farther down Seventh Avenue, at the corner of 21st Street, a biker came roaring down the avenue on his chopper—you could hear him coming for blocks—and sat idling at the light. He was hugely fat, hairy, tattooed, with a tiny helmet atop his head. The thunderous rumbling of his engine shattered the relative calm of the morning.

An older man, somewhat disheveled in T-shirt and jeans, was walking along, and when he heard the chopper, he stuck his fingers in his ears. A look of intense irritation on his face, he strode right over to the curb and yelled, "Hey asshole, you think you got it loud enough?"

The biker turned and looked at the older man. He couldn't hear over the din of his bike. "Excuse me?" he yelled back.

"You think you've got it loud enough, asshole?" the old man repeated.

The biker shook his head in disbelief and, as the light changed, put the chopper in gear and roared off.

The Last of the Superstars:
Edie Sedgwick and Rene Ricard
at the Chelsea

On the night of the big fire, Susan and I snuck up to our room to make sure things were okay. Of course they were. So we decided to go back down and hang out in the lobby. As we made our way down the stairs, the smell of smoke was strong. Water was streaming down the stairwell in the middle of the hotel, flowing all the way down into the lobby. There was a crowd of firemen coming up the stairs, dragging their hoses and all their equipment with them. Though we were clearly in their way and they all gave us dirty looks, they didn't say anything to us as we slipped by them and scampered down the stairs. But no sooner had we got past them than who should we see coming down the stairs behind us but the old Warhol superstar Rene Ricard. A man is his sixties, tall, thin, his face drawn and gaunt, his nose aquiline, Rene was a flamboyant figure in porkpie hat, red pants, and plaid jacket. A former dancer, he skipped lightly, gracefully, down the stairs.

Annoyed by all these residents underfoot, the fire chief said, crossly, "You can't come this way just now. Go back to your room."

Rene didn't miss a stride. He raised his hand with a theatrical flourish and said imperiously, "Fuck you! Use the service elevator."

Poet, artist, actor, dancer, critic, jack-of-all-trades and all-around wild man, Rene Ricard was born in 1946 and grew up in New Bedford, Massachusetts. He ran away to Boston at age sixteen, where he supported himself by working as an artist's model, and by eighteen he was in New York City, becoming involved with Andy Warhol's Factory scene. Warhol soon cast Rene in a movie, *Kitchen*, in which he spends most of his time with his back to the camera, washing dishes while Edie Sedgwick sneezes and runs a malted machine to cover up the fact that she's forgotten her lines. Rene had a better role in 1965's *Chelsea Girls*, in which he stars in the "Boys in Bed" episode, rolling around in his underwear with two other boys in a room at the Chelsea Hotel. In his (and Edie's) last film for Warhol, *The Andy Warhol Story*, Rene embarks on a speed-fueled diatribe, rattling off every nasty thing he can think of to say about Andy. This is the kind of part Rene was born for, and surely it must have been his finest role, but sadly the film has been lost. An art critic in the eighties, in 1981 Rene published "The Radiant Child," the first major article about Jean-Michel Basquiat, in *Artforum*. Rene has published four books of his poetry: *Rene Ricard* (1979), *God with Revolver* (1989), *Trusty Sarcophagus Co.* (1990), and *Love Poems* (1999), and was portrayed by the actor Michael Wincott in Julian Schnabel's 1996 film *Basquiat*. Rene brought out a book of his art in a limited edition in 2003. He has lived at the Chelsea since the early nineties.

The king of the Chelsea eccentrics, Rene gives one the sense of a being not of this world. He flits around the hotel fairylike, ethereal, skipping lightly on a cloud of his own creation. Tall and gaunt with a wispy goatee, a porkpie hat atop his head, he's a bundle of nervous energy, unable to sit still. Rene is quite learned and knowledgeable about art and culture and many other subjects besides. When he speaks he's agitated, restless, wringing his hands, almost frantic sometimes—though often he positively bubbles with good humor. His speech can best be described as a sort of off-the-cuff intellectual rant. Though what he says is never uninteresting and you'll always want to hear more, he speaks quickly and is gone. Blink, and you might miss him. If you're lucky enough to run into Rene on the elevator, he will sometimes share a poem, often an obscene or ribald one. The floor of Rene's tiny room at the Chelsea is piled high with papers and pornographic magazines, leaving scarcely a path on which to traverse the thicket. Overflowing ashtrays crowd every raised surface. The mind immediately turns to thoughts of fire.

———

When we got down to the lobby, several of our fellow residents were gathered, passing around a bottle of wine, as the firemen tramped in and out with their equipment. We talked of fires of the past, the most infamous of which was set by Edie Sedgwick in 1967.

Born in 1943, Edie came from a prominent old money family with a history of mental illness. Two of her brothers committed suicide in the early sixties, and Edie herself spent time in a mental hospital for treatment for anorexia in 1962. Edie was beautiful and photogenic, and she had a bubbly personality—aided by various forms of speed—that made everyone love her. She met Andy Warhol early in 1965 and soon became his sidekick, dying her hair platinum blond to match his wig. Andy put her in several of his movies, including *Vinyl, Poor Little Rich Girl, Beauty No 2, Inner and Outer Space,* and of course *Kitchen* and *The Andy Warhol Story,* both also featuring Rene Ricard. (Edie was set to star in *Chelsea Girls* as well, but her part got cut when she and Warhol had a falling out.) Edie was the toast of the town for a couple of years. In Jean Stein's *Edie: American Girl,* an eighteen-year-old Rene Ricard describes Edie's meeting with Mick Jagger at the New York club the Scene:

It was an extraordinary moment! Edie Sedgwick, the most famous girl in New York, and Mick Jagger, the most famous singer and the one everyone wanted to fuck! And there he was. . . . She said, "How do you do? I just love your records." Well, what *do* you say? And he said, "Oh, thank you." Then, all of a sudden there was an explosion of people and every corner of the Scene emptied into the tiny vestibule where we were standing. People were pushing and banging up against each other. The flash bulbs were blinding. Edie was able to get into the ladies room. The poor thing! She was appalled by the crush.

Crumbling under the pressure of fame and substance abuse, Edie parted ways with Andy in March of 1966. She immediately took up with Bob Dylan, whom she believed would put her in a movie. Although it's a good question as to whether or not Dylan ever actually had an affair with Edie, he wrote several songs about her: "Leopard Skin Pillbox Hat," "Just Like a Woman," and "Like a Rolling Stone" among them. (In the last Dylan seems to be accusing Andy of exploiting Edie.)

Edie made one more film, *Ciao! Manhattan,* though Dylan didn't have anything to do with it. He was also long gone from the Chelsea by the time Edie checked in, though she adopted a cat that was apparently the offspring of the cat Dylan had while he was here.

Though Edie was a speed freak, she took downers to sleep, and these didn't mix well with the candles she insisted on burning all around her room. She passed out in her room at the Chelsea and the flames went up around her. Waking up to discover the room on fire, she hid herself in the closet to escape the blaze. When that didn't work, and the smoke came into the closet, she crawled across the room on her hands and knees and managed to get out the door, burning her hands on the doorknob in the process. Unfortunately, the cat, aptly named Smoke, did not survive the fire.

Edie left the city soon after the fire, retreating to her hometown of Santa Barbara, where she was in and out of mental hospitals, undergoing shock treatment as dramatized in *Ciao! Manhattan*. She married a man named Michael Post, whom she met in the hospital, and died of a drug overdose on November 15, 1971.

Our neighbor Sally Singer, an editor at *Vogue,* writes in that magazine (January 2006) of bringing the actress Sienna Miller to visit the Chelsea. Sienna was at the time portraying Edie Sedgwick in the movie *Factory Girls* and wanted to get a feel for the raving lunacy the Chelsea in order, I suppose, better to portray a raving lunatic. Stanley Bard told them that Rene Ricard had some film footage of Edie at the Chelsea, and they unwisely decided that they needed to see it. Rene is notoriously volatile and unpredictable, and, a simple phone call having failed to get through, they were trying to figure out how best to approach him:

> "You can't go up there," Bard says. "He's paranoid." He turns to a passing hotel resident. "This is the girl who's going to play Edie," he says. "Can you take her up to see Rene." The tenant edges toward the elevator. "No, man, I just got back from Europe today. I can't. He's crazy." I ask another. "Don't ruin my day," he replies. "He's crazy." Finally, another painter—a young Texan who sits all night in the lobby working on a picture of the lobby—strides over and says to Sienna, "I'll take you up ma'am. I can do this."
>
> The two women then ride the elevator up with the Texan and wait on a bench near the elevator while he

bangs and kicks furiously at Rene's door, only to come back and announce:

"He's not here. Or he's not answering."

As luck would have it, I was in the lobby that day, passing by the front desk as Stanley and the two women were discussing the matter, and I got on the elevator and rode up with them. I didn't recognize Sienna, because, if I remember correctly, she was disguised in a floppy hat and sunglasses, looking slightly mad, as if she belonged here. Bernard Crosley, a poet and art collector, was one of the people they asked to approach Rene. They didn't ask me directly, as far as I remember, though I do remember laughing at the very idea. The painter who finally agreed to go up there was a young man named Bradley, who always wore a trucker hat and, as Sally said, used to paint in the lobby. (In fact, he's the guy who painted himself into the Chelsea. And yes, his gambit succeeded and he did get in. I think it was the titanic literalism of his metaphor that ultimately did the trick.) The way I remember it, the women (wisely) got off on a lower floor. "Hell, I don't care," Bradley said as we proceeded up. "What's he gonna do?"

Bernard and I both shook our heads at the folly of youth. "I can't believe these people are so naïve!" Bernard exclaimed when we got off on our floor. "Drugs and money, that's what'll get his attention! I like Rene fine," he added. "But I'll see him when I see him. Far be it for me to awaken the sleeping beast."

Now in his sixties and still at the Chelsea, Rene is nothing if not a survivor. But his fast-paced lifestyle has taken its toll. You'll see him dragging himself out onto the streets in the morning, irritable, uncommunicative, his face haggard, his eyes concealed behind dark glasses. On such occasions it's best to keep your distance.

But whatever Rene's faults, and though on at least one occasion Stanley has tacked an eviction notice to the poet's door, our illustrious proprietor is not likely to get rid of the one-of-a-kind Rene Ricard, the Chelsea's last remaining link to the Warhol era. As legend has it, Stanley threw Warhol and his crew out of the hotel halfway through the filming of *Chelsea Girls,* only to come to regret it later, as Warhol filmed the rest of the movie in a mock-up of a Chelsea Hotel room somewhere else. As Stanley has learned over the years, a little bit of craziness helps keep this place interesting, and he's not liable to make the same mistake again.

2006

Chelsea Revenants

Something Like an Eternal Debate

I was talking to the painter Michael Bell and the poet Sheryl Rubenstein at the party for the one-year anniversary of *Living with Legends,* our Chelsea Hotel blog. The New York light, orange at sunset, was streaming in through the west-facing window much as it would have seventy years before when Thomas Wolfe lived in this very room.

There was a reporter, Lisa Chamberlain from the *New York Times,* at the party, taking notes. "It's nice that someone is finally paying attention to all this," Michael said with a sweep of his arm, "all this creativity going on around here."

United in our thankless plight, we all agreed that it was patently unfair, this misunderstood toiling in obscurity that we seemed doomed to endure.

"Who do you think has it worse," Sheryl asked, "writers or artists?"

"Well," I said, "at least people don't think they could just crank out a painting like they think they could sit down and write a novel if they felt like it."

But Michael said, "Oh, yes they do. They think they can just throw down paint. They don't think there's anything at all to color theory or technique."

"But it's so much more obvious that you're creating something," I protested. "An object of beauty. I know damn well I could never paint anything. But people use language every day and they probably figure their office memos are just as good as anything I write."

I thought Sheryl would back me up, but strangely, she agreed with Michael. "They especially say that about abstracts," she said. "When they see one they say, Oh, if you like that you should see what my child paints!"

"Yes, but that's almost a cliché," I said. "People have been saying that for years. But these days, of course, they're joking."

"I don't think so," Sheryl said, and she and Robert both chuckled. I was facing right into the streaming light in such a way that I could scarcely make out Michael's and Sheryl's faces for the glare. I saw merely their dark silhouettes: they were shaking their heads back and forth in unison. I broke out in a sweat, less from the sun's heat than from the realization that they were right.

I sighed. "You know, there was a lady in the lobby saying that very same thing just the other day," I said. "I don't think it was your painting, Michael, but maybe it was Philip Taaffe's. Besides that, she was a nice lady, from North Carolina, a tourist of course. And now I'm feeling really bad about this. Because I just burst out laughing right in her face."

The real highlight of the party didn't come, however, until much later in the evening when most everyone had gone home. An Irish lady who was staying next door popped her head out of her room to tell us how nice it was that there were still hotels like this left. She drank a glass of wine with us and showed us her room—the other half of Thomas Wolfe's old suite, now renovated as one of the nicer rooms in the hotel—and what should we discover there but the fashion designer Charles James's ancient drafting table! As mentioned earlier in the book, not having enough room in our apartment, Susan and I reluctantly set this table out in the hallway many years ago with a note attached describing what it was. We've been wondering ever since who might have retrieved it, and now we know: Stanley Bard! He has it nailed securely into a wall-mounted bookshelf, so that no one can ever again throw it in the trash.

The Lost Art of Angling

Capitol Fish Tackle, which had been in its present location on the ground floor of the Chelsea Hotel for sixty-five years, was moving at the end of July 2006. Since we'd never been in there before, Susan and I figured we should visit the store at least once and maybe even buy something to show our support.

On our way out the door we noticed that, as happens frequently at the Chelsea, preparations for a movie shoot were under way. There were cones set up on the street in front of the hotel, blocking off every possible parking place anywhere near the Chelsea. One lone man guarded the cones, sitting in his cloth chair under the shade of the scaffolding to escape the ninety-eight-degree heat of the afternoon.

Inside the tackle store, we looked at various lures and bobbers and sinkers and finally decided on a cheap rod and reel to use to play with the cat who lives on our floor. At the register a tall, gaunt man with red, curly hair rang up our purchase, scarcely even glancing at us.

"I heard you guys were moving," I said. "What happened? Did Stanley raise the rent on you?"

The man looked up. In an angry, incredulous tone, he quoted an exorbitant figure as the amount of his rent increase.

"He's raising it on a lot of us tenants too," I said.

"He's got a good thing here, good people," the man said in a Brooklyn accent. "Why's he want to screw it up? He don't know what he's gonna get with the new people, he don't know who's gonna move in here." The man seemed bitter.

"At these prices he's going to have to provide luxury accommodations," I said, half-jokingly.

"Yeah. And this place is fallin' apart. You don't know the kind of shit we've had to put up with here. It's just greed. Greed is all it is." He shook his head in disbelief. "Sixty-five years," he said. "Why would he want to ruin a good thing?"

II: IRRITATION

Outside the temperature was topping out at a hundred, and the shit had hit the fan. A man roared up in a gray SUV and parked right in front of the hotel, knocking several cones out of his way. One of the cones became stuck in the underside of the car.

The guard got up from his chair and walked up to the window of the SUV: "Hey man, what are you doing? You're running over my cones."

The driver sat rigidly in the car with his hands clutching the wheel. He stared straight ahead and didn't roll down the window.

"You're disrespecting me by running over my cones, man," the cone guard said.

The driver threw open his door and got out. He was a short, thin, tightly wound man. "You can't just set up cones in front of the hotel!" he declared, irately. He then proceeded down the line of cones, kicking several of them up onto the sidewalk.

The driver was being an asshole, but I could understand his frustration, and I felt that ultimately he was in the right.

The usual cursing and yelling ensued as the two men squared off. "You better be glad I don't react!" the driver exclaimed.

"React! Go ahead, react!" the cone guard said. He was husky and muscular and could have throttled the driver with one hand. The reason for the SUV man's visit became clear when the artist Joshua Thurman emerged from the hotel lugging a huge canvas. Cheerful and easygoing, Joshua had his usual smile on his face despite the heat, though it turned to a frown when he saw what was going on. With a wisdom that comes only from a lifetime of dedication to one's art—or maybe he's into yoga or something as well—Joshua chose to stay out of the dispute. He set down his painting for a moment, opened the back hatch of the SUV, and then loaded the painting in. Giving one last glance at the two men arguing, he shrugged his shoulders, shut the hatch of the SUV, and went back into the hotel.

Amazingly, but probably because he didn't want to lose his job, the cone guard ultimately backed down and retired to his seat under the scaffolding. Grimly triumphant, the driver got into his SUV and drove off with the cone still wedged in the underside of the vehicle.

III: A BIG FISH

Back on our floor at the Chelsea, I couldn't wait to try out my new toy. I unwrapped the reel—a Shakespeare!—and fastened it to the rod, then threaded the string through the eyelets and tied it to a plastic casting plug. But the cat was nowhere to be found.

It was sweltering inside the hotel as well. Susan and I went out to the stairwell, and I hung the rod over the edge and let the plug drop the eight stories down to the first floor landing. "Works pretty good, eh?" I said as I reeled it back up.

Somebody came into the stairwell on the second floor and started down the stairs. "I'll freak this dude out!" I said, and I let the plug drop.

As I reeled it back up, a gray-haired man stuck his head over the railing and looked up at me. "Oh, shit!" I said, ducking back out of the way. "It's Stanley Bard!"

Susan laughed, and said, "Quick, do it again!"

I let the plug drop. This time our illustrious proprietor was on the final flight of stairs before the first-floor landing. When he heard the plug hit the ground he reached out for the line. I jerked it out of his way but he ran down a few stairs and grabbed the plug as I was reeling it in. He was surprisingly spry for a seventy-year-old man.

"Oh, we caught a big one!" Susan exclaimed.

Plug in hand, Stanley looked up and called out, "Why are you doing that?"

I was at a loss to explain it. "We're practicing for our fishing trip to Montana," Susan said. Sounded good enough for me.

"Well, stop it!"

My rod bowing, I jerked at the plug and tried to reel it back in, but Stanley didn't want to let go. I think he was trying either to break the line or to untie the plug, but I had it on there pretty good. Finally, he released the plug, and it shot back skyward.

Stanley came up in the elevator. "It's you!" he said with surprise when he saw me.

"Yes," I replied.

"You could hurt somebody with that."

"I'm just dropping it straight down," I said. The first-floor landing is enclosed by the railing, and nobody can get in there.

"A little kid could stick his head out and get a concussion," Stanley said.

Whoops. I didn't think of that. Seemed unlikely, the plug was too light, but he did have a point. "Okay, I'll stop it," I said.

Stanley Bard: patron of the arts, sworn enemy of fishing. I guess he has to put up with a lot around here, too. As I mentioned before, Stanley has quite a bit of pressure on him from his board of directors. And now, to top it all off, here's one of the inmates casting a fishing reel down the stairwell! What next?

Thanksgiving Greetings from Montana

We heard them come in late last night; several people checked into the transient room next door and all had to go to the shared bathroom in the hallway, one after another. The next morning I met the last of them as he was clearing out, a thin man in his late thirties dressed in rugged winter gear with an Afghani hat and carrying a green army duffle bag. He said he was from Montana, which (maybe) would explain the getup, and that they had driven three thousand miles in thirty-three hours to get to New York. "Sounds peaceful," I said, meaning Montana, not the drive. They had one more night in New York, he said—though not, apparently, in the Chelsea—and then it was back on the road, back to Montana. (Maybe they came to see the Macy's Parade.)

"I know this building has lots of history," the Montanan said.

"You have no idea," I replied and took that opportunity to hand him a blog card.

"Come here," he said, leading me back into the transient room, "I want to show you a letter I left on the desk here."

Ever the suspicious New Yorker, I thought, Oh shit, it's going to be one of those goddamn chain letters and now I'm going to be cursed if I don't send it to a hundred people. Instead, he had left a pen, a stamped envelope, and a notepad with a note on it that said: "Write that letter today. You know which one I'm talking about. You'll feel better if you do." "That's nice," I said, thinking, hell, nobody from New York would ever think to do that, we're all too selfish, too caught up in our own lives. The man said he had checked into a hotel several years back and had seen a note just like this sitting on a desk, and that it had led to a bout of soul-searching, with the end result that he had sat down at that desk and written a long—and long-overdue—letter to his father (he left the details to the imagination). Since then, he said, whenever he checks out of a hotel room he always leaves the note and the rest of the stuff.

He asked if the maid would leave the note and I said yes, though actually I wasn't quite so sure; it was just that I didn't want to say no, since it was such a touching gesture in such a godforsaken place as this that I didn't want him to take it back. For the next few hours I listened for the maid and when I heard her rustling around over there, I rushed over just in time to see her closing the pen up in the notepad and getting ready to take it away. She said she didn't know what on earth that was all about, but I told her she was supposed to leave the things, and I believe she did.

Oh, one more thing: I told the guy that I had just been to my cousin's wedding in Montana this summer, though I couldn't remember the name of her town. Now I remember. So in case you're reading, guy from Montana, it's Lewistown.

Stanley Bard's Long-Lost Son

The two desk clerks were laughing when I came into the lobby, though one of them, Morgan, was laughing the loudest. "What's so funny?" I asked.

"Henry just said a transvestite came in last night and said he was Stanley Bard's son," Morgan said.

When I heard that I cracked up too.

"So what did he look like?" Morgan asked Henry.

"He was tall," Henry said, indicating with his hand.

"Was he dressed in women's clothes?" Morgan asked.

"No, but he had on all the makeup and everything."

"Did he look like Stanley?" I asked.

Henry seemed to be tiring of the interrogation. "Well, he was the same color."

"I wouldn't just dismiss it out of hand," I said.

"Yeah, you never can tell what kind of weird shit goes on around this place," Morgan said. "You'd have to get a DNA test to rule it out."

"He didn't have one of those," Henry said, irritably.

"Are you sure it wasn't David?" I asked, naming Stanley's actual, known son and probable successor as manager of the hotel.

"No!" Henry cried. "I know what David looks like!"

"So did you give him a room?" I asked.

"Joe talked to him," Henry said, naming one of the night

managers. "He was going to rent him one, but I guess he didn't like the price, so he went away."

"I'm gonna call Joe right now and ask him about this!" Morgan exclaimed, snatching up the phone.

I didn't wait around to hear from Joe. As the elevator arrived, I said, "Hard to believe you can't get a decent rate these days even when you're the owner's son."

Ghosts and Legends:
Hiroya's "De De" Paintings

Hiroya, the crazy Japanese graffiti painter, left several paintings behind in the hotel when he died. Two of them, replete with crosses, caskets, and the symbolism of death and heavy on Japanese text, have long intrigued us because they seemed to tell the story of Hiroya's falling out with his friend. We have been waiting for a Japanese person to happen by and translate them for us, and finally we found one in Miho Sakai, who directs documentaries for Japanese public TV (she was making one about the Chelsea at the time). The yellow painting that hangs in the stairwell between the seventh and eighth floors is rather poetic and reads approximately as follows:

> From here it's heaven,
> Heaven is a forest.
> Drink Rum in the morning,
> Everyone dance.
> Beyond Death: darkness, time, space, land of God.
> De De Land.

The orange painting that hangs in the stairwell on the first floor, though it touches on a similar theme, tells more of a story:

> De De Land. In heaven I meet De De and Barbara. De
> De always thinking something very deeply. The job of

Barbara is reading "pustory" ("poetry"?) to De De. De De makes blueberry jam. He writes a poem on the pink chalkboard. My job is after he finish writing a poem, put the poem into drawing. My girlfriend Marcia take picture of the drawing and record to De De Land's diary. End of day at De De Land. De De Land is very good feeling (comfortable), mellow world.

Instead of writing in actual Japanese, Hiroya is transliterating his English words, and Miho says his English is not very good, ungrammatical. Yeah, that's Hiroya all right. He took a perverse pride in his poor English-language skills. The "De De" in question is the punk rocker Dee Dee Ramone. Barbara is Dee Dee's wife. Marcia is the photographer Marcia Resnick. The story of the paintings is that Dee Dee paid Hiroya $500 to make two paintings of the Chelsea Hotel for the front and back cover of Dee Dee's novel, *Chelsea Horror Hotel*. Hiroya took the money, but then started to have second thoughts about whoring himself like that and so couldn't bring himself to complete the paintings. This led to a falling out between Dee Dee and Hiroya, but in the end Dee Dee insisted that Hiroya at least owed him two paintings of some sort, and these are what Hiroya came up with.

It was Dee Dee who introduced Hiroya to drugs. Dee Dee died in the same way as Hiroya, of an overdose, proceeding him in death by a year.

It's rather sad that Hiroya couldn't make it back to the Chelsea. I envision his ghost wandering the halls of the Gershwin, confused, disoriented, thinking: Where am I? What is this place? It looks kind of like the Chelsea, but not really. No, not exactly.

So the rumor I want to start is that as part of the memorial service at the Chelsea, we dumped Hiroya's ashes from the top of the Chelsea Hotel stairwell. A lot of people at this hotel believe in ghosts: the Chelsea, with its faded grandeur, with all the famous, tormented geniuses and larger-than-life characters it's held over the years, seems to be conducive to the belief. And so I would like us all to start seeing Hiroya walking around the hotel late at night, painting in the halls, accosting tourists, performing bizarre Butoh skits, and in general being his good old annoying self. Maybe in this way we can conjure him up, and he can haunt the halls of the place where he really belongs. For what else is a ghost, anyway, except the traces of a person in someone's memory, reflected through visions and dreams.

So if you don't mind, please spread this rumor. This is how legends often start, after all: somebody says something crazy, as a joke or whatever, and then someone else repeats it as fact. From there it's on its way to a life of its own, and even its creator can no longer deny it. It is elevated to mythical status and becomes, for all functional purposes, the truth.

A legend is kind of like a ghost in this respect and kind of like the Chelsea itself: it's what's in the mind that's important.

Afterword

The end of an era is finally upon us. On the evening of Thursday, June 14, 2007, our illustrious proprietor, Stanley Bard, was seen staggering out of his office in stunned disbelief upon being given the news that he was to be replaced as manager of the hotel after fifty years at the helm. Though the Bard family is the majority shareholder in the hotel, a judge ruled against them due to (at this time) undetermined improprieties. The hotel's Board of Directors, led by Marlene Krause, moved swiftly to replace Stanley with BD Hotels, NY L.L.C., a management firm that specializes in converting residential hotels into high-priced boutique hotels. Monday, June 18, was set as Stanley's last day at the helm.

However, when Monday morning came and the corporate suits descended upon the hotel, sizing it up floor by floor with an eye to replacing the idiosyncratic layout with cookie cutter boxes to maximize square footage, a funny thing happened: the writers and artists, who are usually too self-involved to say boo to one another, began to flood the lobby in an unprecedented show of support for Stanley and the Bard family. What's more, outside media interest was high, as reporters and photographers from several major newspapers showed up to get the story of the dismemberment of America's last great bohemian outpost. In a failed attempt to avert a public relations disaster, the Board and BD Hotels allowed

Stanley to stay on at the hotel, albeit in a reduced role as "Consultant," or "Goodwill Ambassador.

Sadly, Stanley's son and planned successor David Bard appears (at this time) to have become the sacrificial lamb. Told there would be no place for him in the new order, he was seen dejectedly carrying boxes of his stuff out to his car late Monday afternoon. It's a shame he never got the chance to run the place himself.

The market forces of gentrification have chewed up the poor and the working class since the real-estate boom began in the late nineties, and these forces are now gnawing their way up through the middle classes. Perhaps the Chelsea Hotel is where we fed-up New Yorkers will finally draw our line in the sand. A Chelsea Hotel Tenants Association was born on the rooftop garden of the hotel that Monday evening, as we have all banded together to fight for our unique enclave. But as BD Hotels is no doubt quite familiar with such tactics, we will need a spotlight of outside interest in order to keep our home.

We will also require a constant, tasteless, and hopefully grating, barrage of sophomoric humor:

Top Ten Questions for BD Hotels:

10. Where's Stanley?
9. Where's the hotel bar?
8. Here's my art portfolio. Can I get a room?
7. Can we go up on the roof?
6. Did Harry Smith really keep a Zombie in his closet?
5. Can you get the junky out of my bathroom?
4. Do you plan to take down all the art?
3. Do you know who the bloggers are?
2. Can we stay in Sid's room?
1. Do I really have to pay my rent now?

References

CHELSEA HOTEL

Robert Baral, *Turn West on 23rd: A Toast to New York's Old Chelsea*, Fleet Publishing Corp., New York, 1965

Rita Barros, *Chelsea Hotel: Fifteen Years*, Lisboa, Camera Municipal, Cultura, 1999

Claudio Edinger, *Chelsea Hotel*, Abbeville Press, New York, 1983

Florence Turner, *At the Chelsea: A Personal Memoir of New York's Most Famous Hotel*, Hamish Hamilton, London, 1986

Sarah Vowell, "Chelsea Girl," in *Take the Cannoli: Scenes from the New World*, Simon and Schuster, New York, 2000

RYAN ADAMS

Ryan Adams, "Conversation with Jim Derogatis's Answering Machine," posted January 7, 2004, http://www.mp34U.com

Jim Derogatis, "Note to Ryan Adams: Wish You Were Anywhere But Here," *Chicago Sun-Times*, December 15, 2003

Jim Derogatis, "Readers React on Adams, Empty Bottle Cancellation," *Chicago Sun-Times*, January 2, 2004

Michael Hoinski, "Three Times a Crybaby," *Village Voice*, January 24, 2006

Tricia Romano, "Crudités Anyone?" *Village Voice*, January 20, 2004

Various Authors, "Ryan Adams," *Wikipedia, the Free Encyclopedia*, http://en.wikipedia.org

MICHAEL ALIG

Leslie Felperin, "Film: Angels with Dirty Faces . . . ," *The Independent* (London), October 10, 2003

Joseph P. Fried, "In Setback, Prosecutors Forced to Drop a Key Witness . . . ," *New York Times,* January 31, 1998

Frank Owen, *Clubland: The Fabulous Rise and Murderous Fall of Club Culture,* St. Martin's Press, New York, 2003

Frank Owen, "Nightclubs, Downtown and Dirty . . . ," *The Washington Post,* February 14, 1998

Frank Owen, "Will Gatien Get Off?" *Village Voice,* February 17, 1998

Alix Sharkey, "Death by Decadence," *The Guardian* (London), April 19, 1997

CHARLES BUKOWSKI

Charles Bukowski, *Women,* Black Sparrow Press, Santa Rosa, 1978

Neeli Cherkovski, *Hank: The Life of Charles Bukowski,* Random House, New York, 1991

BEN LUCIEN BURMAN

Ben Lucien Burman, *Heaven on Earth,* Kessinger Publishing, Whitefish, Montana, 2005 (reprint of Grosset and Dunlap, 1929)

Michelle Cousin, "The Burmans at Home," from *Ben Lucien Burman: Tributes and Mementoes,* Jake Elwell, ed., Harper Collins, New York, 1992

C. Harvey Gardiner, "Ben Lucien Burman, the Man and His Writing," from *Ben Lucien Burman: Tributes and Mementoes,* Jake Elwell, ed., Harper Collins, New York, 1992

John Iams, "By His Own Reckoning, Ben Lucien Burman . . . ," United Press International, October 28, 1980

No byline, "Author Ben Lucien Burman Dies of a Stroke," Associated Press, November 12, 1984

No byline, "Ben Lucien Burman, 88, Author of 22 Books," *New York Times,* November 13, 1984

No byline, "Ben Lucien Burman and Alice Caddy Burman Papers," Tulane Manuscripts Department, Literature and Literary Organizations, www.tulane.edu

No byline, Article from the Associated Press, November 18, 1981

GERALD BUSBY

Gerald Busby, "Time in Place," *Living with Legends: Hotel Chelsea Blog,* www.hotelchelseablog.com

Jason Victor Serinus, "There and Back Again; Gerald Busby, Composer now 70, Is Alive and Cooking," *Gay City News,* vol. 4, 49, December 8–14, 2005, www.gaycitynews.com

No byline, Program for Gerald Busby's 70th Anniversary Concert at Carnegie Hall

STORMÉ DELARVERIÉ

David Carter, *Stonewall: The Riots That Sparked the Gay Revolution,* St. Martin's Griffin, New York, 2005

Leslie Feinberg, *Transgender Warriors: Making History from Joan of Arc to Dennis Rodman,* Beacon Press, 1997

Mack Friedman, *Strapped for Cash: A History of American Hustler Culture,* Alyson Publishing, Boston, 2003

Charles Kaiser, *The Gay Metropolis: 1940-1996,* Houghton Mifflin, Boston, 1997, 198

Rita Kempley, "Presenting the Provocative; Michelle Parkerson's Cinematic Battle . . . ," *Washington Post,* May 2, 1987

Various Authors, "Stonewall Riots," *Wikipedia, the free encyclopedia,* http://en.wikipedia.org

No byline, "'In the Life' Spotlights 20th Century's Gay and Lesbian Trailblazers," *Between the Lines News,* 1227, July 1, 2005, http://www.pridesource.com

No byline, "Stormé DeLarverie," *Equality Forum,* http://www.equalityforum.com

ETHAN HAWKE

Dan Halpern, "Another Surprise . . . ," *The Guardian* (London), October 8, 2005

Patrick Mulchrone, "Uma: My Hurt Over Divorce," *The Mirror,* October 10, 2005

Maeve Quigley, "Love . . . The Long and Short of It . . . ," *Sunday Mirror,* July 25, 2004

HERBERT HUNCKE

Ann Charters, ed., *The Portable Beat Reader,* Viking Penguin, New York, 1992

Herbert Huncke, "Again—The Hospital," Broadsheet, Heaven Poster Series #23, White Fields Press, Louisville, 1995

Benjamin G. Schafer, *The Herbert Huncke Reader,* William Morrow, New York, 1997

Robert McG. Thomas Jr., "Herbert Huncke, the Hipster Who Defined 'Beat,' Dies at 81," *New York Times,* August 9, 1996

CHARLES JAMES

Gary Alston, "Charles James," in *The Glamour Years,* http://www.highheelsnewsletter.com/GlamourYears.html

Richard Martin, "Charles James," in *Universe of Fashion,* http://www.designerhistory.com

JACK KEROUAC

Patrick Fenton, "Kerouac in Queens; Jack the Wizard . . . ," *Newsday* (New York), April 1, 1990 (*On the Road* written in Queens)

Irene Lacher, "A Critical Eye; In the Hands of Gore Vidal, A Pen . . . ," *Los Angeles Times,* October 30, 1995

Cathleen Miller, "Chelsea Moaning; In NYC, Bunk with the Ghosts . . . ," *Washington Post,* January 24, 1999 (*On the Road* written at Chelsea Hotel)

Gerald Nicosia, *Memory Babe: A Critical Biography of Jack Kerouac,* University of California Press, Berkeley, 1994

NYO Staff, "A Major Announcement," *New York Observer,* November 8, 2004

Matt Schudel, "End of the Road; Jack Kerouac, King of the Beats . . . ," *Sun-Sentinel* (Fort Lauderdale, FL), October 23, 1994

Deirdre R. Schwiesow, "*On the Road* in a Bohemian Generation's Footsteps," USA Today, June 17, 1996 (*On the Road* written at 454 W. 20th Street)

Thomas Swick, "Beat City: In the Cool of the Night . . . ," Sun-Sentinel (Fort Lauderdale, FL), February 22, 2004

Spenser Williams, "Straight Acting in Gay New York," http://www.advocate.com

No byline, "10 Great Places to Get on the Road and Feel the Beat," *USA Today,* http://USATODAY.com (*On the Road* written at Chelsea Hotel)

No byline, "Jack Kerouac: The Official Web Site," http://www. jackkerouac.com

ARTHUR MILLER

John Heilper, "Memories of Arthur Miller, Take-Out, TV and Olivier," *New York Observer,* February 21, 2005

Arthur Miller, "The Chelsea Affect," *Granta 78: Bad Company,* Summer 2002, pp. 235–254

No byline, "Synopsis: Death of a Salesman," Utah Shakespeare Festival, http://www.bard.org

DEE DEE RAMONE

Legs McNeil and Gillian McCain, *Please Kill Me: The Uncensored Oral History of Punk,* Grove Press, New York, 1996

Dee Dee Ramone, *Chelsea Horror Hotel,* Thunder's Mouth Press, New York, 2001

Dee Dee Ramone with Veronica Kofman, *Poison Heart: Surviving the Ramones,* Fire Fly Publishing, Wembley, England, 1997

Various Authors, "Dee Dee Ramone," *Wikipedia, the Free Encyclopedia,* http://en.wikipedia.org

EDIE SEDGWICK AND RENE RICARD

Callie Angell, Program Notes for May 16 and 17, 1998, showing of *Chelsea Girls* at American Museum of the Moving Image

Gary Comenas, *Warholstars,* http://www.warholstars.org

Frank Green, ed., "Poet Rene Ricard," *Frank 151,* book 22

F. L. Guiles, *Loner at the Ball: The Life of Andy Warhol,* Bantam Press, London, 1989

Jack Kroll, "Underground in Hell," *Newsweek,* November 14, 1966

Jonas Mekas, column in *Village Voice,* September 29, 1966

Yvonne Rainer, "Don't Give the Game Away," *Arts Magazine,* April 1967

Rosalyn Regelson, "Where Are the Chelsea Girls Taking Us?" *New York Times,* September 24, 1967

Julian Schnabel (director), Film: *Basquiat,* 1996

Robert Shaw, "Carrie Bedsore's Curious Chelsea Factoids," *Living with Legends Hotel Chelsea Blog,* December 4, 2005, http://www.hotelchelseablog.com

Sally Singer, "Just Like a Woman," *Vogue,* January, 2006

Jean Stein, *Edie: American Girl,* Grove Press, New York, 1982

No byline, Article on Rene Ricard's 1981 "Radiant Child" article about Jean-Michel Basquiat, *Artforum,* 2001

No byline, Biography of Albert "Rene" Ricard, from *Trusty Sarcophagus Co.,* Inandout Press, 1990

HARRY SMITH

Paolo Igliori, *American Magus: Harry Smith, A Modern Alchemist,* Inanout Press, New York, 1996

PATTI SMITH

Anne Glusker, "Patti Smith, Mom and Pop . . . ," *Washington Post,* July 28, 1996

Virgil Thomson

Anonymous Chelsea Bloggers, "Virgil Thomson's Secret Coq au vin Recipe," *Living with Legends: Hotel Chelsea Blog,* http://www.hotelchelseablog.com

No byline, "Composer Virgil Thomson Dead at 92," United Press International, September 30, 1989

No byline, "Virgil Thomson (1896-1989)" and "Virgil Thomson – Vignettes of His Life and Times," Virgil Thomson Foundation, http://www.virgilthompson.org

Sid Vicious

Jessica Berens, "Sid Vicious Didn't Want to Sniff Deodorant," *The Times* (London), October 1, 2004

Maurice Chittenden, "Note Says Sid and Nancy Had a Death Pact," *The Gazette* (Montreal, Quebec), May 8, 2000

Adrian Dannatt, "Obituary: Rockets Redglare," *The Independent* (London), June 16, 2001

John Kifner, "Sid Vicious, Punk-Rock Musician, Dies, Apparently of Drug Overdose," *New York Times,* February 3, 1979

Deborah Orr, "Nancy and Sid: A Punk Mystery Story . . . ," *Independent on Sunday* (London), October 12, 2003

Alan Parker, *Vicious: Too Fast to Live: The Authorized Biography of Sid Vicious,* Creation Books, London, England, 2004

Charlotte Robinson, "25 Up: Punk's Silver Jubilee; So Tough: The Boy Behind the Sid Vicious Myth," *Pop Matters Music,* http://www.popmatters.com

Paul Scott, "Sid, Nancy, and a Vicious Conspiracy," *Sunday Herald Sun* (Melbourn, Australia), February 29, 2004

No byline, "Pistols Play in Death Hotel," *Scottish Daily Record & Sunday Mail Ltd.,* August 19, 2003

No byline, "The Smoking Gun: Sid Vicious' Biggest Hit," http://www.thesmokinggun

ARNOLD WEINSTEIN

Adrian Dannett, "Obituary: Arnold Weinstein; Dazzling Playwright and Librettist," *The Independent* (London), September 27, 2005

Anne Midgette, "Arnold Weinstein, 78, a Poet and Collaborator on Operas," *New York Times*, September 6, 2005

THOMAS WOLFE

David Herbert Donald, *Look Homeward: A Life of Thomas Wolfe*, Fawcett Columbine, New York, 1987.

C. Hugh Holman, "Thomas Wolfe," North Carolina Collection, UNC, Chapel Hill, http://www.lib.unc.edu

Ted Mitchel, "Thomas Wolfe: A Biography," Biographical Sketch of Thomas Wolfe, Details & Trivia, Thomas Wolfe Society homepage, http://www.thomaswolfe.org

Thomas Wolfe, *Look Homeward Angel*, Charles Scriber's Sons, New York, 1929

Thomas Wolfe, *You Can't Go Home Again*, Dell Publishing, New York, 1934

Thomas Wolfe, *The Web and the Rock*, Dell Publishing, New York, 1937

No byline, "Thomas Wolfe Biography," Thomas Wolfe Web Page, http://www.library.uncwil.edu

Acknowledgments

Thanks to my girlfriend, Debbie Martin, who conceived the idea for the blog *Living with Legends* and did much of the research for this book; to my agent Bob Shuman, who came up with the idea of integrating the history of the hotel into the book; to Keith Wallman, who edited the book; to copy editor Lara Comstock; to Victor Bockris, Rita Barros, Claudio Edinger, Julia Calfee (who also hosted the one-year anniversary party for the blog), Greg Kitchen, and Linda Troeller, Chelsea residents who contributed photographs to the book; to Wendy Dorsett at Anthology Film Archives; to Susan Swan, Gerald Busby (who also interviewed us for http://tribecaradio.net), Willem van Es, and Stormé DeLarverié, who provided feedback on various chapters; to Luke Joerger and his assistant Will Squibb, who produced a video series based on my stories; to the actors who starred in that video series, including Elizabeth Pugh, David Combs, J. L. Cutler, Scott Widener, and Mario Corry as "the paintah"; to all the Chelsea guests and residents, past and present, who contributed to the blog, including Lisa Ackerman, Hawk Alfredson and Mia Hanson, Joe Ambrose, April Barton, Blair Bauer (BlairWear), Julia Bell, Bettina, Dan Bern, Nick Bienes and Rhea Gallaher, Anders Bramsen, Stefan Brecht and Rena Gill, George Chemeche, Judith Childs, Henry Chung, Andre Codrescu, Rachael and Merrilee Cohen, David Combs, Dan

Courtenay of Dan's Chelsea Guitars, Alan Grubner, Dee Dee Halleck, Sparkle Hayter, Charlie Huston, Robert Lambert, Bruce Levingston, Merle Lister, Eileen Myles, Artie Nash, Tony Notarberardino, Pat Padua, Jean Pearson, Daniel Reich, David Remfry and Caroline Hansbury, Libby Johnson, Mary Ann Rose, Bruce Russell, Robert Shaw (our Australian correspondent), Mikkel Straup, Tim Sullivan, Kyle Taylor, Lothar Troeller, Arthur Weinstein, Holly Williams, Bill Wilson, Bruno Wizard, and Michelle Zalopany; to the journalists who wrote articles about the blog, including Adam Cohen and Lisa Chamberlain of the *New York Times,* Paul Berger of *Metro New York,* Vivienne Leheny of *Chelsea Now,* and Sherry Mazzocchi of *BlogChelsea;* to the filmmaker Michael Maher of Australian Broadcasting Corporation, and his cameraman, Tim Bates, for documenting our work on the blog; to Miho Sakai of NHK Enterprises America Inc. (who also provided the translation of Hiroya's paintings), and her cameraman Robin Adams; to Martina Buttler of German Public Radio; to Coffin Ed, Jay Katz, and Miss Death of the Australian radio station FBi 94.5; to Dashiell at *Gawker;* to all the other bloggers who have linked to our blog over the years, including Jen Carlson of *Gothamist,* Lauren Cerand of *Luxlotus,* and the folks at *Curbed, New York Magazine, Hotelchatter, Gridskipper, Maudnewton,* and *Grumpyoldbookman;* to historian Sherrill Tippins and her medium; to Cindy Gallop for providing controversy and a good cocktail party; to editors Larry Lerner and Nicole Davis of *Chelsea Now* for keeping the Chelsea Hotel in the news; to David Bard; and last but not least, to the Chelsea Hotel's illustrious proprietor, Stanley Bard, without whom this bizarre and wonderful institution would have never been possible.

About the Author

Ed Hamilton was born in Atlanta, Georgia, and grew up in Louisville, Kentucky. He earned a bachelor's degree in philosophy and psychology from the University of Kentucky, and a master's degree in philosophy from the University of Louisville. His fiction has appeared in dozens of small magazines, including *Modern Drunkard, SoMa Literary Review, Journal of Kentucky Studies, Exquisite Corpse, River Walk Journal, Lumpen Times,* and *Limestone: A Journal of Art and Literature.* Ed contributes to *Living with Legends: Hotel Chelsea Blog* (http://www.hotelchelseablog.com), *BlogChelsea* (http://www.blogchelsea.com), and the *Huffington Post* (http://www.huffingtonpost.com), and writes regularly for the community newspapers *Chelsea Now* and *The Villager.* He has lived at the Chelsea Hotel for twelve years.